Engendering the Word

Engendering the Word

FEMINIST ESSAYS
IN PSYCHOSEXUAL POETICS

Temma F. Berg
Editor

Anna Shannon Elfenbein
Jeanne Larsen
Elisa Kay Sparks
Co-editors

With a Foreword by
Sandra M. Gilbert

UNIVERSITY OF ILLINOIS PRESS
Urbana and Chicago

PS
152
.E5
1989

The contributors to *Engendering the Word* wish to acknowledge the generous support of Gettysburg College.

This book is printed on acid-free paper.

Library of Congress Cataloging-in-Publication Data

Engendering the word: feminist essays in psychosexual poetics /
   Temma F. Berg, editor; Anna Shannon Elfenbein, Jeanne
   Larsen, Elisa Kay Sparks, co-editors.
     p. cm.
   ISBN 0-252-01555-X (cloth: alk. paper). ISBN 0-252-06016-4
(paper: alk. paper)
    1. American literature—History and criticism. 2. Women and
literature. 3. Feminism and literature. 4. Psychoanalysis and
literature. 5. English literature—History and criticism.
I. Berg, Temma F., 1943–
PS152.E5 1989
810'.9'9287—dc19
                                                 88-4881
                                                   CIP

To All Our
Strong Mothers

Contents

PART THREE *L'Écriture féminine*: **The Language of Women**

SANDRA M. GILBERT

Foreword: Of Circles and Circles

What is the relationship between gender and genre, between sexuality and textuality? How do such relationships get dramatized in poems, and historicized in the lives of poets? These are a few of the questions to which *Engendering the Word* responds, and they are questions that had me going around in circles when I wrote the syllabus for the course in American Sexual Poetics out of which the book has arisen. I planned this class, which I taught at the School of Criticism and Theory in the summer of 1984, not just with care but, to be frank, with some anxiety, because I knew that, as the editors of this collection of essays point out, it was to be the school's first offering in feminist theory; in fact, I was to be the first woman appointed as a full-time core faculty member.

Like most American feminist critics, I define myself as both a theorist and a practical critic—specifically, a historian and analyst of a female literary tradition. I wanted, therefore, to trace the interactions of gender and genre empirically, in a comparatively "controlled" situation, and *then* to speculate more generally about the ways in which "masculinity" and "femininity," as constructed in our culture, get inscribed in texts. Do men and women read and write differently? If so, is that because they experience language differently, because they understand history and "tradition" differently, because they inhabit genres differently, or all (or none) of the above? I set out to develop a course that would help me and my students begin to answer these questions.

Well, "students": the concept doesn't apply. As the essays included in *Engendering the Word* reveal, the participants in my seminar were truly colleagues, no matter what their official professional standings were—and these ranged from graduate student to tenured professor. Indeed, they were among the liveliest, most thoughtful, and most creative colleagues I have ever had. Together, we undertook not only to theorize about some of the toughest issues contemporary thinkers confront but also to read some of the most difficult texts recent critics have had to deal with as well as to *re*read some of the most familiar writings of our time (perhaps the hardest task of all).

In order to establish a canon that would allow us significant opportunities for empirical study, I had decided to pair male and female American poets from the late nineteenth century to the present. Some examples: we compared crucial innovators—Whitman and Dickinson; major expatriates—T. S. Eliot and H. D.; important *non*expatriates—Wallace Stevens and Marianne Moore; always tracing stylistic, generic, and thematic similarities as well as differences. But at the same time, in order to formulate theories that might (or might not) illuminate the works of these artists, I assigned or suggested readings in T. S. Eliot, Virginia Woolf, and Harold Bloom; in Sigmund Freud, Jacques Lacan, and Nancy Chodorow; in Hélène Cixous, Luce Irigaray, Julia Kristeva, and other contemporary French feminists as well as in the works of American feminist critics from Elaine Showalter to Joanne Feit Diehl, from myself and Susan Gubar to Margaret Homans and many others. I knew we had a lot to do, but I was sure, too, as soon as I had my first meeting with these new colleagues, that it would be exciting, even electrifying, for us to do it together.

And indeed, I was not wrong, for as is the case with any *simpatico* group of people in a seminar or workshop, it was possible for us to think and do things together that would have been a lot more problematic for each of us separately. Fairly quickly, we developed what I suppose I must call a "discourse of our own." One particularly striking phrase that I remember was "The resurrection trope strikes again!"—though, to be honest, I don't think I could translate it very accurately at the moment. But we all knew what it meant at the time: our rhetorical codes were extremely useful and helped us cut through tangles that would have been far more knotty without such seminal seminar shorthand. Fairly quickly, too, we learned how to admit, and ultimately resolve, our confusion over interpretive "cruxes" like the riddling last stanza of Dickinson's "My Life had Stood—a Loaded Gun" or the ambiguous conclusion of Moore's "Marriage." And if it took a little longer to gain the courage to float free of "received" readings like the explications of "Prufrock" or "Sunday Morning" that most of us had internalized in graduate school, that was probably all to the good. We needed to figure out how to live with multiplicity, how to negotiate between our relatively recent sense that these texts were significantly "engendered" and our comparatively long and complex education in more standard historical/critical contexts.

Were we "marginalized" at the School? Here I tend to disagree with the editors of *Engendering the Word*; I don't think we were. To be sure, the intellectual and social adventures of our communal summer were sometimes stressful. I have to confess that occasionally I felt as though I, personally, was in Evanston, Illinois, to represent not just feminism but womankind—a nasty feeling for a critic committed to the plural rather than the monolithic, to the liberating variety facilitated by cultural constructionism rather than the false unity imposed by biological essentialism. But how much of that uncomfortable feeling was simply my own self-consciousness and how much was really inflicted by the situation? I suspect more was due to the former than to the latter, and I suspect it because many of the issues that were crucial to our seminar were also central to most of our other colleagues at the school.

We were concerned, for instance, to define the use(s) of "theory" —"*high* theory," if you will—to feminism, and we were absorbed with questions about the future (and meaning) of "evaluation," in particular, of course, its relevance to the whole process of canon formation. We were anxious to define the pleasures and pains of the literary text, as well as the relationship of those enigmatic forces to cultural and psychological contexts. Who (and what) we are as speaking subjects, how and why we write as we do: these were matters that continually fascinated us, as they fascinated everyone else who attended the crowded, energetic, often contentious symposia at which the whole school met weekly in Evanston.

And clearly it is out of persistent, intense attention to such matters that *Engendering the Word* has risen. For as all the essays collected here demonstrate, we cannot understand who we are and how we behave as producers of language without also trying to grasp who and what we are as "masculine" and "feminine" linguistic subjects. The texts of our selves, as much as the texts we write or read, are variously but inexorably marked by the imperatives of gender, at least as much as by those of class and race, whether or not we bring any of these cultural edicts to consciousness. I don't want to be excessively smug about the virtues of feminism and its *contents/contents*, but I do believe that this rich collection exists, and is the first full-length book to come out of the school, because analyses of the relationship between gender and genre, between sexuality and textuality, force critics to focus on such key imperatives.

To elaborate a metaphor that the editors of this book emphasize in their introduction, I am delighted that the circle in which we sat and exchanged ideas that summer in Evanston has generated such a powerful and empowering recirculation of ideas, delighted, indeed, to see my colleagues circling back to the questions I had myself sought to put in circulation when I wrote my syllabus and assembled my reading list. And I am even more pleased to think that our circle will now continue to widen and perhaps even to help us all go on deconstructing hierarchical notions of the distinction between "margin" and "center." At the end of her superb *Trilogy*, H. D.—one of "our" poets—granted Kaspar the Magus, a kind of protoliterary critic, a vision of "the Hesperides . . . the circles and circles of islands/about the lost centre-island, Atlantis. . . ." Whether or not there is or ever was a "lost centre-island," I think that most of us, that summer, had such a vision of "circles and circles" of islands, and ideas, as we sat in our own eager, embattled, charmed circle.

TEMMA F. BERG and JEANNE LARSEN

Introduction

> These familiar flowers, these well-remembered bird-notes, this sky
> with its fitful brightness, these furrowed and grassy fields, each with a
> sort of personality given to it by the capricious hedgerows—such things
> as these are the mother tongue of our imagination. . . .
>
> George Eliot
> *The Mill on the Floss*

This book begins (and ends) with questions. Do women and
men use language differently? What effects does gender have on the
experiences of reading and writing? How can theories of psycho-
sexuality—theories about the nature and origin of sexual identity—
help us understand the grounds of *poesis*? How can feminist scholars
retain their commitment to the study of neglected literatures while
exploring the new theoretical approaches that have become important in critical writing today? Can the words of the fathers help us
find the mothers we have lost, help us continue to uncover a tradition
of our own? Can a book of essays retain a clear focus while reflecting
honestly the authors' differences in backgrounds and beliefs? What
must be done to ensure that the synergistic value of collaboration
does not conflict with the energy and insight that come from setting
oneself outside whatever circle one is in? And how do we best make
use of that collective literary space that has proven so appropriate
for the purposes of contemporary American feminist criticism—the
anthology?

The space of the anthology duplicates the kind of space women
as critics often seek to inhabit, a space characterized by both unity
and diversity. The frequent insistence of feminist literary critics on
the ability of feminist criticism to include contradictions without
losing cohesiveness has been one of its greatest advantages. Even a
brief look at a sampling of feminist anthologies reveals the force of
this ongoing concern with the tension between variety and unity,
theory and practice.

In one of the earliest anthologies of feminist literary theory,

Images of Women in Fiction: Feminist Perspectives, published in
1973, Susan Koppelman (Cornillion) expressed her sense of pluralism in a pragmatic way: "The people who have written this book
range in age from twenty-one to the late sixties. Some of us haven't
gone in for formal education beyond high school and some of us have
Ph.D.'s. Some have been published before and some of us have never
written before. Some are married, some single, some divorced. All
of us are trying to belong to ourselves. About half of us are parents
with children ranging from infancy through adulthood. Many of us
are teachers, some are students, some are writers, some librarians,
some waitresses, some full-time mothers at home. We are from all
over the country and are all excited and happy to have found one
another" (pp. xi–xii). The energy and exhilaration of the early stages
of the second wave of feminism can be found throughout Koppelman's book. There was joy in discovery and in sharing and validating
personal experience, a joy that acknowledged and valued difference.
However, in this and in other early anthologies, feminism avoided
theory.

In 1977, when Arlyn Diamond and Lee R. Edwards published
their anthology, *The Authority of Experience: Essays in Feminist
Criticism*, the commitment of feminism to a new perspective was
emphasized in the title as well as throughout the book. Attempting
to circumvent institutional modes of analysis and evaluation, feminists felt freer to exercise the authority that comes from personal
experience. New powers as readers and writers emerged. However,
despite their emphasis on divergence, Diamond and Edwards also
sought convergence: "That there is as yet no universally acceptable,
definitively formulated feminist aesthetic is neither surprising nor
particularly depressing; in a world which still argues about what
Aristotle meant, such purported critical monuments disappear like
Ozymandias' tomb. . . . If feminist literary criticism does not con-
note a school of criticism with a rigidly defined methodology, the
term does imply a general orientation, an attitude toward literature
which can turn a wide variety of existing techniques to its own ends"
(p. xii). Feminism had begun to ask what uses it could best make of
the techniques of critical theory in dealing with difference.

Like Diamond and Edwards, Catharine R. Stimpson and Ethel
Spector Person insisted on the need for many perspectives when in-

troducing their 1980 anthology, *Women: Sex and Sexuality*: "Since female sexuality exists within specific contexts, within matrices of the body and the world, no single perspective, no single discipline, can do intellectual justice to it" (p. 2). Another book that came out in 1980 used its title—*The Future of Difference*—to express its commitment to a plurality of perspectives. As Editor Hester Eisenstein wrote in a Post-preface to the book's 1984 edition: "The issues surrounding women's difference and differences among women are, if anything, more acute now [1984] than then [1980], in a time when feminist optimism has been sorely tested by current political realities" (p. xiii). Difference/differences: though women share a common sense of difference, this shared difference cannot eradicate the many differences of class, culture, ethnicity, sexuality. In her *Prelude*, Associate Editor Alice Jardine also reflected on the issue of difference and sameness as it shaped their book: "The conference [with which the book originated] was organized as a space for a multiplicity of voices investigating difference in very different ways. But this multiplicity of voices is also a common voice, which crosses cultural, political, and linguistic boundaries. It is a constantly renewed voice, which, in spite of or perhaps because of difference, will continue to reject the metaphor of woman as a detour on the way to man's truth" (p. xxvii). In both books, theoretical frameworks were used to explore the questions of difference and sameness. Difference and sameness, we were learning, could not be placed in opposition to one another; they had to be seen as interactive: we are the same, we are different. Out of our differences emerges our common voice. Our common voice encourages us to express our differences.

In their introduction to *Women and Language in Literature and Society* (1980), Editors Sally McConnell-Ginet, Ruth Borker, and Nelly Furman stressed the interaction between the theory of commonality and the practice of difference: "To see diversity in kinds of use [of language] leads us to expect that sex will interact with language in a variety of different ways that link back to particular use" (p. xiii). To avoid the reductive tendency of any single theory, McConnell-Ginet, Borker, and Furman used "a variety of sophisticated methods . . . to study language in relationship to women" to answer one "fundamental" question: "*what can a focus on language tell us about women in literature and society?*" (pp. xi–xii). In their book, McConnell-Ginet, Borker and Furman made it clear that the relationship between the generalities of theory and the particularities of experience is indeed complex.

Although in 1980, McConnell-Ginet, Borker, and Furman found critical theory essential in their pursuit of answers to questions about difference, by 1985, some feminists found themselves struggling against such "fathers" of theory as Sigmund Freud, Jacques Lacan, and Jacques Derrida. In *The (M)other Tongue: Essays in Feminist Psychoanalytic Interpretation*, Editors Shirley Nelson Garner, Claire Kahane, and Madelon Sprengnether presented their work as a re-vision of Freud. They wanted to emphasize what Freud overlooked: "On the whole, oedipally organized narrative (as well as interpretation) that is based on the determining role of the father and of patriarchal discourse tells a different story from preoedipal narrative, which locates the source of movement and conflict in the figure of the mother" (p. 10). Their ultimate goal, as the title of their anthology suggested, was that common language we have not yet learned to speak: "Feminists working from a number of critical approaches are concluding that it is time to learn, to begin to speak our mother tongue . . ." (p. 29). Again, feminist literary theory, while insisting on the need for critical pluralism, suggested the paradoxical interdependence of sameness and difference. Although we need to use a plurality of critical approaches and to question the words of the fathers, the mother tongue we seek may be singular.

Feminist theory has always, it seems, been pulled between a desire for, and a repudiation of, system. Elaine Showalter, in her Introduction to *The New Feminist Criticism: Essays on Women, Literature and Theory* (1985), exemplified this tension. On the one hand, she seemed, like other feminist theorists, to deplore overarching systems: "[T]he essays in this book are not pieces of a single large critical system, but rather represent a variety of positions and strategies engaged in a vigorous internal debate" (p. 4). On the other hand, she sought one: "It is now clear that what we are demanding is a new universal literary history and criticism that combines the literary experiences of both women and men, a complete revolution in the understanding of our literary heritage." Perhaps this "new universal literary history and criticism" would be able to respect difference but the use of the word *universal* tends to make that possibility seem problematic.

Gayle Greene and Coppélia Kahn, the editors of *Making a Difference: Feminist Literary Theory* (also 1985), saw Showalter's desire for closure as one side of a continuing tension in feminist theory: "[Sydney Janet] Kaplan [one of the contributors to their anthology] sees the diversity of feminist criticism, its eclecticism and ability to incorporate a variety of approaches, as its strength, but she points out the tension between this tendency—[Annette] Kolodny's 'playful pluralism'—and the movement towards a monolithic theory advocated by Showalter" (p. 37). However, most feminists are likely to agree that the tension is not only between people like Showalter and Kolodny, but also within each of them, each of us.

In their Preface to *Gender and Reading: Essays on Readers, Texts, and Contexts* (1986), Editors Elizabeth A. Flynn and Patrocinio P. Schweickart also addressed the issue of theory's tendency to limit pluralism, but they went on to suggest the value of such limitation: "On the one hand, it is important to convey the multiplicity of interests and experiences that make up the female perspective and, more importantly, to avoid the repressive assimilation of the perspectives of more vulnerable groups. On the other hand, generalization is essential to theory formation: if we wish to examine the implications of gender, we must assume that there is some common ground in the experiences and perspectives of different kinds of women that sets women apart from men" (pp. xiii–xiv). Schweickart and Flynn obviously believed that the questions raised by critical theory and the issue of gender were inextricably connected: "[W]hat is clear is that for us theory and gender intertwined. The need to comprehend the ramifications of gender deepened our passion for theoretical work and the intense critical attitude and intellectual honesty demanded by the theoretical enterprise made the issue of gender inescapable. Many questions, we saw, cannot be fully answered without addressing the issue of gender" (p. vii). Practice/theory. Difference/sameness. Does using theory make it difficult to take into account all the differences that separate women? When women use theory, do they risk being used?

In the Preface of *Gender and Reading*, we can see the persistence of the feminist consideration of the usefulness and the hazards of theory. We can see, too, how necessary it is for feminist theory to resist enclosure within a system. In their Preface, Schweickart and Flynn explained how their book, like ours, grew out of participation in the School of Criticism and Theory (SCT). But, as they noted, their concerns were not "on the official agenda"—in 1981 (p. vii). However, by 1984, feminist concerns *were* part of the agenda. Our book developed from the first feminist seminar sponsored by SCT. But our acceptance within that institution was still somewhat precarious. Though feminist concerns had been recognized, we still had occasion to feel marginalized, still struggled for acceptance, were still prone to paranoia. Perhaps, in the end, such marginality is necessary to stoke the energies of feminist literary theory, or, at least, we can turn it to good use. Provoked by what we sometimes viewed as our displacement in the institution of critical theory, we experienced a solidarity that grew as the summer proceeded. As privileged as we were in many ways, as close to the center as we might have seemed, we were still part of the long struggle to be heard. It is partly because of this eccentricity that we think of our anthology as ongoing, incomplete, open-ended.

Our seminar with Sandra M. Gilbert in "American Sexual Poetics" took place during the summer of 1984 in a room at Northwestern University, and met for certain hours on certain days of the week. But, in part because of Gilbert's encouragement and the model of her creative collaboration with Susan Gubar, it was not restricted to that time and place. We learned, as Barthes suggests, that the space of a seminar is in some way a fictive enclosure. "It is," he tells us, "only the space of the circulation of subtle desires, mobile desires. . . ."[1] Certainly our seminar and our desires did not stop when we left the room we were assigned. They continued to circulate in the angled hallways and the clustered lounges of the dorm we made our home that summer, as we Eco-ed through the stacks of the university library, as we danced, drank, skinny dipped, played charades.

We agreed with each other. We disagreed. We asked each other questions; we had a few angry encounters. One of us revised the school's unofficial motto that summer to reflect our continuing sense of engagement with Papa Freud and the patriarchy: "Summer at Fort Da" became "Summer at Fort Ma." We decided, on the last night, that we would not let the seminar be confined even by the summer's limits. We wanted to stay in touch with the Strong Mother (the *fort* Ma) we had created, the matrix of support we had generated. We would continue to work together, to create a tribute to our experience of collaborative inquiry.

This book's unity, then, lies in its origin in our common experience and discussion. At the same time, it reflects our thinking as we have responded in different ways to a number of germinal ideas in contemporary theory. Though the ideas that circulate through the chapters in this book have their genesis in the seminar, they are also the product of our individual changes over the last three years. They have developed further as a result of new developments in literary theory and as a result of suggestions and criticisms from each other. We have circulated these essays among us and, in the process, we have grown as our book has grown.

This book underlines both our diversity (of ethnicity, gender, social class, sexual orientation) and our joy in shared discovery. The texts discussed here have a wide cultural range and they reflect many different genres: dreams, novels, letters, critical writings, poems. We investigate women's and men's use of language in texts from Hélène Cixous's "Laugh of the Medusa" to T. S. Eliot's "Tradition and the Individual Talent," from Delmira Agustini's "Serpentina" to Emily Dickinson's letters. *Engendering the Word* maps our differences as well as our samenesses. We seek to express, each in our own way, our mutual indignation at the way language has been used to exclude some of us from its power and to obscure the forces of oppression at work in our world.

One of our common assumptions is that language and psychosexual identity are deeply interconnected. Researchers like Nancy Chodorow and Carol Gilligan have questioned the use of a male model of identity formation as the only human model.[2] Similarly, some of us are beginning to suspect that insistence on a language and a rhetorical praxis that are fixed, rational, orderly, impersonal, teleologically motivated, and aimed toward climactic closure may be another such straitjacket. Women need to claim, reclaim, and proclaim a sense of identity, a language, a style of our own. We need to subvert the structures that are already in place. As Rachel Blau DuPlessis tells us in "For the Etruscans," "If it's really the forms, the language, which dominate us, then disrupting them as radically as possible can give us hope and possibilities."[3] In *Engendering*, we often try to say things in a new way. As we write about the ways women have subverted the dominant discourse in the past, some of us experiment with ways to subvert the dominant discourse in the present. Others use a voice that will sound familiar to you, but we believe that what each of us has to say has the sound and the spirit of subversion. We do not want to say what has always been said even if we continue to speak in the voice you have always heard, and we will not limit ourselves to that voice. We, like feminist theory in general, seek to incorporate the differences we write about.

We have divided the book into three sections. This seemed useful for our readers and even necessary (since we were so different from one another), but it took some doing (since we were so very much alike). One icy night in Morgantown, West Virginia, three of us sat on the floor sorting slips of paper bearing essay titles, trying to separate into categories the tightly woven web of what we had to say. We wanted bridges, not boundaries; we wanted to connect our several answers to the questions we asked during the course of our seminar (germinar?). *Engendering* is our intertextual dialog with each other and with our readers. Our investigation is part of an ongoing exploration, and we invite you to join in the conversation. We do not want a period at the beginning or the end of our work. We want an ellipsis, that curious form of punctuation, indicating either exclusion or inclusion, omission or extension.

The first section of the book looks at different models of the relationship between sexuality and textuality, models provided by both writers labeled "theorists" and writers labeled "creative." In the opening essay, "Suppressing the Language of Wo(Man): The Dream as a Common Language," Temma F. Berg explores the question of sexual difference in language by examining the varying perspectives provided by the work of Sandra M. Gilbert and Susan Gubar, Luce Irigaray, Julia Kristeva, and Sigmund Freud. She ends her essay by designating the dream as a possible common language. Using condensation and displacement, the passionate and primordial language of the dream empowers us. As the mother tongue we seek, it gives us access to what has always been suppressed, and gains (rather than loses) force from its need to act subversively. The dream, Berg tells us, is the language we must use if we want to lose (or use) our sexual difference.

An alternative elaboration of difference is provided by Adriana Méndez Rodenas in "Tradition and Women's Writing: Toward a Poetics of Difference." Méndez Rodenas examines the concepts of text, tradition, and temporality that build T. S. Eliot's and Octavio Paz's masculine poetics. To this tradition she contrasts Hélène Cixous's *écriture féminine* and the subversive poetics of Kristeva in order to ask whether women's writing closes the gap of difference. Méndez Rodenas asserts difference rather than sexual opposition, for opposition merely serves to deny women a place in literary partnership, as in Julio Cortázar's arbitrary division between the male and female reader. Like Virginia Woolf's androgyny and Cixous's bisexuality, difference is redefined as a textual phenomenon, as the (in)difference of writing that displaces relentless binarisms with the ambivalence of parody and erotic word play. Although Méndez Rodenas joins women's writing to other plural approaches to the text—such as the fiction of the Argentine Manuel Puig and the Cuban Severo Sarduy —she concludes by replacing woman in her own "sexuality."

In "Old Father Nile: T. S. Eliot and Harold Bloom on the Creative Process as Spontaneous Generation," Elisa Kay Sparks explores the issue of woman's relationship to the special languages of both theory and lyric poetry, and decides that women's frequent exclusion from both suggests that there is something in the structural assumptions underlying literary criticism that does not accommodate the feminine. She demonstrates how it is elided by patriarchal theory. By anatomizing Bloom's and Eliot's critical metaphors, Sparks illuminates their ambivalence toward the feminine (an ambivalence that sometimes becomes virulent contempt). By setting their metaphors alongside Virginia Woolf's, she suggests ways feminist criticism could ease women's access to the canon, to theory, and to lyrical poetry.

In the last essay in the first section, "The Gaze of the Other Woman: Beholding and Begetting in Dickinson, Moore, and Rich," Leigh Gilmore looks at the struggles of the three women poets to achieve a lyrical poetic vision of inclusion within a tradition that works to exclude them. In speculations that look beyond Lacan and Freud, she locates a poetics of beholding and begetting that allows her to circumvent the familiar oedipal story of literary inheritance. Gilmore finds that by reinscribing a female version of the gaze, Dickinson, Moore, and Rich write within (without [perhaps] regarding it) a new critical and poetic tradition.

The second section of the book crosses many of the lines we

ordinarily use to mark divisions both within ourselves and between ourselves and the Other. In the process, we learn how difficult and treacherous it can be to cross lines, but also how necessary it is to approach the borders that threaten to close us out (and in).

In " 'This Woman Can Cross Any Line': Power and Authority in Contemporary Women's Fiction," Marilee Lindemann explores the quest for linguistic power and cultural authority in works by women of such diverse backgrounds as Leslie Marmon Silko, Gayl Jones, and Marilynne Robinson. All three writers, Lindemann finds, empower readers by using narrative strategies that initiate readers into female processes of knowing and telling, processes grounded in female psychosexual identity and authority. These women reject the masculine Worlds Elsewhere of style and pristine self-hood, and create alternative female Worlds Within-and-Out. In the process, the boundaries of the self and the form of the novel become equally fluid. Ultimately, Lindemann seeks to stress the concept of a female identity that cuts across lines of race and class.

Race and class have consistently marginalized one group of female characters in American and British fiction: in "The 'Incredible Indigo Sea' within Anglo-American Fiction," Laura Niesen de Abruña argues that the energy of the Caribbean woman, whether Creole or Afro-Caribbean, has been consistently and resolutely repressed. When the woman is "dark"—either by complexion, or nationality, or race—she is more easily targeted as the "Other," the foreign, the alien, the "bad." Fictional devices in William Faulkner and James Fenimore Cooper can then be seen to express imperialistic-patriarchal society's dis-ease with its exploitation of other cultures. Niesen de Abruña hopes that the redemption of the dark woman in Jean Rhys's *Wide Sargasso Sea* can help us find a way to validate and liberate the cultural self-identity of the Caribbean woman. We need to learn how to let her enter the conversation of Anglo-American discourse without killing her for interrupting.

In "Feminine Voices in Exile," María Rosa Olivera-Williams shows the gradual awareness of Latin American women writers of their voice and role in the creation of literature. In order to cross the border imposed by culture (women are to be the objects of creativity, not the creators), writers like the Uruguayan Delmira Agustini and the Argentine Alfonsina Storni had to struggle long and hard against the assumptions behind the traditionally male Latin-

American canon. In her essay, Olivera-Williams seeks to return to these women the feminine voice that has been denied them by their (primarily) male interpreters. However, while she is able to help Latin American women writers come slowly out of their exile, she still finds herself exiled as a literary critic. There are more obstacles placed in the way of the literary critic trying to write as a woman than there are placed in the way of the literary creator.

If it is hard, as Olivera-Williams suggests, to move out of exile from the feminine, "Testing the Razor: T. S. Eliot's 'Poems 1920,'" by Stephen H. Clark, confronts the difficulties of circumventing a masculine psychosexual identity. Starting from a position adjacent to feminism, aware of its debates but trying not to encroach upon it, Clark asks whether a man can escape from the exile of the masculine, especially when reading such violently repudiatory images of sexuality as those that can be found in Eliot's early poetry. "Poems 1920" has customarily been treated as a critique of social degeneration into which a language of misogyny has accidentally seeped. Clark reverses these priorities and reads the collection as an articulation of sexual fear and desired retaliation. He argues that for the male reader the ideal of aesthetic impersonality is itself a form of complicity and an evasion of the need to challenge the dominance model of masculinity that the very visceral force of these texts, if honestly confronted, compels him to acknowledge.

The last section, *L'Écriture féminine*: The Language of Women," emphasizes women's linguistic generativity by investigating the connections between womanly power and voice. In " 'How Lovely Are the Wiles of Words!'—or, 'Subjects Hinder Talk,' " S. Jaret McKinstry demonstrates how Dickinson's manipulation of language in her letters empowers her to create and speak herself. Destitution becomes Dickinson's wealth; her indirection becomes a power of interpretation. The Master letters simultaneously stress and transcend difference, while the Higginson letters allow Dickinson to continue her child's role, even as she anticipates and controls her correspondent's responses. Dickinson, according to Jaret McKinstry, "effectively inverts female humility so that it conceals irony and reveals power in female disguises."

Continuing McKinstry's discussion of Dickinson's linguistic experimentation, Anna Shannon Elfenbein's "Unsexing Language: Pronominal Protest in Emily Dickinson's 'Lay this Laurel' " demonstrates how Dickinson extends the meaning of the elegiac quatrain "Lay this Laurel" beyond the parameters of engendered language. The quatrain, like many of the poems in which Dickinson undermines traditional English grammar through her unconventional use of pronouns, directs attention to the patriarchal bias of the English language. The poem protests the connection of gender and fame/success/social esteem codified by language. "Deathless" and veiled, the laurel of Dickinson's poem, unlike the laurel garlands employed to deck the great men of history, transcends and transvalues gender. Bestowing the laurel of her poem, rather than claiming it as her due, Dickinson takes her stand outside the patriarchal procession of great men and great male poets.

Like McKinstry and Elfenbein, Carolyn A. Durham is intrigued by the intersection of sexuality and language. Her essay, "Linguistic and Sexual Engendering in Marianne Moore's Poetry," explores three distinct stages in Moore's poetic career: the critique of male sexual and linguistic oppression, the creation of a female language and literary tradition, and the identification of language itself as a poetic instrument that mediates the false dichotomies of gender. According to Durham, Moore's poetry is characterized by radical self-reflection and self-generation and alters etymology and lexicography, whose cultural and linguistic forms have predominantly served the male poet, to reassign linguistic primacy and power to the female. Moore's restructured language allows her to rewrite gender and undermine our very notion of masculine or feminine by eliminating the structure of opposition that has traditionally allowed us to define the two categories.

In the last essay, "Text and Matrix: Dickinson, H. D., and Woman's Voice," Jeanne Larsen continues the search for, and the celebration of, a liberating womanly language. Larsen applies the concept of l'écriture féminine to H. D.'s "The Flowering of the Rod" and to several of Dickinson's poems. Larsen's discussion of "The Flowering" reveals the value of a psychosexual reading of H. D.'s radical reversal of masculinist image systems in Christian myth; the poem celebrates the female, the oral, and the creative powers of the mother. Dickinson's work inscribes her refusal to be silenced: she claims the powers of speech through fictions, circumlocutions, lies; through her deconstruction of phallogocentric language; and through her hesitant, sly, triumphant assertion that a new tongue may be born. Larsen's essay also reminds us that the feminist critic may sometimes choose to speak in a language other than that of linear, logical, scholarly discourse. As a daughter to these female precursors, she "descants to the mother's tune."

Thus, this essay, like the book it introduces, comes full circle back to the questions that began it. What is the effect of gender upon language? What is the effect of language upon gender? What is the effect of men's and women's different relationships to the developing literary tradition? How, that is, does one's psychosexual identity affect the way one writes, or reads, or writes about what one reads? And is the difference within or without? We attempt in the following essays to share with each other, and with you, some of our concerns about language, literature, power, authority, traditions, canonicity, inheritance, gender, dominance, subversion. Though we try to de-scribe a circle, we do not forget that a circle is also a sign of omission; it is both hole and whole. We invite you to continue our dialogue, to fill in the places we left empty, to empty the places we temporarily filled and so to re-new them. We want the circle (circulation) of our desires to continue to extend . . .

NOTES

1. Roland Barthes, *Roland Barthes by Roland Barthes* (New York: Hill and Wang, 1977), p. 171.
2. The list of books that challenge prevailing models of identity formation and personality development is growing, but we would also like to note here the valuable work of Mary Field Belenky, Blythe McVicker Clinchy, Nancy Rule Goldberger, and Jill Mattuck Tarule in *Women's Ways of Knowing* (New York: Basic Books, 1986).
3. Rachel Blau DuPlessis, "For the Etruscans," *Feminist Criticism: Essays on Women, Literature and Theory*, ed. Elaine Showalter (New York: Pantheon Books, 1985), p. 287.

PART ONE

Toward a Feminist Psychosexual Poetics: Theoretical Groundwork

TEMMA F. BERG

Suppressing the Language of Wo(Man): The Dream as a Common Language

> No one lives in this room
> without confronting the whiteness of the wall
> behind the poems, planks of books,
> photographs of dead heroines.
> Without contemplating last and late
> the true nature of poetry. The drive
> to connect. The dream of a common language.
>
> Adrienne Rich
> *The Dream of a Common Language*

During the past twenty years, feminist literary critics have become less concerned with images of women in literature and polemical attacks on macho authors and phallic critics, and more interested in questions of sexual and textual difference. In this essay I would like to look at the ways contemporary feminist critics specify the difference, but, at the same time, I want to pursue the argument that there is no difference. While it is impossible not to agree with the argument that women's writing has always been suppressed, I would like to explore an alternative argument that demonstrates that woman's writing has never been completely suppressed.

I use the words *woman* and *women* in the preceding paragraph deliberately, and I will continue to use them carefully, for I want them to indicate the difference I am trying both to elaborate and eradicate. When I use the word *woman*, I want to indicate what I think Jacques Lacan means when he uses *"La femme."* "There isn't any *'La femme'* since . . . in her essence, she isn't everything [she is not-all]" (*Encore* 68). ["*Il n'y a pas La femme puisque . . . de son essence, elle n'est pas toute.*"] I use the word *women* to indicate the historical, cultural dimension—that is, actual living women. In many ways, contemporary feminist criticism is an ongoing argument about the meaning of these two words.

To attempt to describe all of the current arguments would be an impossible task. I will limit myself to the work of Jacques Lacan, Luce Irigaray, Sandra M. Gilbert and Susan Gubar, Julia Kristeva, and Sigmund Freud, for I believe that through an exploration of their work, we will be able not only to come to an understanding of the terms of the debate but also to a suggested (dis)solution of the difference about which they speculate.

To understand Lacan's view of woman and her relationship to language, it is first necessary to understand his view of the Oedipus. It is, of course, impossible to locate a definitive description of the Lacanian Oedipus. However, there are suggestive allusions. "Thus the Oedipal identification is that by which the subject transcends the aggressivity that is constitutive of the primary subjective individuation" (*Écrits: A Selection* 23). For Lacan, the Oedipus is a process of socialization. It is separation from the mother and acknowledgment of the Law of the Father and the use of language as entrance into the symbolic order:

> This is precisely where the Oedipus complex—in so far as we continue to recognize it as covering the whole field of our experience with its signification—may be said, in this connexion, to mark the limits that our discipline assigns to subjectivity: namely, what the subject can know of his unconscious participation in the movement of the complex structure of marriage ties. . . . The primordial Law is therefore that which in regulating marriage ties superimposes the kingdom of culture on that of a nature abandoned to the law of mating. . . . This law, then, is revealed clearly enough as identical with an order of language. For without kinship nominations, no power is capable of instituting the order of preferences and taboos that bind and weave the yarn of lineage through succeeding generations. . . . It is in the *name of the father* that we must recognize the support of the symbolic function, which, from the dawn of history, has identified his person with the figure of the law. (*Écrits* 66–67)

Through language the child successfully detaches himself from the mother (as Freud's grandchild Ernst did, according to Lacan, with his use of the now famous *"fort/da"* game [*Écrits* 112n]). Through language, the child regulates his sexual desire and, by accepting the taboos signified by kinship nominations, suppresses his incestuous desires. There is, as Lacan notes, a limit to how much we can consciously know of our abandonment of our primordial nature, but society, law, culture, all depend on our submission.

I have, in the above paragraph, used male pronouns because it is nearly impossible to insert the woman into the oedipal process as outlined by Lacan. Many of Lacan's translators and defenders have covertly acknowledged this difficulty. In her commentary on Lacan, Anika Lemaire unintentionally betrays Lacan's exclusion of woman even as she tries to include her: "The Oedipus is the drama of a being who must become a subject and who can only do so by internalizing the social rules, by entering on an equal footing into the register of the symbolic, of Culture and of language; it is the drama of a future subject who must resolve the problem of the difference between the sexes, or the assumption of his or her unconscious desires by means of a development which presupposes the transition from natural man to man of culture" (91–92). While Lemaire attempts to explain Lacan's theory without emphasizing sexual difference, she cannot. The careful use of such neutral terms as "subject" or such phrases as "his or her" becomes, in the end, "man"—"from natural man to man of culture." Lemaire elsewhere writes, "For the young child whose ambition is to seduce its mother, to be for her the phallus, the unique object of her desire, to succeed in sublimating the Oedipus is in fact to accept reality: differences in age, time and generation. It means accepting that he has a real penis and limited power. It means internalizing the Law of the Father (the super ego) and waiting for biological maturity in order to be able to fulfill his wish" (179–80). Again, the neutral words "the young child" and "its" are replaced by the image of a little boy with "a real penis" who must grow up before he can use it on mother, or her substitutes. Though some of these syntactical difficulties might be the result of the vagaries of translation, they cannot all be. Some must be traced back to the man who could not see woman as other than Other. Though Lacan may have denied woman's mystery (that is, seen its source in man's need to project his Otherness onto another), he also perpetuated it (woman as God, death, Other; unable to talk words, things, or herself; always already escaped from any discourses meant to contain her).

In *Feminine Sexuality: Jacques Lacan and the école freudienne*, Juliet Mitchell and Jacqueline Rose share Lemaire's difficulty. In fact,

translator Rose openly acknowledges her difficulty with Lacan's pronouns (or, with trying to subvert his insistence on the masculine):

> In translating from the French, I have chosen for the most part to
> follow the predominant English usage of the masculine pronoun in
> cases where gender was grammatically determined in the original. My
> early attempt to correct this throughout by the consistent use of "he/
> she," "his/her," or of "she/her" alone, produced either an equality or
> a "supremacy" of the feminine term, the absence of which this book
> attempts to analyse and expose. Within this limit, however, wherever
> it was possible to use "he/she" as the acknowledged reference to male
> and female subjects, I have done so. (59)

Throughout their book Mitchell and Rose seek to defend Lacan.
They believe that "femininity cannot be understood outside the
symbolic process through which it is constituted" and that Lacan
best understands this symbolic process. However, granting their
argument—that Lacan described (and did not prescribe) the situation
of woman/women in a linguistic structure ruled by the name of the
father and the phallus—is there not now some need to change this
situation? Is there not a need to go beyond description to subversion? Also, is there not a need to see Lacan as a man caught in the
symbolic process he describes?

While some of Lacan's critics and defenders believe he is inten-
tionally ambiguous in his attitude toward women and celebrate his
wit,[1] there are moments when his wit turns to sarcasm and his ambiguity to contempt: "There is no woman but excluded by the nature
of things which is the nature of words, and it has to be said that if
there is one thing about which women themselves are complaining
at the moment, it is well and truly that—it is just that they don't
know what they are saying, which is all the difference between them
and me" (*Encore* 68). Elsewhere in *Encore*, he writes, "There is one
thing which vividly demonstrates this *pas-tout*. See how, with one
of those nuances, of those oscillations of signification which language produces, the *pas-tout* changes meaning when I tell you—my
colleagues, the lady analysts, have told us nothing ['*pas-tout*'] about
feminine sexuality . . . *pas tout*! It is quite striking. They haven't
advanced by one bit the question of feminine sexuality. There must
be an internal reason, tied to the sexual organs [*l'appareil de la jouissance*]" (*Encore* 54). With regard to this last attack, it is interesting

to note that, according to Luce Irigaray, she was ousted from Lacan's school when she proposed a course on feminine sexuality.[2] It would seem that in this case the Law of the Father ("The lady analysts have told us nothing. . . .") could not be violated.

As further evidence of the Lacanian attitude toward women, I would like to offer the tale of Lacan's exclusion from the International Psychoanalytic Association (IPA) as given by Stuart Schneiderman in *The Death of an Intellectual Hero*. This will require an extensive amount of quotation, but I believe the reader will find it pertinent in both its intentional and unintentional revelations. Throughout the excerpt, Schneiderman, who believes he is exonerating Lacan, frequently incriminates both his hero and himself:

> Of course there were important theoretical issues in question [in Lacan's exclusion from the IPA], especially concerning Lacan's attack on the theory of ego psychology and his practice of the short session. But the crux of the issue seemed to be the sentiments of Marie Bonaparte, who at first sided with Lacan and his group and who later turned against them to side with the group led by Sacha Nacht. The groups were divided over questions of who was to teach what. But the deciding factor in Lacan's exclusion was the about-face of the Princess, as Marie Bonaparte was called. Wild rumors circulated that Lacan had made a pass at Mme Bonaparte; other more lucid wits answered that her reaction could only be explained by the absence of any such pass. Lacan, though, attributed her behavior to the fact that, when he drew up the by-laws for a new institute, he neglected to give her an honorary position and title in the organization. He felt that this gesture of disrespect had drawn her wrath. Teaming up with the Princess was none other than Anna Freud, and during the discussions held by the executive committee of the IPA the opinion of these two *grandes dames* held sway.
>
> A keen observer of these things, Philippe Sollers, told me that Lacan was expelled because he did run afoul of the matriarchy. How does one go afoul of a matriarchy? In the words of Anna Freud, Lacan washed his dirty linen in public. After respectability, the second most important characteristic for a psychoanalyst is discretion, and Lacan was notoriously indiscreet. Conflicts in the world of psychoanalysis in Paris did not stay within this world; they became public events. By the time Lacan had become a "national monument," the splits in the world of French analysis were major news events.
>
> And Lacan's indiscretion was not limited to psychoanalytic affairs;

there were whisperings that Lacan was involved in other kinds of
affairs, and that he did not limit these to furtive dalliances. Rumor
had it that his mistresses were almost as legion his followers [sic].
The matriarchs do not mind these manifestations of masculine libido;
they do mind when they are not permitted to ignore them. If these
rumors are true, and I am sure that future biographers will find out
all there is to know about them and more, then the cardinal sin is not
washing one's dirty linen, but dirtying it in public. (13–14)

In Schneiderman's story, Lacan becomes the naughty little boy
trapped by the contradictory desires of inconsistent, egotistical,
hypocritical, wrathful matriarchs. While it is difficult to glean
Lacan's attitude toward the two *grandes dames*, or toward matriarchy
in general, it does seem legitimate to wonder if the intellectual hero
might not have contributed some of the irony in the worshipper's
voice.

In sum, Lacan's work on woman is the story of her lack, exclusion, subordination to subjectivity, and abandonment to ignorance
of her own condition. Though Lacan's description of woman's position might seem to place her in an extremely negative light, Irigaray
is able to take this sexual difference Lacan insists on, this lack (or
"*pas tout*") of woman, and turn it into a positive statement about
woman's need for a language of her own. If, as Lacan asserts, women
do not know what they are saying, that may be, according to Irigaray,
because they speak a language men do not know how to listen to,
for they speak a language that is, like them, fluid and open. If men
know what they are saying, it is because they use a language that
is, like them, hard and closed. Though women have been trained to
use men's language and taught to suppress their own, they need to
recover this language of their own, which men do not understand.
If, as Lacan asserts, the child accepts the Law of the Father when
(s)he enters language, and passes over from nature to culture when
(s)he represses desire for the mother into an unconscious desire for
the Other, then Irigaray believes her task as a feminist is to return
to the preoedipal moment and to find a language that will enable
her to extend that moment into the world from which it is excluded.
Interestingly, though Lacan, his French interpreter, virtually ignored
the preoedipal, Freud was struck by its importance: "Our insight
into this early, pre-Oedipus, phase in girls comes to us as a surprise,

like the discovery, in another field, of the Minoan-Mycenean civilization behind the civilization of Greece."[3] Like Freud, and unlike Lacan, Irigaray is fascinated with the preoedipal; it has much to do with woman's sexuality and with the kind of language she believes women need to learn to use.

The fluidity of the preoedipal union with the mother offers the daughter an image of her body and of the language she needs to learn to use. Defined by woman's sexual difference, woman's language would be fluid, disorderly, sensual: "The multiplicity of woman's erogenous zones, the plural nature of her sex, is a differentiating factor that is too rarely considered by the male/female polarity, especially as far as its implications for 'signifying' practices are concerned" (*Speculum of the Other Woman* 103n). A reexamination of how woman uses language as well as how woman has been used by language will lead to the subversion of the closure of traditional Western metaphysics. In *Speculum of the Other Woman*, woman's sexuality/language decenters the male discourse of philosophy. Using the speculum of a deconstructive praxis, Irigaray explores the underside of Western philosophy, releasing the force of the subversive feminine, which has been systematically repressed. Using her woman's language, Irigaray enables us to reenter Plato's cave, from which the "good" male philosopher has expelled us. The cave becomes the womb, the womb from which we seek consciously to escape and to which we struggle unconsciously to return.

By writing with and about that which was once unmentionable—menstrual blood, breast milk, wombs, vaginas, the lips of the clitoris—woman's language writes the body. The woman's body, no longer idealized, conventionalized, as in men's writing, is apprehended in all its physical difference and is able to disrupt discourse as we know it. Personal and open, the language of woman, according to Irigaray, seeks to achieve the fluidity[4] it writes about by making the meanings of words elusive. Woman's writing escapes confinement through interpretive mastery. It will signify shamelessly. The reader cannot seek ascendancy over the text. Moreover, neither can the author. The author cannot control the reverberations or oscillations of meaning her text will give rise to:

> To put it another way: there would no longer be either a right side or a wrong side of discourse, or even of texts, but each passing from one to

the other would make audible and comprehensible even what resists the recto-verso structure that shores up common sense. If this is to be practiced for every meaning posited—for every word, utterance, sentence, but also of course for every phoneme, every letter—we need to proceed in such a way that linear reading is no longer possible: that is, the retroactive impact of the end of each word, utterance, or sentence upon its beginning must be taken into consideration in order to undo the power of its teleological effect, including its deferred action. (*This Sex Which Is Not One* 80)

The ordinary, straightforward, hierarchical way of writing/reading will be replaced by an agglutinative networking that reaches out to include as much as possible, to resonate endlessly. Woman's writing will look, sound, feel very different from men's writing.

At first glance, collaborative critics Sandra M. Gilbert and Susan Gubar seem to agree with Irigaray that men and women use language differently. However, though they flirt with French "feminology" in their essay "Sexual Linguistics," they end by dismissing it: "both in France and in America a number of feminist thinkers remain uneasy with what we call feminologist re-Joycings; a number refuse to be Mollified" ("Sexual Linguistics" 6, hereafter "SL"). Gilbert and Gubar distrust any equation of avant-garde (Joycean) language with the mother tongue. To simply oppose feminine fluidity to masculine rigidity does not, Gilbert and Gubar suspect, tell us as much as we need to know about women's writing. Moreover, Gilbert and Gubar believe that when feminists laud a new language that has never been written or that, if it has, has been written by men as often as by women, they miss the historical point. There has always been an *"écriture féminine"*; it has just been overlooked. Indefatigable in their efforts to nurture women's writing, Gilbert and Gubar find it more productive to unearth and appreciate the texts we have, to write a history of our own, rather than to insist on a new language.

Insisting that a tradition of male misogynistic response has always attended women's desire for linguistic release, Gilbert and Gubar suggest that in defense women sought "to come to terms with the urgent need for female literary authority through fantasies about the possession of a mother tongue" ("SL" 16). This mother tongue would more adequately describe women's experience and would enable women writers to reach those aspects of their experience that remain hidden and unnamed in men's writing. Sought and exploited by women writers as diverse as Emily Dickinson, Zora Neale Hurston, Gertrude Stein, Christina Stead, Willa Cather, and Virginia Woolf, this mother tongue is not unlike the language Irigaray describes. It is primordial, passionate, powerful, private. New words, a new language, to express what has never been expressed before, the woman's experience. A subversive language powerful enough to subvert patriarchal power.

Though Gilbert and Gubar understand the impulse behind such fantasies—the woman writer's need to survive in a man's *linguisterie*[5]—they insist that they are fantasies. However, they are less harmful than the fantasies men use to disable women. There are, according to Gilbert and Gubar, two prongs to men's attack on women's writing. First, men have constantly belittled and scorned the "scribbling" of women. Drawing on the writings of Nathanael West, William Faulkner, T. S. Eliot, and others, Gilbert and Gubar powerfully demonstrate the relentless hostility of this attack. Second, and more importantly, men have used various techniques to prevent women from using the power of language. In the past, men privileged themselves by using the classical languages and by denying women the world of classical education; now, they privilege themselves by using the obscure language of critical theory and by excluding feminist theory from it.

Gilbert and Gubar draw on the work of Walter Ong to explain how men used the languages of classical education to disenfranchise women. By speaking Greek and Latin, the *patrius sermo*, and, at the same time, by preventing women from gaining access to these languages, men, according to Ong, kept women from sharing intellectual authority. Women's education was second rate and so, necessarily, was their writing.[6] During the Middle Ages, and on into the twentieth century, Latin was, according to Ong, "a sex-linked language" (*Fighting for Life* 130). However, when the daughters of educated men entered institutions of higher learning in greater numbers, at the beginning of the twentieth century, emphasis on the classical languages diminished. When men could no longer exclude women by using the *patrius sermo*, it became obsolete. Gilbert and Gubar use this observation of Ong's to draw a conclusion of their own, that contemporary critical theory has revived the exclusionary practice of the *patrius sermo*. Obscure, unnecessarily difficult, the language of critical theory, Gilbert and Gubar believe, is adopted primarily by men in an effort to exclude women once again.

At one point, Gilbert and Gubar draw on Tennyson to develop their case against the language of current critical theory. Critical theory uses a language as difficult and private as the one Merlin uses in his book of charms: "Writ in a language that has long gone by. . . . / And every margin scribbled, crost, and crammed / With comment, densest condensation, hard. . . . / And none can read the comment but myself; / And in the comment did I find the charm."[7] According to Gilbert and Gubar, the language of critical theory is, like Merlin's secret language, difficult, crabbed, obscure. However, this description of Merlin's secret language could also be used to describe the language of the women writers they admire. The writing of Dickinson, Hurston, and Stein is also condensed, hard, crammed, criss-crossed with the commentaries we read in an effort to unravel their writings.

It seems to me that though Gilbert and Gubar seek to differentiate between them, the mother tongue and the *patrius sermo* of critical theory are more alike than unalike. Both hide their message. Both condense and distort. Both are private and difficult. From Emily Dickinson to Jacques Derrida, writers have sought to occult language. Writers strive to forge a language that will capture experience in all its unmediated intensity.

Of course, Gilbert and Gubar know this, and at one point they allude to a mother tongue that "is common to both genders" ("SL" 32). However, when Gilbert and Gubar close their paper on sexual linguistics with an enthusiastic and invigorating call for "feminist *puissance*," they seem to move away from the idea of one maternal language common to all back to the lingering binary opposition their paper almost eliminated—"For at last, in spite of feminist doubt and masculinist dread, we can affirm that woman has not been sentenced to transcribe male penmanship; rather, she commands sentences which inscribe her own powerful character." Do women have a sentence of their own or not? Do they write in special characters that empower them as women or not? On the one hand, Gilbert and Gubar say yes; on the other hand, they say no. While Gilbert and Gubar suggest the existence of a common language, it remains unnamed, unexamined, overshadowed by the persistent possibility of a language of women's own.

If we turn to Julia Kristeva, another critic active in this debate about the possibility of a woman's language, we find less ambiguous sightings of a language beyond misogyny and feminist doubt. Kristeva relishes the same linguistic disorder that Irigaray seeks and that Gilbert and Gubar seem alternately to praise as woman's language and to deplore as man's disguise, but Kristeva does not confine this poetic language to a sexual difference. It is the language of the semiotic, the language that must be repressed to preserve the Law of the Father. The Oedipus is, in fact, the repression of the semiotic (the instinctual desire for the mother) to ensure the continuance of society—"society may be stabilized only if it excludes poetic language" (*Desire in Language: A Semiotic Approach to Literature and Art* 31).[8] Though the semiotic must be repressed, Kristeva assures us that it has never stopped erupting. In her work, Kristeva traces its force at work in Bakhtin's carnivalesque, in the avant-garde, in the heterogeneity of poetic language, in the *jouissance* of *le sémiotique*, and in the mysterious space of the *chora*, the space that Irigaray and Gilbert and Gubar alternately allude to and elude, the space of the unconscious, the common language of the dream, the poetry we all read/write.

According to Kristeva's reading of Mikhail Bakhtin, when medieval society moved from the symbol (fixed transcendence) to the sign (and its sliding ambivalence), carnival entered to disrupt: "Carnivalesque discourse breaks through the laws of a language censored by grammar and semantics and, at the same time, is a social and political protest. There is no equivalence, but rather identity between challenging official linguistic codes and challenging official law" (*Desire* 65). Bakhtin's discovery of the dialogic, what Kristeva calls the text as "a mosaic of quotations," was essential to his stance as a revolutionary. When Bakhtin discovered that the late nineteenth- and early twentieth-century novel was able to transgress conventional linguistic codes, to move beyond both fixed and theological epic grandeur and the dogmatic novelistic real (monologistic because it adhered to a single truth) to a dream discourse of poetic polyphony, he discovered, according to Kristeva, the principle of revolutionary defiance and disorder.

This defiant stance of the Bakhtinian dialogic is also the position taken by the avant-garde, according to Kristeva. The avant-garde unsettles and displaces. In fact, to all who seek to find a way to discriminate between ordinary and poetic language, Kristeva offers this disruptiveness as the difference itself: "'[P]oetic language' . . . through the particularity of its signifying operations, is an unsettling process—when not an outright destruction—of the identity of meaning and speaking subject, and consequently, of transcendence or, by derivation, of 'religious sensibility'!" (*Desire* 125). Whether she is speaking about carnivalesque, the avant-garde, poetic language, or *le sémiotique*, through all her many permutations, Kristeva is always seeking to name the difference. The difference is sexual, but it is not exclusively sexual. Men as well as women unleash the subversive force of poetic language.

On the one hand, Kristeva wants to place the source of poetic language—the *chora*, the mysterious receptacle of the maternal body —beyond sexual difference: "The true guarantee of the last myth of modern times, the myth of the feminine—hardly the third person any longer, but, both beyond and within, more and less than meaning: rhythm, tone, color, and joy, within, through, and across the Word?" (*Desire* 158). The feminine becomes the realm of the artist of either sex: a realm of the Word itself. The feminine is what fills and empties meaning. On the other hand, there are indications that Kristeva, like Irigaray, sees the feminine as a special difference that functions in a woman's practice. Only a woman can seek the will-of-the-wisp of the "subject-in-process," for only a woman is aware "of the inanity of Being" (*Desire* 146). Nevertheless, the woman must not allow herself to fall into the fold of sexual difference:

> After the saccharine whirlwind of Jocastas and Antigones, next to a quietude fascinated with the self-indulgent whims of hysterics, the negative awakens within the body and language of the other so as to weave a fabric in which your role is tolerated only if it resembles that of women in Sade, Joyce, and Bataille. But you most certainly must not consider yourself either as the weaving or as the character against whom it is woven. What is important is to listen to it, in your own way, indefinitely, and to disappear within the movement of this attentiveness. (*Desire* 166)

Kristeva wants women to be tolerant, indefinite, shifting, and attentive, for to draw one thread too tightly through the fabric of all the languages we listen to and write would unnecessarily and prematurely cut us off from the infinite set of possible differences.

As much as Kristeva wants to discover the poetic language common to both genders, she seems as unable to name its source as Irigaray, who doubts that it exists,[9] or Gilbert and Gubar, who glimpse it fleetingly. The language common to both genders is the one language we cannot locate. At once a myth to be spelled and dispelled, this language is a practice that has both suppressed and expressed woman. What is this linguistic space that we all can inhabit, yet that seems to elude us? Where are we to find a language that is at once fluid, nonteleological, crammed, condensed, subversive, erupting with the power of the repressed? I would suggest nowhere but in the language of the dream, the space within which Freud, according to H. D., sought the cure of humanity's ills: "The picture-writing, the hieroglyph of the dream, was the common property of the whole race; in the dream, man, as at the beginning of time spoke a universal language, and man, meeting in the universal understanding of the unconscious or the subconscious, would forgo barriers of time and space, and man understanding man, would save mankind."[10] The language of dreams is the primordial language that shares all the characteristics of both the *patrius sermo* (which is motivated by a desire to occult language and separate self from other) and the mother tongue (which we desire to use to express self directly and to connect self with other). Significantly, it is the language that would most closely fit the description in the citation from Tennyson, especially one line of it that Gilbert and Gubar omit—"And none can read the text, not even I. . . ." Perhaps Gilbert and Gubar omitted this line because it complicated their binary opposition. According to this line, even men can be powerless before the condensed distortion of this charmed language. However, this line serves as a wonderful gloss on the language I am trying to identify, for the dream is the only text that even the dreamer cannot read directly. The dreamer can only read the commentary, the language used to transcribe the dream, the narrative that can never hope to capture the dream. Carnivalesque and dialogic, the dream exceeds any commentary that seeks to contain it. A dark undercurrent, it can serve as the speculum with which we see not only woman's hidden sex but all our private parts. In the dream what is repressed (outlawed) returns.

In his *Die Traumdeutung*, Freud sought to relocate and re-assemble the lost preoedipal wholeness of mankind. What some feminists are beginning to claim as women's territory on which a man can only trespass—the unconscious—Freud sought to claim for us all. In the primal language [11] of the dream, there is no sexual difference. Or, if there is a difference, it becomes so diffuse and incoherent that we cannot build any linguistic or psychic binarisms on it. Rather, the space of the dream opens to us all—women and men —indifferently. Using condensation, displacement, metaphor, symbolism, and narrativization, we can all become poets of the imaginary. We can all go underground to plot the only revolution that will probably ever succeed.

Irigaray suggests this link between the dream and the subversive politics of psychoanalysis when, toward the end of *Speculum*, she deconstructs Plato's myth of the cave, and in a brilliant interpretive maneuver links Plato's cave with the womb and the night of our dreams, and points out their inevitable clash with the imperative to satisfy the daylight needs of the City. The prisoners in the cave are in a "dark room where projects of shadows, of course—are fed by an almost magic lantern. . . ." They are by analogy linked to the analysand in analysis:

> Anyone who devotes himself to describing and memorizing such a show is certainly not without merit, and he deserves his reward. But on what grounds? And what risk would the City run if all the people got caught up in that game? Stayed, endlessly, in that *psychē* analysis that distracts them from more useful duties. Attended to phantoms, fakes, fantasies, that turn them away from more objective realities. Not even realizing that they are under the spell of thaumaturges, because they are unable to turn round and take measure against the "shadows" that bewitch them. Which, in any case, they perceive as being in front of them, opposite. (350)

Though Irigaray might at first seem to be condemning the underground world of the cave, and, by analogy, psychoanalysis, since they both detain us from "more useful duties" and "more objective realities," Irigaray is, clearly, being ironic, doubly ironic. Speaking as Socrates, she uses Socratic irony against itself. For, unlike Socrates and his Plato (or Plato and his Socrates), Irigaray (and Freud) prefer the darkness of the cave and its flickering shadows to the busy daylight world of the City. Irigaray and Freud prefer to linger in the night-world of our dreams, our common ground, our original home. Exploring the labyrinthine connections of our dreams is, for both Irigaray and Freud, our most subversive activity. Our preoedipal prehistory, our eternal return to union with the mother, our repressed, disorderly unconscious, the dream is the place where we all can exceed our ordinary bounds and use every night the primal language that completes and competes with our everyday discourse. And if we enter psychoanalysis, we enter to unleash this creative though sometimes destructive power.[12]

Clearly, Freud believed we all needed to reach and exploit our repressed unconscious, but he was ambivalent about the consequences. Writing the common language of the dream brings us closer to the mental and sexual bisexuality that, throughout his life, Freud believed was the ground of our psychic being.[13] But submerging oneself in one's dream life (one's bisexuality?) can also bring psychic disintegration. I will attempt to demonstrate this disintegration in Freud's mental process by looking at one particular dream—what I have come to call the "*She* Dream"—and its interpretation. Significantly, at the end of this dream and interpretation, Freud notes that he wakes up in a mental fright. He finds this fright inexplicable since he believes the dream has successfully worked through fears of death and expressed his sense of achievement. However, his mental fright is very explicable if we look at the dream and its interpretation as a series of highly condensed images of the dissolution of sexual difference and its linguistic consequences. The dream could, of course, be interpreted in other ways. The ideational life, as Freud tells us and experience reassures us, is incredibly rich. However, in my reading I want to limit myself to the way the dream sets up and erases sexual difference.

The dream begins with a scene of dissection: "Old Brücke must have set me some task; STRANGELY ENOUGH, it related to a dissection of the lower part of my own body, my pelvis and legs, which I saw before me as though in the dissecting-room, but without noticing their absence in myself and also without a trace of any gruesome feeling. . . . The pelvis had been eviscerated and it was visible now in its superior, now in its inferior, aspect, the two being mixed together."[14] Since the pelvic region is eviscerated and something is absent, this dissection is clearly a castration. But since a man would presumably view his own castration as "gruesome," it would seem that Freud in the dream is a woman. Only a woman would view her castration calmly, for only the woman's castration is an absence that is not an absence. Thus, Freud becomes, in the first part of his dream, a castrated woman. However he is not only a castrated woman, he is also a woman examining her sex (and, in the process, denying her castration?): "Thick flesh-coloured protuberances (which in the dream itself, made me think of haemorrhoids) could be seen." Finally, Freud, the castrated woman examining her own sex, becomes a woman giving birth: "Something which lay over it [the pelvis] and was like crumpled silver-paper had also to be carefully fished out."

While the first part of the dream displaces the anatomical difference about which Freud was usually quite certain, the second part of the dream displaces him in another way. Freud, the man/woman, becomes Freud the about-to-be-born infant: ". . . I took a cab. To my astonishment the cab drove in through the door of a house, which opened and allowed it to pass along a passage which turned a corner at its end and finally led into the open air again." In a footnote Freud suggests that the cab scene took place "on the ground-floor of my block of flats where the tenants keep their perambulators. . . ." It would seem he is at once the child being hurried through the birth canal and the child being taken out for a walk in the pram.

The third scene of the dream portrays Freud following an Alpine guide to a "small wooden house at the end of which was an open window. There the guide set me down and laid two wooden boards, which were standing ready, upon the window-sill, so as to bridge the chasm which had to be crossed over from the window." Freud variously interprets this small house as the grave or the coffin itself. However, this house can also be seen as another variation on the womb. This time Freud sees the womb in reverse. The child (man?) looks at it from without. The window from which he has just exited is the window he now seeks to reenter, but this time the journey is more perilous than before (across a chasm) because while we know what happens after a child is born, we do not know what happens after death. Freud is obviously correct when he interprets this small wooden house as the grave, for, at this point, a return to the womb *is* a turn to the tomb.

Outside the house or hut are two sleeping children who make, according to Freud, his crossing over the chasm, his transition from life to death (from death to life?) possible. It would seem that Freud is able to die once he has produced the children who will outlive him and provide him immortality, but that is not how Freud interprets the dream. According to Freud, the dream demonstrates that he is able to die once he has succeeded in surpassing his father. Freud wants to interpret the dream as yet another example of his successful resolution of the oedipal struggle. However, the last line of his analysis leads to a very strange ambiguity: "Accordingly, I woke up in a *'mental fright,'* even after the successful emergence of the idea that children may perhaps achieve what their father has failed to—a fresh allusion to the strange novel in which a person's identity is retained through a series of generations for over two thousand years." Here, Freud wants to suggest that the idea that a child may achieve what a father has failed to is an allusion to the novel *She,* which is an important part of the dream because during the dream day (the twenty-four hours preceding the dream) he discussed the novel with Louise N. Though much in this dream does seem to develop from the novel, it is unclear how the child's achieving what the father failed to is a "fresh allusion" to it. Moreover, if you have been successful, why awaken in a mental fright?

Freud says he wakes in a mental fright because although he has turned his vision of death into a positive occurrence (transforming "the gloomiest of expectations into one that was highly desirable" —the expectation of being buried in an Etruscanlike tomb), he yet could not change the affect (". . . a dream can turn into its opposite the *idea* accompanying an affect but not always the affect itself"). Therefore, he awakens frightened at the prospect of his own death. However, I would like to suggest that this fright was (as Freud says about the earlier cab scene) "over-determined in several other ways." The dream not only alludes to a successful resolution of the Oedipus and retention of identity, but it also alludes to just the opposite. Freud has not resolved his Oedipus or successfully retained his identity. And it is his relationship to the mother, to the pre-Oedipus, that has frustrated his success in both instances. Rather than suggest a successful retention of identity, the dream presents a man who *cannot* retain his identity. It presents a man so bewildered by the dissolves of the dream that he is alternately uncertain of his sex, his age, his place. Is he alive or dead? Old and infirm or young and strong? Is he man or woman?

In his dream, Freud becomes a woman; he gives birth; he is the passive object of a dissection/castration (but without any sense of absence or gruesome feeling); he is the child he gives birth to; and he follows a guide on a perilous journey. Both analyst and analysand, Freud both follows and directs, exhibiting the passive and active behaviors of the bisexuality he believed was the ground of our common mental life. Why then does he wake in a mental fright? I have already indicated that his fright may be determined by his failure to retain his identity, a feat at which Ayesha (also called "She" in the novel) is very successful. At this point I would like to suggest that it is also determined by Freud's encounter with another "She"—Louise N.—during which a different kind of failure to retain identity takes place. Significantly, Freud refers to this encounter as "the occasion of the dream."

During the course of her visit to Freud the day before the dream, Louise N. asks him for a book to read. " 'Lend me something to read,' she had said. I offered her Rider Haggard's *She*. 'A *strange* book, but full of hidden meaning,' I began to explain to her; 'the eternal feminine, the immortality of our emotions. . . .' Here she interrupted me: 'I know it already. . . .' " Freud wants to tell Louise N. about the eternal feminine, through the loan of *She*, which he curiously makes parallel to "the immortality of *our* emotions" (my emphasis), but that, she says, she already knows. *What* does she already know? The novel? The immortality of our emotions? The eternal feminine? The fortuitous but sound apposition of all three? Whatever she knows, Louise N. does not want to read Haggard, she wants to read Freud. "Have you nothing of your own?" she asks him. He protests that his own "immortal works have not yet been written." He is being, I suppose, gently ironic. However, Louise N., by means of a sarcastic thrust, goes on to compound Freud's irony with interest. "Well, when are we to expect these so-called ultimate explanations of yours which you've promised even *we* shall find readable." Her sarcasm upsets Freud. "At that point I saw that someone else was admonishing me through her mouth and I was silent."

Why is Freud silenced by Louise N.'s sarcasm? Is it because she is able to accomplish what he could not? He had wanted to tell her about the eternal feminine, but she would not listen. She interrupted him. However, he is forced to listen to her. And, with her use of the two "we's," Louise N. covertly taunts Freud with the sexual difference he seeks to name (perhaps in those "so-called ultimate explanations") but cannot. Or can he? Who is that someone who admonishes him through Louise N.'s mouth and, in the process, renders him speechless? The answer could only be Freud himself. That is why he becomes silent. She has taken over his voice. Silenced by (speaking through) the woman, Freud now understands an important part of his dream-thoughts: "I reflected on the amount of self-discipline it was costing me to offer the public even my book upon dreams—I should have to give away so much of my own private character in it. . . . The task which was imposed on me in the dream of carrying out a dissection *of my own body* was thus my *self-analysis* which was linked up with my giving an account of my dreams."

Freud connects his dream analysis to Louise N.'s ventriloquism and suddenly feels the need to defend himself because he wonders what this woman, who not only can take over his voice but who can overtake him on his quest to name the eternal feminine, thinks of his dream analysis, which is also a dissection, which is also a castration, which is also a becoming woman. What does Louise N. think of this task of self-analysis at which she assists in the dream? Does she see Freud as the manly scientist disciplining himself to dissect his dream? Or does she see him as a woman, exhibiting herself, looking at herself again and again in the mirror of the dreams that she herself has given birth to, projected? Is he merely reflecting, in his analyses of dreams, the eternal feminine in one of its least appealing aspects—turning the mirrored self into a fetish? Is dream interpretation merely a kind of regressive narcissism?

It is difficult to determine from the dream and its interpretation exactly what is the relationship between Freud and Louise N. Is she a patient? Has Freud analyzed any of her dreams? Is she a family friend? Is she a therapist in training? According to Freud, it is extremely difficult to determine the difference between a patient and a student analyst when the therapist in training is a woman: "The wish to get the longed-for penis eventually in spite of everything may contribute to the motives that drive a mature woman to analysis, and what she may reasonably expect from analysis—a capacity, for instance, to carry on an intellectual profession—may often be recognized as a sublimated modification of the repressed wish" ("Femininity" 589). What a mature woman can expect from analysis is not a cure, but the capacity to carry on the profession of psychoanalysis. Small wonder Louise N. helps Freud in his self-analysis/dissection within the dream. Even smaller wonder that he loses his sex in the dream. The woman/therapist/patient has so successfully helped him in his work that she has not only taken away his voice, she has also finally obtained the longed-for penis.

Not only does the penis, the material embodiment of the signifying phallus, disconcertingly shift place, but so does the eternal feminine. Perhaps Freud cannot find the eternal feminine because he wants to look for it in the wrong places. He seeks it in literature and in hysterical patients, and though it may be there, he will not be able to see it clearly until he looks for it in its original and final home—within himself. In the end, there is no outside the eternal feminine just as there is no outside the dream. Whether he is analyzing his own dreams or his patients' dreams, he is always dissecting himself. And, in the process, his identity becomes so fluid and contingent that it threatens to slip away from him entirely and leave him without any words. In analyzing dreams, or the eternal feminine, in trying to re-member the maternal body, the dreamer and the dream interpreter, woman and man, are one, and in that condensation and displacement annihilation lurks. Freud thought he was exiled from the unconscious, from the womb, the dream, the body of the mother, but he was wrong. To dissect his and his patients' dreams was to return to the womb, to submit to castration, and to become woman.

In *Desire in Language*, Julia Kristeva speculates about *her* exile, and what she has to say about exile and language helps us further understand Freud's problem/(dis)solution. She suggests that because "Yalta" exiled her into French, she now speaks that language as a stranger and can therefore look at it differently than a native. She can explore the depths of what she calls its heterogeneity with greater impunity.

> This heterogeneous object is of course a body that invites me to identify with it (woman, child, androgyne?) and immediately forbids any identification; it is not me, it is a non-me in me, beside me, outside of me where the me becomes lost. This heterogeneous object is a body, because it is a *text*. I have written down this much abused word and insist upon it so that you might understand how much risk there is in a text, how much nonidentity, nonauthenticity, impossibility, and corrosiveness it holds for those who chose to see themselves within it. A body, a text that bounces back to me echoes of a territory that I have lost but that I am seeking within the blackness of dreams in

Bulgarian, French, Russian, Chinese tones, invocations, lifting up the
dismembered, sleeping body. Territory of the mother. (163)

Like Kristeva, Freud thought exile gave one a special place from
which to explore the heterogeneity of the text. Because he was a
man, he was exiled from the matrix of the dream's creativity and
therefore in a better position to explore this new language of the
maternal body, the unconscious, the eternal feminine. However, as
the dream he interpreted told him, and as Kristeva suggests above,
there is no such privileged exile. Though there is exile, it does not
privilege, because exclusion is not simple. As Kristeva suggests, the
text, the body, the dream, repudiates identification but also invites
it. It is not-me but also in me. Both inside and outside the text, alternately resisting and being seduced by it, we are never completely
exiled from the language we must sometimes forget to re-member.

Like Kristeva, who knows she can never be completely outside
the language she uses (exploits), Freud knew he was not exiled from
the place of the woman, the site *he* sought to exploit. Even as he
objectified women, he identified himself with them—not only with
Louise N., but also with the heroines of Haggard's novels, and, as
he suspected, such identifications could prove very dangerous: "In
both novels the guide is a woman; both are concerned with perilous
journeys; while *She* describes an adventurous road that had scarcely
ever been trodden before, leading into an undiscovered region." Like
these heroines, Freud is a guide into undiscovered regions and under-
takes a perilous journey as he charts the unconscious. Furthermore,
like Ayesha, the heroine of *She*, he risks annihilation: "The end of
the adventure in *She* is that the guide, instead of finding immortality for herself and the others, perishes in the mysterious subterranean fire. A fear of that kind was unmistakably active in the dream
thoughts."[15] What Freud suspected and what frightened him was that
his was not a privileged exile from the unconscious, the place of the
mother, the primal imaginary. In the dream he could always return,
but such a return entailed danger, for not only is the dream the place
where you return to the mother, it is also the place where you become the mother. It is the place where you lose your distinct sexual
difference and where you find yourself not knowing the difference
after all.

The mysterious subterranean fire in which Ayesha perishes,

and that Freud fears, is like the fire in Plato's cave, the mysterious subterranean source of our dreams. Projecting entrancing shadows, such fires consume and imprison us away from the cool, clear daylight of the sun (son). Though we may fear enthrallment, we also covertly desire it, for by tapping this language, which recreates itself ceaselessly every night, we release a creative, subversive potential. A potential, which, if we knew how to use it, might enable us to do more than just dream of a common language.

NOTES

1. See, for example, Jane Gallop's delightful reading of Lacan in *The Daughter's Seduction* (Ithaca, New York: Cornell University Press, 1982). Gallop believes that by flaunting the privilege and authority of the phallus, Lacan paradoxically undermines the authority of the masculine: "The prick does not play by the rules; he (she) is a narcissistic tease who persuades by means of attraction and resistance, not by orderly systematic discourse. The prick, which as male organ might be expected to epitomize masculinity, lays bare its desire. Since the phallic order demands that the law rather than desire issue from the paternal position, an exposure of the father as desiring, a view of the father as prick, a view of the father's prick, feminizes him. Lacan, inasmuch as he acts gratuitously nasty, betrays his sexualized relation to his listeners. The phallic role demands impassivity; the prick obviously gets pleasure from his cruelty. The evidence of the pleasure undermines the rigid authority of the paternal position" (37–38).

2. See *This Sex Which Is Not One*, where Luce Irigaray explains her removal from Jacques Lacan's school after she proposed a course about feminine desire, female sexuality, and "the difference between the sexes and its articulation in language": "In a departure from the usual practice, this question [What do you propose to do in your teaching?] was addressed to instructors by the 'Department of Psychoanalysis' of the University of Vincennes before its 'restructuring' in the fall of 1974. A commission of three members named by Jacques Lacan wrote me without further explanation that my project 'could not be accepted.' I who had been an instructor in the department since the founding of the University of Vincennes thus was suspended from my teaching. These clarifications would not have been necessary if a version contrary to the facts had not been circulated both in France and abroad" (167n).

3. "Female Sexuality," *SE*, XXI, 226.

4. In a fascinating chapter titled "The 'Mechanics' of Fluids," Irigaray links feminine writing with the science of fluids, for both have resisted incorporation into male rationality. In this respect, the mechanics of fluids are very unlike the mechanics of solids. "Solid mechanics and rationality have maintained a relationship of very long standing, one against which fluids have never stopped arguing" (*This Sex* 113). Irigaray contends that because the fluidity of woman (and her writing) disrupts signification, psychoanalysis has failed to see the fluidity of woman in its need to justify the solidity of man: ". . . the failure to recognize a specific economy of fluids—their resistance to solids, their 'proper' dynamics—is perpetuated by psychoanalytic science" (114).

5. When Lacan uses the term *linguisterie* in *Encore*, he uses it to indicate what the unconscious says (92). I use it as a general term. Just as *menagerie* means a collection of animals, I use *linguisterie* to indicate a collection of linguistic operations.

6. Perhaps this is why the debate about the level of Shakespeare's education has always been important to literary historians. If Shakespeare could achieve greatness without classical training, perhaps a woman could. On the other hand, if greatness depended upon a classical training, then women could be depended upon not to be great.

7. "Merlin and Vivien," in *The Poems of Tennyson*, ed. Christopher Ricks (London: Longman Group Limited, 1969), 1613. Cited in "Sexual Linguistics." The passage occurs at the beginning of a long dispute between Merlin and Vivien. This dispute, which forms the substance of the "Idyll," ends when Vivien has won her battle and Merlin has given her the "charm" he at first refused her. Significantly, once she has won the charm from Merlin, the narrative voice accepts Merlin's earlier estimation of the wily woman. Earlier Merlin had used the word *harlot* when addressing Vivien; now the narrative echoes him: "Then crying, 'I have made his glory mine,' / And shrieking out, 'O fool!' the harlot leapt / Adown the forest, and the thicket closed / Behind her, and the forest echo'd 'fool.' " Likewise, when the forest ambiguously echoes her words, it seems to call her fool. Obviously, it is not easy for a woman to use certain "charms."

8. Of course, the semiotic is not simply poetic language. It is that which struggles against "scientific language." However, Julia Kristeva does not want to set up a binary opposition. Rather than oppose one another, the semiotic and the scientific (or symbolic) condition and make one another possible. "The semiotic activity, which introduces wandering or fuzziness into language and, *a fortiori*, into poetic language is, from a synchronic point of view, a mark of the workings of drives (appro-

priation/rejection, orality/anality, love/hate, life/death) and, from a diachronic point of view, stems from the archaisms of the semiotic body. Before recognizing itself as identical in a mirror and, consequently, as signifying, this body is dependent vis-à-vis the mother. At the same time instinctual and maternal, semiotic processes prepare the future speaker for entrance into meaning and signification (the symbolic). But the symbolic (i.e., language as nomination, sign, and syntax) constitutes itself only by breaking with this anteriority, which is retrieved as 'signifier,' 'primary process,' displacement and condensation, metaphor and metonymy, rhetorical figures—but which always remain subordinate—subjacent to the principal function of naming-predicating. Language as symbolic function constitutes itself at the cost of repressing instinctual drive and continuous relation to the mother. On the contrary, the unsettled and questionable subject of poetic language (for whom the word is never uniquely sign) maintains itself at the cost of reactivating this repressed instinctual maternal element" (*Desire* 136). Using the semiotic means risking incest (dalliance with the mother). Using the scientific, or symbolic, rescues us from incest and from "fuzziness," but it also alienates us from our instinctual desires.

9. There are times when Irigaray acknowledges that writers of either sex may enjoy the special language she elaborates—"A cave [the space of the mother] explored, or even exploited, and for their loss, by painters and poets who can accept the figuration of repetition—and *hysterical mimesis*—but only by good citizens" (*Speculum* 356). While here Irigaray seems to suggest that artists regardless of gender exploit their hysteria—their link to our common womb, the receptacle of the mother, the *chora*—elsewhere she seems to reserve this space for the woman: "It is already getting around—at what rate? in what contexts? in spite of what resistance?—that women diffuse themselves according to modalities scarcely compatible with the framework of the ruling symbolic. Which doesn't happen without causing some turbulence, we might even say some whirlwinds, that ought to be reconfined within solid walls of principle, to keep them from spreading to infinity. Otherwise they might even go so far as to disturb that third agency designated as the real—a transgression and confusion of boundaries that it is important to restore to their proper order" (*This Sex* 106).

10. H. D., *Tribute to Freud* (New York: New Directions, 1956), 71. Of course, I wish I could explain H. D.'s insistent use of the word *man* in the above passage. Is she being ironic? Does the harsh rhythm created by the recurrence of the word express some kind of discomfort? How can we be sure?

11. Though Freud did not use the term *primal language*, he was interested in the existence of more primitive "picture" languages. Freud would often relate these languages to the language of dreams. See "Uncertainties and Criticisms," his final chapter on "Dreams" in his *Introductory Lectures on Psychoanalysis*: "The coalescence of contraries in the dream-work is, as you know, analogous to the so-called 'antithetical meaning of primal words' in the most ancient languages" (*SE*, XV, 229). Freud goes on to remark, "The one certain gain we have derived from our comparison is the discovery that these points of uncertainty which people have tried to use as objections to the soundness of our dream-interpretations are on the contrary regular characteristics of all primitive systems of expression" (*SE*, XV, 232). In "The Antithetical Meaning of Primal Words" (*SE*, XI), Freud explores the issue in greater depth, quoting extensively from the work of philologist Karl Abel. He concludes, "In the correspondence between the peculiarity of the dreamwork mentioned at the beginning of the paper [that is, dreams often represent thoughts and feelings by their contraries] and the practice discovered by philology in the oldest languages, we may see a confirmation of the view we have formed about the regressive, archaic character of the expression of thoughts in dreams. And we psychiatrists cannot escape the suspicion that we should be better at understanding and translating the language of dreams if we knew more about the development of language" (161). In "The Uncanny" (*SE*, XVII), Freud explores the way the word *heimlich* "develops in the direction of ambivalence, until it finally coincides with its opposite, *unheimlich*" (226). Interestingly, he proceeds to connect this coincidence to repression: "It may be true that the uncanny [*unheimlich*] is something which is secretly familiar [*heimlich*], which has undergone repression and then returned from it, and that everything that is uncanny fulfills this condition" (245). I would like to thank Lis Møller, from the University of Copenhagen, for pointing out the above references.

12. Though here I am linking Freud and Irigaray and emphasizing their harmonious agreement, elsewhere Irigaray attacks him relentlessly as the Victorian phallocrat. She thus gives us, despite her acknowledgment of the gaps in his argument, a perversely univocal reading: "So we must admit that THE LITTLE GIRL IS THEREFORE A LITTLE MAN. A little man who will suffer a more painful and complicated evolution than the little boy in order to become a normal woman! A little man with a smaller penis. A disadvantaged little man. A little man whose libido will suffer a greater repression, and yet whose faculty for sublimating instincts will remain weaker. Whose needs are less catered to

by nature and who will yet have a lesser share of culture. A more narcissistic little man because of the mediocrity of her genital organs [?].
More modest because ashamed of that unfavorable comparison. More
envious and jealous because less well endowed. Unattracted to the
social interests shared by men. A little man who would have no other
desire than to be, or remain, a man" (*Speculum* 26). In *The Daughter's
Seduction*, Jane Gallop offers an intriguing reason for the narrowness
of Irigaray's reading of Freud: "The Freud Irigaray both uses and questions is based on Jacques Lacan's reading of Freud" (*Seduction* 80). I
would agree that Irigaray's reading of Freud suffers from its indebtedness to Lacan.

13. "In mental life we find only reflections of this great antithesis [passive/
active]; and their interpretation is made more difficult by the fact, long
suspected, that no individual is limited to the methods of reaction of
a single sex but always finds some room for those of the opposite one.
. . . The fact of psychological bisexuality embarrasses all that we have
to say on the subject and makes it more difficult to describe" ("An
Example of Psychoanalytic Work" 89).

14. The full dream and analysis can be found in *The Interpretation of
Dreams*, trans. James Strachey (*SE*, V, 452–55).

15. In his analysis of the dream, Freud refers mainly to She, or Ayesha,
the heroine of *She*. He scarcely mentions the other Haggard heroine—
Maya—at all. One significant aspect of her history might explain why
Freud is reluctant to identify with her. Maya is the last in a long line
of Indians who hope to overthrow the yoke of Spanish domination and
regain control of Mexico. Her retention of identity is thus more natural than Ayesha's; it is the preservation of a royal bloodline. However,
as her story opens, her people are losing rather than gaining numbers.
Freud, who, according to H. D., sought immortality through his children ("He would live forever like Abraham, Isaac, and Jacob, in his
children's children, multiplied like the sands of the sea. That is how
it seemed to me his mind was working, and that is how, faced with
the blank wall of danger [Nazism], of physical annihilation, his mind
would work" [*Tribute* 62–63]), might have feared identifying with
Maya. For, not only are her people dwindling away, but, as the story
ends, she inadvertently destroys the remaining few and any chance of
revitalizing her race. Though identification with Ayesha threatens his
own annihilation, identification with Maya threatens annihilation of
his children and his people.

Tradition and Women's Writing: Toward a Poetics of Difference

"Women who write have for the most part until now considered themselves to be writing not as women but as writers. Such women may declare that sexual difference means nothing, that there's no attributable difference between masculine and feminine writing. . . . Most women are like this: they do someone else's—man's—writing, and in their innocence sustain it and give it voice, and end up producing writing that's in effect masculine" (Cixous, "Castration or Decapitation?" 51–52).

This quote from Hélène Cixous exposes the paradox of women's writing within the broader critical gesture of French feminism, which is the positioning of woman within the psychoanalytic postulate of sexual difference (Kuhn, "Introduction" to Cixous's "Castration or Decapitation?" 36–37). A woman's text reads as a copy of the set of works that compose a masculine Textual Law, what in more traditional terms is called Tradition. But at the same time literature written by women bears the (birth)mark of a second body, that Second Sex postulated by Simone de Beauvoir.

Are women authors of their own text or must they parody a male model of writing? If, to argue with Cixous, we recall de Beauvoir's definition of womanhood as a fundamental alterity (43–45, 48–49), then this essential Other-ness complicates a woman's entry into literature. I will sketch here my thoughts on how woman as Other appropriates the language of the One or dominant symbolic order so as to gain access to textuality. In order to be read, the female novelist, short-story writer, or poet is forced to assimilate the norms governing the canon of Master-Works. From the corners of "a room of one's own," a woman peers through the looking-glass of literature in order to transform her individual experience into Imagination.

Yet she finds that her only mirror is a language transparent on one side and opaque on the other. Like her male counterpart, the female subject is at once positioned and structured by language, but the difference lies in that a woman's relationship to language remains paradoxical, as the word is simultaneously foreign and familiar to her. By forming part of a linguistic community (*parole*), woman necessarily assimilates a *langue* or system. But, at the same time, she lives outside of language, dwells in a foreign tongue, because she has been excluded from the textual code that writers transmit to each other from generation to generation. The cultural past is composed of works written by Male Masters and heavy with the weight of intertextuality—the notion of Tradition as Archive.

Can an alternative tradition be set up, a labyrinth of works produced by the Female Imagination at the turning points of history and in specific linguistic contexts? Or, within the confines of difference, must women's writing be assessed and interpreted in conformity to the dominant literary canon? In order to determine whether Cixous's proposal of a sexually marked writing is, in fact, a viable alternative, I will review two "traditional" definitions of Tradition, those offered by T. S. Eliot and the Mexican poet Octavio Paz.

In his classic essay "Tradition and the Individual Talent," T. S. Eliot defines tradition as the artistic sensibility that a nation unified by a common language manifests over historical time. Let us redefine Eliot's view of tradition to include the legacy of styles, genres, and literary forms practiced in a specific geographic setting, as well as in a restricted time frame. In other words, I am expanding Eliot's term to imply a tradition of writing or *écriture*. For Eliot, Tradition is inseparable from the "critical turn of mind" (3), since criticism is the invisible current that determines the flow of creative literature. The analysis of sacred and secular works orchestrates a textual canon, but it is the critic who writes the score. To place a work within tradition means to examine its relation to a legacy of writing; it also means determining to what extent convention has influenced literary form. This step necessarily involves submitting the work to critical evaluation in order to judge its stylistic features against the background of *écriture*.

With this definition in mind, I want to show how this "two-way mirror" of tradition affects the possibility of women's writing. Poet-critics like T. S. Eliot and the Mexican Octavio Paz consider tradition

in terms of a continuous fluctuation between artistic experiment
and conformity to preexisting textual models. I will explore how
both Eliot and Paz ground their poetics on the notion of Tradition as
an ideal and almost static order of books, a pillar of masterworks. In
my view, this is the building block of a masculinely connoted poetics
—what Cixous calls a *"marked* writing" (Cixous, "The Laugh of the
Medusa," 249)—whose sexual stamp is the emphasis on Textual Law.
How do Eliot and Paz conceive the inheritance of poetic language
and the exchange of literary models among writers? Within the erect
tower of books, is there "a room of one's own" for a feminine textual space? These questions will lead us to the trace of a feminine
poetics left by Cixous and Kristeva (I am using the adjective in the
French sense of *écriture féminine,* based on the postulate of a specificity of women's writing. Hence this usage absorbs the distinction
made in English between the social construct implied by *feminine*
and the biological mark signaled by *female,* so as to convey both
gender and sex with the same term [Moi 97]. My gesture recuperates
"the feminine" to describe the imaginative invention of womanhood
through literature, in the Spanish sense of *lo femenino* as essence
and experience). How is Tradition en*gender*ed—and encoded—from
the *other* side of difference? Is there a written or a blank page across
the biological divide?

In "Tradition and the Individual Talent," T. S. Eliot reveals
the contradiction inherent in the concept of literary tradition. On
the one hand, the work of art must yield to the accepted conventions of reading and writing; but, on the other hand, the literary
artifact should strive for originality. In his essay *Children of the
Mire* Octavio Paz explores the paradoxical "tradition against itself"
of modernity in terms of a temporal discontinuity. What constitutes the modern tradition is the constant renewal of literary forms,
as contemporary textual practices either reject established literary
models or else, in reverse motion, privilege certain dominant genres,
styles or verse patterns (3–4).

The constant ebb and flow of forms seeks to establish, in turn,
an *alternative* tradition, a "tradition against itself" defined precisely
by the renewal of cultural conventions or by textual play; in Paz's
words, by "rotating signs" in perpetual innovation (1–2). In the same
way that Eliot incorporates a "critical turn of mind" within tradition,
so Paz discovers in modernity the radical, subversive function of

criticism. "What distinguishes our modernity from that of other ages is not our cult of the new and surprising, . . . but the fact that it is a rejection, a criticism of the immediate past, an interruption of continuity. Modern art is not only the offspring of the age of criticism, it is also its own critic. The new is not exactly the modern, unless it carries a double explosive charge: the negation of the past and the affirmation of something different" (3).

Both Eliot and Paz gloss a *temporal* concept of tradition, since their poetics have as points of departure the influence of past literary models and simultaneously the imperative of formal experimentation. Though separated by their respective linguistic and cultural universes, both poets are united in a shared concern for the literary *avant-garde*. Whereas Paz accentuates change, Eliot reinforces convention, making both extremes a part of the paradoxical concept of tradition. Eliot, however, puts emphasis above all on the continuity of literature, on its preservation as a semistatic or seemingly atemporal order. Hence Eliot's definition of the term *tradition* absorbs the very sense of temporality on which it is founded: "Tradition is a matter of much wider significance. It cannot be inherited, and if you want it you must obtain it by great labor. It involves . . . the historical sense, . . . and the historical sense involves a perception, not only of the pastness of the past, but of its presence . . ." (3).

In a "masculinely marked" poetics, such a historical perspective is attained when the poet strikes up active dialogue with his precursors, not only with poets of his own speech (*parole*), but also with the poets of classical antiquity and the European mainstream. This dialogue-in-the-imagination with preceding generations of poets conditions the modern poet's "historical sense." At the same time, and paradoxically, it foments in the poet of today a sensation of permanence, a taste for the nontemporal, which, in turn, characterizes his contemporaneous "tradition-ality:" "This historical sense, which is a sense of the timeless as well as of the temporal and of the timeless and of the temporal together, is what makes a writer traditional. And it is at the same time what makes a writer most acutely conscious of his place in time, of his own contemporaneity" (4). Eliot's conclusion sets the tempo of that contradictory lapse between past and present implicit in the concept of tradition. Modern poetry is written in an "off-beat," for, in order to feel the pulse of *his* own history, the poet has to go back in time and follow the measure of his precursors.

At first glance, the temporal view of tradition that Eliot advances reads as a "neutral" concept, charged as it is with universal implications. To echo Eliot's own appraisal of "Tradition and the Individual Talent," he appears to formulate an "Impersonal theory of poetry" (7). But when he affirms that "the historical sense compels a man to write not merely with his own generation in his bones," he obviously thrusts creative endeavor onto the male gender (4). Though Eliot aspires to "depersonalize" art, his approach to poetry denies woman the right to a poetic inheritance. Eliot's imaginary patrimony has no room for the woman poet, just as it excludes non-European traditions marginal to the Arch-Text of the West.

If from Eliot's perspective we conceive an alternative tradition of women's writing, it becomes apparent that the accepted notion of Tradition implies an (un)conscious rejection of woman. Not only is the woman writer condemned to marginality, but also the solitude of her creative act is greater, because she is not supported by a literary community in the same way as the "individual talent" of the male writer. Although Eliot speaks of an imaginary dialog among poets, this "intertextuality" is constructed, nevertheless, on the transmission of knowledge from one school of literature to another. A woman is less able to write "with her own generation in her bones," as Eliot conjectures, because women writers, as a general rule, do not congregate in "clans" and literary groups as do their male counterparts. Paraphrasing Virginia Woolf, critic Elaine Showalter claims in *A Literature of Their Own* that "each generation of women writers has found itself, in a sense, without a history, [and has been] forced to rediscover the past anew, forging again and again the consciousness of their sex" (11–12).

Woman is forbidden access to her own tradition, precisely because "traditionally" women's writing has been considered a forbidden book, a literature enclosed within four walls, an abandoned and forsaken body. In *A Room of One's Own*, Virginia Woolf recalls the way in which Jane Austen hid her pages from the eyes of servants, visitors, and relatives (70). "For masterpieces are not single and solitary births; they are the outcome of many years of thinking in common. . . ," remarks Woolf (68–69). She traces the emergence of a narrative tradition in nineteenth-century England to the pioneer women that had based their material existence on the craft of writing the century before (68). Still, Woolf recognizes the difficulty that women writers have to insert themselves in an imaginary relationship with a literary past. Speaking of the Brontë sisters and of Jane Austen, Woolf claims that "they had no tradition behind them, or one so short and partial that it was of little help." (79). Unlike Eliot's hypothetical poet, women's literary experience is marked by discontinuity and lack: "For we think back through our mothers if we are women. It is useless to go to the great men writers for help, however much one may go to them for pleasure," adds Woolf (79).

In contrast to the Male Canon available to men, in British literary history the woman writer has recourse to the "great tradition" of women's literature (as Elaine Showalter has named it): Charlotte and Emily Brontë, George Eliot, and Jane Austen (Woolf 69; Showalter, "Literary Criticism," 439). Each of these four writers "revolutionized," in Paz's words, the genre of the novel. As Woolf points out in *A Room of One's Own*, for Austen, Eliot, and the Brontës to do this, they literally had to "steal" the book from men, because male models of writing did not offer the flexibility needed to de-scribe difference. In order to translate feminine intimacy into literature, a fundamental instrument of writing was needed: the sentence itself (79–80). Woolf explains how the rhetorical pattern practiced in the literature of the period gives rise to "a man's sentence" and hence to a distinctively masculine mode of writing (79). The "masculine" sentence sums up the peculiar sensibility, world view, and gift of language that testifies to a man's "natural" appropriation of the literary legacy. For Virginia Woolf, it also influences the dominant style that will set the scriptural profile of each successive period in literary history. In other words, Eliot's poetic inheritance is circulated by the vehicle of style, since only a shared *écriture* guarantees a reciprocal influence among writers of the same generation.

Eliot's hypothetical (male) talent is surrounded by a continuum of living and dead poets with whom he can establish literary rapport, through the medium of an "inherited" verbal art. By contrast, women novelists had to begin by finding an adequate syntax, a proper wording, a sentence of their own, for only on this basis could women originate their own textual models. In Woolf's account, this process begins with the woman writer's initial contact with the male canon and the necessary break with it, and culminates with the rise of the nineteenth century novel of feminine authorship. With their respective contributions to the novel form, four British novelists inaugurate the "tradition against itself" that is women's writing. But this "room of one's own" in the edifice of tradition was only partially built on the block laid down by Eliot—the Law that makes tradition not an inheritance but rather an acquisition ("Some can absorb knowledge, the more tardy must sweat for it," Eliot, 6). In Woolf's account of women in fiction, women acquire the mainstream canon only insofar as they assimilate a genre that, like the novel, is adaptable to their needs (80). But the woman writer must carry this legacy further than the male writer, and invent her own grammar, letter, forms, and conventions (80). More than the acquisition of a past history of writing, Woolf believes that the woman writer is formed by life experience (73). Ultimately, however, she argues that woman should write without a consciousness of sex (108)—Woolf's conclusions to *A Room of One's Own* raise the question once more of an alternative tradition of women's writing.

Must the woman writer forge her work unconscious of the narrators, essayists, and poets that preceded her? Although from the nineteenth to the twentieth century women make the transition from Jane Austen's drawing-room to Virginia Woolf's "Oxbridge," the female writer still needs to recuperate those texts that are lost, mutilated, or repressed in her cultural past. This archaic memory of a woman's textual body leaves a trace on the individual writer's "mystic writing pad" (Derrida, "Freud and the Scene of Writing," 106–17). The slow accumulation of text upon text, of woman's scriptural fabric, will gradually deposit the sediment of a Feminine Imagination or creative unconscious. Through the long tunnel of a woman's textual memory, the female writer must go in search of the sentence that will in-scribe her *differently*.

A metaphor of this insertion into the Feminine Imagination can be found in the story "Las islas nuevas" ("The New Islands") by the Chilean María Luisa Bombal. Yolanda, the protagonist, appears to Juan Manuel, the man in love with her, as an elusive medusa, in a scene in which he seeks to find one of the "new" islands that mysteriously vanish from view: "The new islands have disappeared. . . . Where was the first one? Here. No, there. No, here it was. He leans over the water to look for it, convinced however that his eyes could never follow it in its vertiginous drop below, never reach the dark depths of mire and seaweeds to which the island has returned once more" (my translation 80–81). Just like Juan Manuel, the woman writer has to delve into the mirage of Imagination, or creative unconscious, and look for the fleeting "new island" that is her own creative text.

Bombal's description of an undifferentiated, preverbal Imagination situated in an archaic past suggests a "feminine" access to tradition, which is reminiscent of Julia Kristeva's preoedipal "semiotic" mode (Moi 161–62). Contrast this to the "masculine" imagery developed in Eliot's "Tradition and the Individual Talent," where the continuum between past and present poets is represented as stages in the edifice of Tradition. In his essay, Eliot heightens the Textual Tower to encircle the space in which the individual work of art converges with the accumulated canon of texts. This passage can be read as the cornerstone of a "masculine" poetics, for it constructs the metaphor through which the West has thought the Book—as a monument or petrified script that recalls the ancient hieroglyphic:

> The existing monuments form an ideal order among themselves, which is modified by the introduction of the new (the really new) work of art among them. The existing order is complete before the new work arrives; for order to persist after the supervention of novelty, the *whole* existing order must be, if ever so slightly, altered; and so the relations, proportions, values of each work of art toward the whole are readjusted; and this is the conformity between the old and the new. (5)

In Eliot's poetics, and in Paz's "tradition against itself," the same paradoxical concept of a literary canon is operative: an impersonal labyrinth of books, a closed edifice, an immutable wall that cracks open to allow entrance only to the work of genius—by implication, to a *gifted* man. Critic Terry Eagleton "deconstructs" the male notion of tradition as a "tower of texts" that is Eliot's vantage point on literature:

> This arbitrary construct, however, is then paradoxically imbued with the force of an absolute authority. The major works of literature form between them an ideal order, occasionally redefined by the entry of a new masterpiece. The existing classics within the cramped space of the Tradition politely reshuffle their positions to make room for

a newcomer . . . but since this newcomer must somehow have been in principle included in the Tradition all along to have gained admission at all, its entry serves to confirm that Tradition's central values. The Tradition, in other words, can never be caught napping: it has somehow mysteriously foreseen the major works still unwritten, and though these works, once produced, will occasion a revaluation of the Tradition itself, they will be effortlessly absorbed into its maw. (Eagleton 39)

Eliot's contradictory idea of Tradition, trapped as it is between continuity and change, upholds not so much an ideal erection of texts as the individual work of the poet who wants to insert himself into the Borgian "Library of Babel"—that poet being none other than Eliot himself (Eagleton 39). "The Library of Babel" is Borges's metaphoric model for the Western enclosure of Tradition: "The universe (which others calls the Library) is composed of an indefinite, perhaps an infinite, number of hexagonal galleries . . ." (79). Eliot wants to make sure that his rightful place inside the Library is that of Borges's "Man of the Book:" the famous author of the "total book" or single volume that is "the cipher and perfect compendium of *all the rest*" (Borges 85).

A comparison between Eliot and Octavio Paz verifies the continuity of a distinctively "masculine" poetics. In *Children of the Mire* Paz evokes the generational transmission of knowledge in a manner analogous to the "historical sense" postulated by Eliot. But, in contrast to Eliot, the Mexican poet emphasizes not so much the continuity of tradition as its constant "revolt"—in other words, the modern tradition's tendency to accelerate time (5–8). Modernity, situated at the turn of the century and projected toward the present, earns its name through the experiments in form and poetic expression that alter the prevailing nineteenth-century literary canon. What Paz calls a "tradition against itself" is the sign of the *avant-garde*, the discontinuous movement of forms and styles that aspires to create a new tradition, that which is defined precisely by the rejection of a literary past (1–3). The mainstay of modernity is, in Paz's redefinition, not the past but rather the present: the plurality of artistic languages, the heterogeneity of forms, the constant renewal of cultural models (8, 17).

In this way, Paz's propositions about modernity carry Eliot's hypotheses to more radical conclusions by asserting artistic experi-

mentation and change over the permanence of Canon. In spite of
this difference, both poets nevertheless structure their poetics on
the same paradoxical principle. In order to belong to tradition, a
work must strike stone; demolish the monument of Masterpieces;
break the Textual Law. For an "individual talent" to enter tradition,
then, it must *renew* the existing order, add another volume to the
Borgian Library. Hence, we render "masculine" a poetics conceived
and defined by the paradoxical time-flow that sustains tradition: an
imaginary link between past and present generations of poets (Eliot);
the disproportionate interval between a static pillar of texts and the
rotating thrust of the innovative work (Paz).

Literature written by women is a question mark to the preceding norm, since it refutes the concepts of text, time, and tradition
diffused by poet-critics like Paz and Eliot. The radical function exercised by women's writing surfaces in Hélène Cixous, the French
theorist who invades the Freudian/Lacanian *phallologocentric* psychology. The term, which Cixous derives from Derrida, results from
the combination of *phallocentrism* and *logocentrism*. The first *centrism* implies the psychoanalytic prescription of the phallus as the
mark of desire and sexual difference (Carolyn Burke 293). In this
direction, Cixous follows Derrida's critique of Lacan in "La question du style," which posits woman as a reversal of lack, her body
the emblem of "anti-castration" (Derrida, *Spurs*, 61; cf. Burke 293).
The thrust of Cixous's "Castration or Decapitation?" is to resist the
Lacanian limitation of woman to a double void ("[s]he lacks lack,"
Cixous 46), thus searching for a femininity outside the "old appara-
tus" of phallocentrism (Derrida, *Spurs*, 61). As pillars of a masculine
Symbolic, both the sign and the phallus are conceptual erections
that jointly edify the notion of a Transcendental Signifier. Cixous's
adaptation of Derrida's *phallogocentrism* virtually makes transparent the mutual implications of the terms *logos* and *phallus*. Only
the abstraction of the linguistic sign can permit the "conception" of
an absolute Letter or signifier, identified with the phallus in Lacanian psychoanalysis (Kuhn 37). The second *centrism* attacked by the
French feminists is, then, the dominance of *Logos* as Word, absolute
Presence, principle of origin, and instrument for the mastery of the
world (Burke 293; Kuhn 37n4).

Cixous's reflective/creative texts slowly transcribe their own
Symbolic, a scriptural grid of the Second Sex:

A feminine textual body is recognized by the fact that it is always endless, without ending: there's no closure, it doesn't stop, and it's this that very often makes the feminine text difficult to read. For we've learned to read works that basically pose the word "end." But this one doesn't finish, a feminine text goes on and on and at a certain moment the volume comes to an end but the writing continues and for the reader this means being thrust into the void. ("Castration or Decapitation?" 53)

To resist this dominantly male order, Cixous thus envisions the power of the feminine "sext"—"an elision of *sexes* ("sexual organs") and *textes* ("texts") (Kuhn 38n6)—an Amazon cut into the writing practices and reading habits assumed to be "natural," but that, in fact, are propagated by the male-influenced cultural tradition.

Women's literature debunks many other myths associated with the masculine notions of Text and Tradition—one of the most resistant is the concept of "passing time" or *Chronos-Logic* (Kermode 46–50). The poetics invented by Eliot and Paz project tradition toward the permanent future of literary fame, epochs that weigh down canonical variations. In contrast, a woman's text alters the paradoxical assumptions of tradition, by violating the temporal sequence that underlies writing; that is, the expectation that a Book be ordered with a beginning and an end (Cixous, "Castration or Decapitation?" 53). Quite the contrary, women's time extends itself in the seriality of repetition, in the delight of cyclic recurrence, to the rhythm of desire and *jouissance* (Kristeva 16). The Feminine Imagination projects itself onto a "monumental temporality" that goes against the static "Master-texts" petrified by Tradition. This (other) symbolic order is composed of those ancestral fertility myths that give coherence to pre-Western cultures: incest, the cult of the earth-mother, resurrection (Kristeva 16–17).

In our own time, women authors and homosexual writers such as the Argentine Manuel Puig and the Cuban Severo Sarduy within the Latin American tradition, work to replace the masculine search for origins with dispersion and fantasy. Puig's *Kiss of the Spider Woman* (1979) dissolves the socially imposed codes of masculine/feminine behavior to rescue Freud's view of an innate bisexuality at the core of the psyche ("'no individual is limited to the modes of reaction of a single sex . . . '"; Freud, "An Outline of Psychoanalysis," as quoted in Heath 62). In this novel, the homosexual character

Molina identifies himself exclusively as a seductive and subservient woman, whereas his cellmate Valentín rejects Molina's submission to the feminine stereotype. Although Valentín represents the hetero-sexual male committed to political action, he enters into a relation-ship with Molina that transcends the prison of sexual difference, both on a biological and social level. Through Molina, Valentín em-braces the "spider woman" within himself. In an essay on her own creative discovery, the Mexican novelist Julieta Campos describes the process of shifting sexual identity dramatized in Puig's novel: "But the feminine and the masculine, present in every psychic struc-ture, perform alliances and combats in each person's inner stage. . . . In that plot that is internally woven and that shapes our self-image, [one's] sexual identifications may or may not coincide, through the various phases of the formation of the psyche, with the bodily sign" (my translation 468).

If Puig invalidates the notion of sexual difference, Severo Sar-duy inscribes desire in the verbal fabric of his texts. *From Cuba with a Song* (1972) is divided into three narrative sections that embody Cuba's racial/cultural heritage in a single triad. Each fiction typifies the language of the island's Chinese, African, and Spanish popu-lations, respectively. The first tale, "By the River of Rose Ashes," opens with a seduction scene that illustrates Sarduy's Lacan-inspired economy of desire. A libidinal Spanish general goes in hot pursuit of Lotus Flower, whose "feminine mystique" is described as erotic mirage.

> Lotus Flower leaps up, and, like the fish that jumping out of water becomes a hummingbird, she flies among lianas. Now she's the white mask striped by shadows of sugar canes, now the flight of a dove, the streak of a rabbit. Try and see her. You can't. Yes! her eyes, two golden slits, snake charmer eyes, betray her. . . . She's mimicry. She's a texture—the white plaques on the trunk of a God tree—a wilted flower beneath a palm, a butterfly embossed with pupils, she is pure symmetry. (243–44)

Like Lotus Flower, Sarduy reconstructs Cuba as pure texture, allure of language, play on words. His fictions polish a linguistic veneer that invalidates the masculine, utopian longing for a return to the source, in a manner that echoes Cixous's definition of the female "sext":

[Feminine texts] work on the beginning but not on the origin. The origin is a masculine myth: I always want to know where I come from. The question "Where do children come from?" is basically a masculine, much more than a feminine, question. The quest for origins, illustrated by Oedipus, doesn't haunt a feminine unconscious. Rather, it's the beginning, or beginnings, the manner of beginning, not promptly with the phallus. . . , but starting on all sides at once, that makes a feminine writing. A feminine text begins on all sides at once, starts twenty times, thirty times, over. ("Castration or Decapitation?" 53)

Instead of the journey to the center of the earth, the seductive appearance of woman on the stage of literature.

Julia Kristeva's "Women's Time" transmits the syncopated rhythm that woman (elle) stirs up in the male temporal order: ". . . female subjectivity as it gives itself up to intuition becomes a problem with respect to a certain conception of time: time as project, teleology, linear and prospective unfolding: time as departure, progression and arrival—in other words, the time of history" (17). Under the protective cover of a progressive temporality, "mankind" makes sure to hide the anxiety of separation, the anguish produced by breaks and discontinuity. Though Paz finds it "disturbing" that "the modern era marks the acceleration of historical time" (6), his pages do not reveal the pain of severing. But the fact is that masculine chronology reflects the rigidity of ordered time in the strictness of syntactical order. In this trap of linguistic perfection, man is only evading his own finiteness, as Julia Kristeva points out: ". . . this linear time is that of language considered as the enunciation of sentences (noun + verb; topic-comment; beginning-ending); . . . time [that] rests on its own stumbling block, which is also the stumbling block of that enunciation—death" (17).

Faced with the rigid language of binary oppositions, feminine expression, parody, and other noncanonical texts delight in Difference. By violating grammatical categories, women's writing stresses ambivalence and plurality, word play and fantasy, thus uncovering the forbidden barrier between the masculine and the feminine. This limit is the very frontier of feeling (and sense), since it is also the stroke that divides the sign in the linguistic logic analyzed by Kristeva; the fine line between "sense" and "non-sense" (nonsense). Spreading out in the intervening space of difference, women's textuality does not preclude the opposite term in the deathly combination of signifier/signified, but, instead, invites exchange and fusion, verbal chant, and the writing of the body (Cixous, "The Laugh of the Medusa" 249–50, 254–56, 264).

And so, women's writing cannot be thought of in terms of an unresolved dilemma between betrayal or compliance to tradition, its rejection of or adherence to a dominant literary canon: "The options polarise along familiar lines: appropriation or separatism. Can women adapt traditionally male-dominated modes of writing and analysis to the articulation of female oppression and desire? Or should we rather . . . forg[e] others of our own? reverting, perhaps, to the traditionally feminine in order to revalidate its forms (formlessness?) and preoccupations—rediscovering subjectivity; the language of feeling; ourselves" (Jacobus 14).

Even though the debate on *écriture féminine* continues in literary criticism, it can be refashioned from another theoretical vantage point. Like the parallel poetics of Eliot and Paz, critical speculation on women's writing (en)genders its own Imaginary, a poetics disguised as paradox that does not contradict, however, the postulate of Difference. From writing that is folded in upon itself like the female sex (Cixous), one shifts to the effect of *difference* based on a double definition. The term implies the biological split between the two sexes, but also the repercussions of this division in the constitution of the subject and the organization of male/female sexuality, as theorized by Freudian/Lacanian psychology (a full discussion of the development of the concept of difference in psychoanalysis can be found in Heath 50–78). Freud's understanding of the connection between the biological and the psychological remains the basis for theoretical speculation on difference:

> We are faced here with the great enigma of the biological fact of the duality of the sexes. . . . In mental life, we find only reflections of this great antithesis. . . . For distinguishing between male and female in mental life we make use of what is obviously an inadequate empirical and conventional equation: we call everything that is strong and active male, and everything that is weak and passive female. ("An Outline of Psychoanalysis" as quoted in Heath 62)

The position ascribed to woman in the order of phallic dominance is that of being *different* from man, a difference in nature that comes to rule social and sexual behavior and fixes womanhood inside an identity (Heath 70–71).

In answer to the psychoanalytic prescription of woman, writer-critics like Hélène Cixous have shown how the opposition male/ female cuts across the symbolic order, sustaining Freud's active/ passive principle and determining cultural roles for gender ("Castration or Decapitation?" 44). Cixous also critiques the Lacanian construct of lack as the missing link of femininity (46). This subversion of phallocentrism leads Cixous to the consciousness that, until very recently, feminine discourse has operated within the limits imposed by a masculine cultural order: "woman has never *her* turn to speak . . ." ("The Laugh of the Medusa" 249).

Cixous's critique of phallologocentrism forces a redefinition of difference in terms other than the Freudian dichotomy. Following Derrida's breakup of the binary pair, Cixous posits woman's "difference" as the assertion of a self-defined "womanly being," a search for authenticity that violates the "closure" of sexual opposition ("The Laugh of the Medusa" 250; Moi 108). "By writing her self, woman will return to the body which has been more than confiscated from her. . . ;" and violate the silence to which she was doomed under phallocentrism ("The Laugh of the Medusa" 250–51). The feminine voice surfaces in a writing that follows the contours of a woman's body. Difference, as redefined by Cixous, must reveal the erotic drive suppressed under patriarchy ("The Laugh of the Medusa" 256–57). A woman must look beyond the phallus, open her eyes, "return [the gaze] of difference against the difference," swoon to her desire (Heath 95; cf. the implications of the phallic position as mastery of the look in Heath 94–99). Cixous's claim for a sexually marked writing leads, then, to the analogy between text and body, script and voice (Moi 114–15).

It is not by chance that homosexual writers like Severo Sarduy have grounded their subversive poetics precisely on the correspondence between text and body. Help and Mercy, a pair of mobile "characters" who function as empty signifiers in *From Cuba with a Song*, go in quest of the Transcendental Signified. To satisfy their bodily and spiritual longing, they accompany a wooden Christ in a historical journey that ends in Havana, the island's political and cultural center. The symbol of divine incarnation, Mortal [Everyman]/

Christ undergoes a process of decomposition, but not before Help
and Mercy inscribe in their bodies the text of their desire for Him:

> [Help] tore her clothes in anger, crossed herself, and
> bought a printing set: (to Him): [sic]
>
> I will make of my body Your book,
> they will read from me!
>
> And Mercy [. . .]:
> Come, children of God:
> Here is the flesh made word!
>
> (319–20)

More than any other writer in the Latin American tradition, Sarduy
reveals the relationship between writing and eroticism that Cixous
asserts for women's writing. Just as language is a constant striving for meaning—the word always an inadequate approximation to
Sense—desire is, too, the perpetual reach for an absolute that eludes
our longing. This parallel sustains Sarduy's metaphorical equation
of writing and travesty in *Escrito sobre un cuerpo* (48), which is
dramatized in *From Cuba with a Song* by Help and Mercy's constant
transformations, changes of costume, cosmetics, and camouflage.
The rituals of impersonation not only hide the lack of a fixed sexual
identity, but they also cover up the insufficiency of language. For
Sarduy the deferment of meaning in the narrative sequence is comparable to the postergation of *jouissance* in foreplay. However, and in
paradoxical fashion, this equivalence suggestively opens up the text
to the charge of multiple connotations. *Difference* is then defined
no longer in terms of gender but rather "as a multiplicity, joyous-
ness or heterogeneity which is that of textuality itself" (Jacobus 12).
Or, in Sarduy's words, "[I]ntersexual surfaces are analogous to the
intertextual layers that constitute the literary object. Surfaces that
. . . respond to and complement each other, that outline and define
one another: that interaction of linguistic textures, that discursive
criss-crossing, that dance, that parody is writing" (my translation,
Escrito sobre un cuerpo, 48).

The recovery of difference as a textual phenomenon permits the
inscription of women's writing within a broader context. If "[w]rit-
ing, the production of meaning, becomes the site both of challenge

and Otherness" (Jacobus 12), then women's literary language is, necessarily, modern, for, in Paz's account, "[m]odernity is never itself; it is always *the other*" (1, author's italics). Where Octavio Paz situates the radical turn of modernity in a historical frame, Paul de Man considers every literary artifact as belonging, in a nontemporal sense, to a "tradition against itself," since each "individual talent" wants to begin literature anew with a work of its own invention (151–52). In this way women's writing would ideally be grounded in de Man's "literary modernity"—the flight away from tradition, the obligatory return of the work to the past and present of literature (152). The *difference* lies in that literature written by women is forced to recognize its contradictory relationship to tradition, understood as the predominance of male-inspired canonical forms. As in Virginia Woolf's account, the feminine work of art takes flight from the conventions and forms of this canon, only "to fulfill itself in a single moment" by giving imaginary form to womanhood (de Man 152).

From this perspective, women's writing can generate a poetics of difference out of its consciousness of being Other. On the one hand, it would formulate the historical experience of woman's alterity, what has been her "tradition" according to de Beauvoir; on the other, it would inscribe sexual difference in the direction traced by Cixous as a questioning of the fundamental Otherness assigned to her. But in either case, woman's literary language will be the word other-than-itself of textual difference or atemporal modernity.

Yet to reinsert women's writing into the mainstream of all literature may blur Cixous's "sexts" into the zone of indifference, the in-difference of writing as objectified script: "There is no specific identity of the feminine in writing. . . . The notion of a feminine writing that would be the property of women poses a principle of sexual identity which the experience of writing precisely calls into question" (Heath 79). On this note, texts written by women are not fundamentally *different from* other plural approaches to the textual body, as in Paz's "tradition against itself" and Sarduy's experimental "travesties." What happens, then, to the belief that women do, in fact, generate a specific—and separate—literary tradition? The poetics of difference appears to be based on as paradoxical a concept as Eliot and Paz's "tradition as monument." And this paradox arises from the interplay between a sexually marked writing, at one extreme, and, at the other, a neutral "degree-zero" of writing that would cancel out all gender distinctions.

In spite of this paradox, criticism must stake the claim of a specificity of women's writing in order to insert women's textual production within the confines of patriarchy. Textual difference cannot erase, completely, the struggle of women to appear on the literary scene, nor should it bury the layers of a Feminine Imagination that have slowly emerged from the past. Rather, the plurality of writing should be geared toward the affirmation of difference—to repeat Woolf, "[the] creative power [of women] differs greatly from the creative power of men. And one must conclude that it would be a thousand pities if it were hindered or wasted, for it was won by centuries of the most drastic discipline . . ." (91). So women's writing would recast the textual Edifice in a double movement, the first of which is the recovery of the Lost Continent of a female tradition along with the inscription of Otherness in the text. A second creative gesture entails the need to break free of patriarchal confines, by subverting the hierarchy of gender and affirming ambivalence or "in-difference" to a fixed sexual identity.

This leads us once more to the close of A Room of One's Own, and to Virginia Woolf's warning of the danger implied in writing from a position exclusive to gender. She proposes the radical alternative of literary androgyny, a nondifferentiated Imagination composed of one female half and another male half as its complement (100, 102–3). In her essay on To the Lighthouse, Gayatri Spivak points out that Woolf's propositions about the androgynous mind are presented through the persona of Mary Beton, and argues that the union between male and female principle remains unfulfilled in Woolf's own fiction (323). Yet A Room of One's Own makes clear that Woolf uses the fictional mode in order to speak, as in that final prophecy of the (be)coming of the woman poet, her belief that the lyrical voices of women today and tomorrow shall redeem the lost vocation of Shakespeare's sister (117–18). So that Woolf dons the narrative mask of Mary Beton to say the dream, to allegorize "an essentially Utopian vision of undivided consciousness" (Jacobus 20) that is the writer's unconscious wish. If the dream is not actualized in To the Lighthouse, but persists, rather, as "a preserved division" and "never [as] an androgynous synthesis," (Spivak 324), this is because the novel dramatizes precisely the woman artist's internal split (Jacobus 20).

Lily aspires to create in spite of her exclusion from art by a male-centered culture, all the while seeking a bond to an-Other force of gravity, the elusive Mrs. Ramsey—Spivak's reading of *To the Light-house* as "an attempt to articulate, by using a man as an instrument, a woman's vision of a woman" (326). In Woolf, as in every writer, the distance between poetics and production provides the clue to her imaginative reach, which is the exposure of the juncture facing women in literature.

At the crossroads, Woolf's concept of androgyny would seem to invalidate Cixous's assumption of a gender-marked writing. Yet Woolf's "man-womanly" and "woman-manly" mind (102) closely resembles Cixous's "classic conception of bisexuality," where the two components of the psyche join together in imaginary harmony ("The Laugh of the Medusa" 254; Moi 109). Moreover, Cixous's proposal for a "new" bisexuality, defined as "non-exclusion either of the difference or of one sex," has been prefigured in Woolf's own fiction ("The Laugh of the Medusa" 254). Is there not an echo here of Woolf's alternating dance between Ramsey and Lily around the charms of Mrs. Ramsey? Difference is sustained, as is also the privileging of the woman/womb as the site of production and reproduction (Spivak 324–26). This *"other bisexuality"* at the core of Cixous's poetics stresses not the balance between sexual extremes but, on the contrary, a strident affirmation and exchange of the polarities of gender ("The Laugh of the Medusa" 254–55; Moi 109).

Woolf's androgyny and Cixous's difference can be reconciled by redeeming them both in terms of the Derridean *différance* operating in language. In this light, the innovations produced by women writers—whether they be in textual models or in the reading experience—owe themselves, in the last analysis, to an (after)-effect of writing (*écriture*) (Jacobus 21). If a possible feminine poetics goes in search of an identity—both sexual and textual (Cixous, "The Laugh of the Medusa," 245, 250)—the stroke of the pen inscribes the image of the female body but it also evokes the return of the repressed. A mobile and ambivalent text would reverse the "phallologocentric" notion of the text as monument or book-of-stone. Hence sexual difference would be erased in the flow of spaces and times with which each "intruder" erodes the sacred pillar of tradition.

In this way the literary androgyny dreamed by Virginia Woolf would graft itself onto the surface of writing as "a body that is radically strange, neither man nor woman," to follow Heath's description of a "zero-degree" of writing (79). The "sext," Cixous's neologism for women's literature, would render textuality "different," new, whether it be a product of a Feminine Imaginary or of other writings that seep out from the cleavage of a binary (male-dominant) discourse. A feminine trace would in this way transcribe a specific textual identity, distill an Imaginary, without betraying the "neuterality" of *écriture*.

The practice of women's writing would also deflate the fallacies with which critics and writers have traditionally downgraded the role of woman as producer and receiver of literary texts. To name a single example from the Latin American tradition, the Argentine Julio Cortázar has proposed categories of readers that perpetuate the cultural stereotype of an active masculine principle versus a female condition trapped into passivity. Cortázar invites the reader to engage in two alternative readings of *Hopscotch* (1963). One would be a traditional, consecutive reading of the novel from the first chapter to chapter 56, an order that includes only the first two parts: "From the Other Side," narrated in Paris, and "From This Side," narrated in Buenos Aires (iii, 1, 217). Cortázar's second reading is far more innovative: he lays out a "hopscotch" or numerical sequence of chapters that permits the reader to "skip" from one part of the text to another in nonlinear succession. This alternative order consists of chapters from yet a third part of the novel entitled "From Diverse Sides," situated in the imaginary "no-man's land" of the writer Morelli's reflections on literature. If we take this second route, we learn that Cortázar's choice of readings corresponds to the theory of the novel elaborated by Morelli, a prototypical author intent on writing a modern "antinovel" (397). Morelli's narrative project sounds suspiciously like Cortázar's own "Table of Instructions" for *Hopscotch*: "To attempt on the other hand a text that would not clutch the reader but which would oblige him to become an accomplice as it whispers to him underneath the conventional exposition other more esoteric directions. Demonic writing for the female-reader (who otherwise will not get beyond the first few pages, rudely lost and scandalized, cursing at what *he* paid for the book), with a vague reverse side of hieratic writing" (my emphasis 396).

The "reader-accomplice" or the "*macho*-reader" is the only one capable of reading the narrative sequences of *Hopscotch* in a nonchronological and simultaneous order, whereas the "female-reader," given her inability to "leap" into the text, is relegated to a conventional, linear reading (Cortázar 453–54). Categories such as these sustain opposition rather than difference, and have served to deny woman a place in literary partnership.

A poetics of difference suggests a new reading of *Hopscotch* that would show how Cortázar's binarism ultimately deconstructs itself. In the first place, the "female-reader" is identified by a masculine gender pronoun (*he*) in the English translation, pointing to the possibility of androgyny and sexual inversion fully exploited in the fictions of Cortázar's generational successor, Manuel Puig. Second, the novel's strict dualistic order cancels itself out in a third alternative. For example, the narrative structure of *Hopscotch* supposedly reflects the split between "civilization" and "barbarism" that has riddled the question of national identity and cultural autonomy for Latin American writers. Oliveira plays *Hopscotch* not only in Paris and Buenos Aires but also in the intervening space between the two cities, which is the "neither here not there" of the third part. The polarity between Europe and America is resolved in the imagination—writing a novel—either Morelli's hypothetical antinovel or Cortázar's concrete *Hopscotch*. As Morelli claims in one of the "expendable chapters (351)," he stands right on "*the threshold* (493)," just as Latin American culture is situated at the margins, the supplement to an industrialized center that, paradoxically, offsets the dominance of European cultural models.

Cortázar's novel maintains, nevertheless, a blatantly *macho* bias against women; for instance, in the derogatory treatment that La Maga receives from the falsely erudite Oliveira and the other members of the Parisian Serpent Club ("It's incredible how hard it is for you to grasp abstract ideas," is a typical Oliveira statement to La Maga [76]). Yet Cortázar also makes of La Maga a symbol of a wisdom that escapes Oliveira in his overly speculative approximation of the world: "Only Oliveira knew that La Maga was always reaching those great timeless plateaus that they were all seeking through dialectics" (25). Better than any Argentine commentator, Sarduy has grasped that

. . . the meaning of La Maga . . . is that of ignorance-knowledge. La Maga ignores everything, her life is a constant interrogation, her novelistic emblem is the question mark. But this quest, as if searching were the only answer, finally inverts her ignorance. The magic of La Maga, her essence that is, is her wisdom. Deep down, she knows everything, not intellectually but mantically, not by information but by intuition. *Her lack of knowledge is a "trompe-l'oeil."* Whereas Oliveira . . . stands on the reverse of the coin: [he represents] knowledge-ignorance. (my translation, *Escrito sobre un cuerpo*, 26)

In this way, in Cortázar's novel La Maga fulfills the ambivalent role ascribed to woman by the male Symbolic:

[I]f patriarchy sees women as occupying a marginal position within the symbolic order, then it can construe them as the *limit* or borderline of that order. From a phallocentric point of view, women will then come to represent the necessary frontier between man and chaos; but because of their very marginality they will also always seem to recede into and merge with the chaos of the outside. Women seen as the limit of the symbolic order will in other words share in the disconcerting properties of *all* frontiers: they will be neither inside nor outside, neither known nor unknown. (Moi 167)

In the last analysis, this positioning of woman at the edge is the meaning of the penultimate square between "Earth" and "Heaven" in Cortázar's *Hopscotch* (476). The line between the "end-game" and the end is also the frontier of difference, the possibility of entry into woman and Otherness, a limit of transcendence significantly marked by the textual beginnings. For the first sentence of *Hopscotch* is the quest(ion) of a lost Oliveira: "Would I find La Maga?" (3).

This question, for the woman writer, translates as "Will I find the 'sext'?" Although Cixous insists that women's writing eludes rigid definitions ("The Laugh of the Medusa" 253), her invention of a "second" sext opens up the boundaries of Imagination—previously circumscribed to the script-in-stone of Tradition—to the domain of women. A poetics of difference suggests the experience of writing as the stretching of the limit, the process of "working (in) the in-between" of "sexual opposition" (Cixous, "The Laugh of the Medusa," 254, 253). Hence the precarious balance between earth and heaven mirrors the margins of the page. In that border, a (future) feminine writing (to be-come), added to the inheritance of texts written by women, will find woman in her place: "into the text—as into the world and into history—by her own movement" (Cixous, "The Laugh of the Medusa," 245).

ELISA KAY SPARKS

Old Father Nile: T. S. Eliot and Harold Bloom on the Creative Process as Spontaneous Generation

As when old father *Nilus* begins to swell,
With timely pride aboue the *Aegyptian* vale,
His fattie waues do fertile slime outwell
And ouerflow each plaine and lowly dale:
But when his later ebbe gins to auale,
Huge heaps of mudd he leaues, wherein there breed
Ten thousand kindes of creatures, partly male,
And partly female of his fruitful seed;
Such vgly monstrous shapes elsewhere may no man reed.
Edmund Spenser The Faerie Qveene, I, i, 21.

In 1977, when Susan Lanser and Evelyn Beck compiled the data for their article "[Why] Are There No Great Women Critics?: And What Difference Does It Make?" they found that only 2.4 percent of the essays in "widely used anthologies of literary criticism" were written by women (79), and that "well over half" of these essays were either androcentric—"men's theories applied to the works of men"—or practical criticism—"essays by novelists on the craft of fiction" (80). What was missing from mainstream, historical anthologies of literary criticism then—theoretical work by women and critical treatment of poetry written by women—is to a large degree still missing now. It is true that there are many more women getting literary criticism published, but only a token few are included in general collections; most work by women theorists and most work about women and lyric poetry is shunted off into volumes or sections labeled with the special interest title of "feminist criticism."

The majority of new anthologies published since 1977 are concerned with modern and contemporary criticism. Charles Kaplan's *Criticism: The Major Statements* is the only historical anthology of literary criticism originally on Lanser and Beck's list that has come out in a new edition. Seven essays have been added. Six are by men (Cleanth Brooks, Terry Eagleton, Roland Barthes, Jacques Derrida, Paul de Man, and Stanley Fish); the seventh is Adrienne Rich's "When We Dead Awaken: Writing as Revision." While it is true that this essay is both theoretical and about women's poetry, its singularity as the only essay by or about a woman in a volume purporting to be representative of the whole history of literary criticism is fairly typical.[1] Robert Con Davis's new anthology, *Contemporary Literary Criticism: Modernism Through Post-Structuralism*, has a more generous allotment of women critics. Out of a total of thirty-four essays, six are by women; however, four of those comprise the section on "The Sexual Dialectic."

Among the more specialized anthologies that have come out, representation by women is higher, but women's contributions tend to fall into thematic patterns similar to Susan Lanser and Evelyn Beck's categories. The more an anthology is concerned with practical, pedagogical issues, the more likely that its contributors and/or editors will be women; anthologies focusing on theoretical developments, especially those with strong philosophical emphases such as hermeneutics or deconstruction, tend to be edited and written by men. As Lawrence Lipking notes, "few women have cracked the admittedly mandarin but highly prestigious bastions of literary theory" (62). A generic hierarchy is also evident: articles about women writing prose fiction appear most frequently in general, male-dominated anthologies; articles about women writing poetry tend to be collected in exclusively feminist anthologies.[2]

Many feminist critics have pointed out the difficulties involved for women writing theoretical literary criticism, especially about lyric poetry. Historically, these problems are seen to have arisen from the cultural fictions that have been perpetrated about the nature of women's thought processes, that roster of stereotypical dichotomies that Elaine Showalter and Lawrence Lipking both call *argumentum ad feminam* (Showalter, *Literature* 73; Lipking 70). In their groundbreaking reappraisal of Virginia Woolf's literary criticism, Barbara Currier Bell and Carol Ohmann provided an early catalog of the supposedly unfeminine qualities of literary criticism: "the conventionally accepted ideals of critical method are linked with qualities stereotypically allotted to males: analysis, judgement, objectivity" (49). Their account of why Woolf's criticism had been ignored by the mostly male critical establishment parallels Lanser and Beck's charge that "Patriarchal culture has grudgingly learned to tolerate the woman artist; yet it continues to resist, denigrate, and mistrust woman as critic, theory-builder, or judge. The tasks which 'literary criticism' subsumes—research, evaluation, and analysis—are still viewed as exclusively male activities requiring 'masculine' powers (logic, judgement, ability to abstract) unlikely and improper in a woman" (79).

Indeed, as Showalter also points out, the pervasive identification of theoretical stances and methodological programs with an abstracting quality essential to masculinity led some early feminist critics to reject the attempt to create a feminist poetics as somehow a contradiction in terms. "For some radical feminists, methodology itself is an intellectual instrument of patriarchy, a tyrannical methodolatry which sets implicit limits to what can be questioned and discussed. . . . From this perspective, the academic demand for theory can only be heard as a threat to the feminist need for authenticity" ("Poetics" 127). A similar roster of innate inabilities predicated on sexual dichotomies is cited as having repressed the female lyric poet. Following Virginia Woolf's lament in *A Room of One's Own* that it is "the poetry that is still denied outlet," a number of feminist critics, most prominently Sandra Gilbert and Susan Gubar, have explored the ways in which "from what Woolf would call the 'masculinist' point of view, the very nature of lyric poetry is inherently incompatible with the nature of femaleness" (Woolf 80; Gilbert and Gubar, *Madwoman* 541).[3]

Historical fictions about the nature of the female mind have not been the only limitations on women writers' access to theory and poetry. Perhaps even more insidious, because more subtle and apparently impersonal, have been the ways in which definitions of the nature of literature have been constructed so as to elide or forbid female participation. There are two generic difficulties most often mentioned in accounts of women's efforts to write lyric poetry. First there is the problem that historically women's writing has been associated with the displaced societal and domestic vision typical of novelists. Margaret Homans points out that it has been particularly difficult to formulate a feminist poetics because "Lyric poetry lacks the novel's representative framework of character and plot, and a theory of feminine imagination appropriate to poetry cannot make use of historical material as effectively as can theories appropriate to the novel" (6).

In a similar vein, Gilbert and Gubar observe that writing lyric poetry demands a self-assertion not easily assumable by the average nineteenth-century woman writer. "The novelist in a sense says 'they': she works in a third person form even when constructing a first person narrative. . . . the lyric poem acts as if it is an 'effusion' . . . from a strong and assertive 'I,' a central self that is forcefully defined, whether real or imaginary. The novel, on the other hand, allows —even encourages—just the self-effacing withdrawal that society fosters in women" (Madwoman 548).

But at an even deeper level, the subject matter and even the metaphysical orientation typical of lyric poetry, especially as it has developed through the English Romantic tradition, cripple the creative impulses of the woman poet. Homans explains that Romantic poetry typically polarizes male and female into opposite roles in its quest for spiritual unity. "Where the masculine self dominates and internalizes otherness, that other is frequently identified as feminine, whether she is nature, the representation of a human woman, or some phantom of desire" (12).

As Janet Montefiore points out, such polarization deprives women of a place to stand, a person to be in the lyric genre: "A poetry that is prone to identify women with 'Woman,' fetishized object of desire (or sometimes of hatred and fear), does not lend itself readily to expressing female subjectivities" (71). Lacking a place to stand, the woman poet cannot move the world, much less speak her own mind. Gubar notes that there is a "long tradition identifying the author as a male who is primary and the female as his passive creation—a secondary object lacking autonomy, endowed with often contradictory meanings but denied intentionality. Clearly this tradition excludes women from the creation of culture" ("Blank" 295). This vision of woman as object rather than subject produces the situation described by Suzanne Juhasz as the "Double Bind of the Woman Poet"—the separation of life, where a woman fulfills the object-roles assigned to her by society, from art, where a woman takes on the freedom of the subject: "If she is 'woman,' she must fail as 'poet': 'poet' she must fail as 'woman' " (3).

What all these meditations on women's exclusion from criticism and poetry suggest is that there is something in the structural assumptions underlying the traditional distinctions basic to literary criticism that does not accommodate the female. There is much evidence that the metaphysical categories on which our canonical literary criticism is based are pervasively misaligned against both women writers and women critics. The recognition of these misalignments constitutes what Jonathan Culler describes as the "third moment" of feminist criticism when, instead of "using the concepts and categories that male critics purport to accept . . . these concepts and theoretical categories—notions of realism, of rationality, of mastery, of explanation—are themselves shown to belong to phallocentric criticism" (61–62).

The concepts and categories that most limit women's access to literary theory and lyric poetry are clustered around the issues of creativity and canon formation. Any woman, any feminist literary critic, who wants to discuss the creative process and the ways in which the individual poet enters and participates in the larger community of literary tradition, who wants to retell the myth of poetic engenderment, must confront T. S. Eliot and Harold Bloom as her two strongest, male critical precursors.

Eliot's Olympian stature as the progenitor of the New Criticism gives his account of the creative process a priority only suggested by the fact that "Tradition and the Individual Talent" is the single most reprinted essay in all anthologies covering any aspect of the history of criticism. Feminist critics have often paid tribute to his authority by alluding to this seminal essay in ways that explicitly reclaim his patronymic legacy. Ellen Moers entitled a chapter in her early classic *Literary Women* "Woman's Literary Traditions and the Individual Talent," prefacing it with a quote from Eliot's essay in which the pronouns are changed to accommodate the female (42). Sandra Gilbert and Susan Gubar frequently refer back to Eliot as the arbiter of masculine genealogy, particularly in their recent article "Tradition and the Female Talent." Based on Eliot's depiction of tradition, Bloom's more Promethean meditations on influence are proving to be equally seminal, inspiring work on female patterns of literary affiliation by not just Gilbert and Gubar but also Elizabeth Abel, Joan Feit Diehl, Margaret Homans, and Annette Kolodny.

The confrontation of Eliot and Bloom is likely to be somewhat painful for feminists, since both critics are powerful models of masculine chauvinism in the field of literary criticism. The story of Eliot's overt misogyny is yet to be fully told,[4] while Bloom's portrayal of the family romance in *The Anxiety of Influence* is exclusively paternalistic and filial. An examination of Bloom's and Eliot's theories and images can, however, provide some insight into the variety of methods that patriarchal criticism has evolved for eliding the feminine from literature. And an explication of these men's critical strategies can additionally supply a "map for rereading" their criticism, illuminating the methods feminist critics could evolve to restore their access to tradition.

At first glance, the oppositions between Eliot and Bloom seem to preclude any possible rapprochement. Bloom repeatedly emphasizes his hostility to Eliot's principles, frequently polarizing Eliot as the epitome of all he finds most unacceptable in the New Critical lineage he founded.[5] For all their apparent differences, Eliot and Bloom do, however, share many of the same basic assumptions about poetry. As many critics have pointed out, Eliot's political polemics do not fully disguise the fact that he retains a basically Romantic conception of the creative process.[6] This sublimated Romanticism produces some subtle but pervasive similarities between two critics who seem at first dogmatically irreconcilable, potentially confirming Homans's thesis that there is something in the Romantic and post-Romantic/Modernist epistemology of the creative process that is *sui generis* hostile to the female.

Although Eliot and Bloom's theories of the creative process are certainly problematic for feminist readers, there are ways in which their theories/attitudes are uniquely enriching for feminist criticism. There are three aspects of Eliot's and Bloom's poetics that are most germane to and productive for feminist analysis, each of which demonstrates a different method for circumventing women writers. First, Eliot's and Bloom's pronouncements about *tradition* elide the female as a member of the historic and social community of authors. Their peculiarly paternalistic use of kinship and genealogical metaphors to describe the nature of tradition, their common agreement on its exclusively masculine origin, contents, and general shape, their similar location of Milton as the crisis point of literary history, and their shared haunting by a competitively demonic or destructive version of the mechanics of intertextuality all conspire to construct the map of a literary territory that is no woman's land.

Second, the institutional elision of the female from history is paralleled by the way in which Eliot's and Bloom's metaphorical descriptions of the *creative process* elide the female as an individual artist. Both critics manifest sexual ambivalences in the mechanics of their metaphors that betray a repressed dis-ease with the necessary acknowledgment of a feminine presence in the process of birth.

Third, this desire to repress or forget the trace of the female on the individual level takes on a metaphysical dimension in the context of Eliot's and Bloom's accounts of the relationship between *literature and life*. Both critics attack categorical manifestations of the feminine in the form of such abstractions as "emotion" and "nature."

Each of these issues and methods can stimulate a different strategy for responding to masculine precursors. (1) Feminist readers and women writers can incorporate and undo male precursors by substituting a female point of origin and otherwise defusing an antifeminine genealogy; this is what is being done with Eliot and Bloom's formulations of literary tradition. (2) We can excavate the traces of the feminine hidden below the surface of male writers' imagery and metaphors; this can be done with Eliot's and Bloom's descriptions of the creative process. (3) We can deconstruct the contradictions involved in logocentric attempts at transcendental self-justification; this can be done by bringing out the paradoxes inherent in Eliot's and Bloom's accounts of literary autonomy and relevance.[7]

Tradition

Eliot's idea of tradition has been a fertile source for many feminist examinations of the mechanisms of literary influence and canon formation for he shares with Bloom various assumptions about the nature, origin, shape, and evolutionary trends of literary tradition. Both see literature as a monolithic unity. Eliot has an organic, almost ecological sense of "tradition" as a complex network of interrelationships between mutually influencing literary works; Bloom says that "the meaning of a poem can only be another poem" (*Anxiety* 71, 94). In both cases, however, there is a masculine exclusivity to the contents of tradition, and in Bloom's case a masculine definition of the mechanisms by which tradition operates and is passed on, that feminist critics must rebel against and substantially revise.

One of the most obvious similarities between Eliot and Bloom is their use of genealogical and kinship metaphors, the way that both describe literary tradition as a patrimony handed down from the father, to be earned by the son.[8] The *locus classicus* for Eliot's definition of tradition is the beginning pages of "Tradition and the Individual Talent" (*Essays* 4–5), where he explains the need for the poet to have "the historical sense" which "compels a man to write not merely with his own generation in his bones, but with a feeling that the whole of the literature of Europe from Homer and within it the whole literature of his own country has a simultaneous existence and composes a simultaneous order" (*Essays* 4). Tradition here is a nearly physical inheritance, a oneness of skeletal anatomy. Eliot then goes on to explain how the "test of value" for a new work of art is how well it "fits in" (5) to the legacy of past forms and ideas: "No poet, no artist of any art, has his complete meaning alone. His significance, his appreciation is the appreciation of his relation to the dead poets and artists" (4).

The famous description of the effect that a new work of art has on the tradition—how the new and old complement and transform each other—once again stresses an idea of order that is hierarchic in its linearity and monolithic in its permanence of structure. "What happens when a new work of art is created is something that happens simultaneously to all the works of art which preceded it. The existing monuments form an ideal order among themselves, which is modified by the introduction of the new (the really new) work of art among them. The existing order is complete before the new work arrives; for order to persist after the supervention of novelty, the *whole* existing order must be, if ever so slightly, altered; and so the relations, proportions, values of each work of art toward the whole are readjusted; and this is conformity between the old and the new" (*Essays* 5).

Bloom's approval of Eliot's "ideal of order" for European and English literature is clearly exhibited in the parallelism between the two critics' accounts of the beginning, the contents, the general shape, and the crisis points of literary tradition. For both, the Ur-father is Homer; Bloom echoes Eliot's "the whole of the literature of Europe from Homer" (*Essays* 4) on several occasions, most noticeably perhaps when he prophesies that "the first true break with literary continuity will be brought about in generations to come, if the burgeoning religion of Liberated Woman spreads from its clusters of enthusiasts to dominate the West. Homer will cease to be the inevitable precursor, and the rhetoric and forms of our literature may break at last from tradition" (*Map* 33).

As Bloom's comment on the women's movement makes clear, both he and Eliot implicitly define literary tradition as having an exclusively male purview. Their acts of canonization work mostly by omission. In all of the many volumes of Eliot's collected prose, there is only one essay devoted to a woman artist, a slight (SE 405–8) appreciation of Marie Lloyd, a music hall performer whom he praises as being "the expressive figure of the lower classes" (407) because of the "moral sympathy" (406) she evoked from her audiences. A search through Eliot's fugitive essays as catalogued by Donald Gallup reveals that out of 681 contributions to periodicals only a handful refer to women writers. Besides reviews of Marianne Moore's poetry (item C150) and Djuana Barnes's novel *Nightwood* (item C420), the only essays about women listed in Gallup are four obituaries honoring Virginia Woolf (C468), Mrs. Harriet Weaver (C656), Mrs. Violet Schiff (C659), and Mrs. Sylvia Beach (C664).

Similarly, in the twelve books of literary criticism Bloom has so far published—books whose major task is the wholesale redefinition of the canons of British and American literature—he has only one essay devoted to a woman writer. His "Frankenstein, or The Modern Prometheus" honors Mary Shelley's novel as "one of the most vivid versions we have of the Romantic mythology of the self" (*Ringers* 122), but nonetheless recuperates her achievement as being of a piece with the symbolic constructs of her husband and his literary companions. The only other woman writer Bloom refers to more than fleetingly is Emily Dickinson who plays an equivalent role in Bloom's version of the American lineage; his essay on "*The Native*

Strain: American Orphism" praises her while placing her entirely in a context defined by male writers (*Figures* 80).

Both critics also see this "masculinist" version of literary tradition inscribing a downward parabola, a movement from the Edenic innocence of Homer to the fragmented experience of the modern world, what Northrop Frye once called "the great Western Butterslide" theory of history ("Angels" 133). Both tell the same story of a fall from grace wherein man's natural unity of soul and self is split by the internalization of a recent historical tragedy. Curiously enough, both also see the gate back to this Edenic wholeness guarded by the same literary precursor, Milton. In "The Metaphysical Poets" (1921) Eliot first named the breakdown of the unified mind the "dissociation of sensibility," saying it happened sometime around the Protestant Reformation (*Essays* 247). Earlier, he had located its origin a bit more specifically; in "Marlowe" (1919) he noted that "After the erection of the Chinese Wall of Milton, blank verse has suffered not only arrest but retrogression" (*Essays* 100).[9] Similarly, Bloom comments on "the giant age before the flood," before Milton when generosity of indebtedness was still possible (*Anxiety* 11).[10]

The link between Eliot and Bloom goes by the hidden path of Northrop Frye, a critic whom Bloom often couples with Eliot as a progenitor of an overidealized or "Platonic" doctrine of influence. In the "Polemical Introduction" to the *Anatomy of Criticism*, Frye explicitly reveals his adoption of Eliot's definition of tradition. Quoting Eliot's "principle that the existing monuments of literature form an ideal order among themselves" as a "fundamental" critical recognition, Frye acknowledges his debt to Eliot's influence by stating that "much of this book attempts to annotate it" (*Anatomy* 18).[11]

Bloom's major quarrel with Eliot and Frye is not with their definitions of the nature, content, or form of tradition; all three define literary tradition as an autonomous, self-perpetuating order of works written by males since Homer. Instead Bloom objects to the mildness of the manner by which this male-generated lineage is passed on. Where Eliot and Frye describe an elegantly civilized game of musical chairs and benevolent entailments, Bloom sees the bloody battle of strong fathers and oedipal sons. In *A Map of Misreading* Bloom attacks both Frye and Eliot's idea of tradition as a "fiction," "a noble idealization . . . a lie against time," saying that Northrop Frye "has Platonized the dialectics of tradition, its relation to fresh creation, into what . . . turns out to be a Low Church version of T. S. Eliot's Anglo-Catholic myth of Tradition and the Individual Talent" (*Map* 30).[12] His major swerve away from his critical fathers thus takes the form of an even more intense masculinization of the dynamics of literary tradition. The use of the oedipal situation as the central trope for the mechanisms of influence leads Bloom to emphasize the defensive, competitive, warlike nature of intrapoetic relationships; because the need for asserting priority and authority involves the young poet or ephebe in an inevitable misunderstanding and belittling of his poetic fathers (*Anxiety* 8–9), the whole process by which tradition is maintained and retained takes on an aura of murderous antagonism. "If the imagination's gift comes necessarily from the perversity of the spirit, then the living labyrinth of literature is built upon the ruin of every impulse most generous in us" (*Anxiety* 85).

Although glancing attacks on Eliot and/or Frye are included in nearly every book Bloom has written,[13] Bloom's whole theory of influence rests on an assumption about the holistic, interpenetrating continuity of the literary universe that he shares with these two critical precursors. Perhaps the most obvious sign of complicity between Bloom and his elided influencers occurs in his formulation of the sixth (last and most powerful) revisionary ratio, Apophrades or "the return of the dead." A "revisionary ratio" is a strategy by which a later poet tries to adjust his relationship to a previous artist, weighing and defining the unequal balance between them. In "Apophrades" the young poet tries to even out the ratio by reversing its two sides, giving his own voice priority over the voice of his precursor so that his echoes of the past are cast back against the flow of history. A successful deployment of this revisionary ratio makes us read the poets of the past with the sense that they are imitating the future: Eliot's writing of "Prufrock" has forever changed the way we read Marvell's "To His Coy Mistress" so that "had we but world enough and time" now sounds like an echo of "there will be time." Bloom defines Apophrades as a troping (or trumping) on the stylistic authority of a precursor, a metaleptic reversal[14] by which the strong new poets "achieve a style that captures and oddly retains priority over their precursors, so that the tyranny of time is almost overturned, and one can believe, for startled moments, they are being *imitated* by their ancestors" (*Anxiety* 141).

His description of the reversal by which a line of Tennyson

or Whitman will suddenly seem as if it were written by Eliot[15] as well as his translation of Apophrades as "the return of the dead" (*Anxiety* 139) are themselves ironical inversions of Eliot's attack on the "prejudice" for originality and individuality with which "Tradition and the Individual Talent" begins: "We dwell with satisfaction upon the poet's difference from his predecessors, especially his immediate predecessors; we endeavour to find something that can be isolated in order to be enjoyed. Whereas if we approach a poet without this prejudice we shall often find that not only the best, but the most individual parts of his work may be those in which the dead poets, his ancestors, assert their immortality most vigorously" (*Essays* 4).

In fact, the appellation "return of the dead" is quite illogical for Bloom's process, which is more nearly an invasion of the dead by the living—indeed, very like what Eliot describes on the next page of "Tradition and the Individual Talent" where Eliot ends his discussion of the continuity of tradition by stating: "Whoever has approved this idea of order, of the form of a European, of English literature will not find it preposterous that the past should be altered by the present as much as the present is altered by the past" (*Essays* 5). Both Eliot and Bloom assert the power of the living over the dead, the way the new poet can reach back and impress the corpse/corpus of the past with his presence.

Feminist critics tend to reread Eliot back into Bloom, restoring the benevolence of the Eliotic idea of works changing each other's meanings as tradition evolves through time. A generous reading of this idea in *The Anxiety of Influence* is made possible by an interesting conflation of Virginia Woolf with the composite precursor-figure of Eliot and Bloom. In much feminist criticism, Virginia Woolf stands as a metonymy for the theories of Eliot and Bloom, her sense that "a woman writing thinks back through her mothers" (101) substituting for the exclusively masculine genealogies set up by Eliot's "idea of order" and Bloom's quest "to re-beget one's own self, to become one's own Great Original" (*Anxiety* 64).

This powerful reversal by which Woolf attains priority over the Eliotic account of tradition works so well because Woolf herself shares many of his crucial assumptions about the nature, origins, and development of literary tradition but is able to develop them in a feminist rather than a masculinist mode. *A Room of One's Own* can be read as a counterstatement to both "Tradition and the Individual Talent" and *The Anxiety of Influence*, one that empowers female writers and feminist readers while denuding the idea of tradition of Eliot's absolutistic aura of authority and Bloom's antagonistic aura of anxiety.

Like Eliot and Bloom, Woolf sees literature as an interactive system of texts, but she takes great care to make sure that system is imaged in figures that stress spontaneity and flexibility rather than hierarchy and rigidity. A number of her descriptions of the relations between women writers sound very like Eliot's and Bloom's pronouncements about tradition: "For masterpieces are not single and solitary births; they are the outcome of many years of thinking in common, of thinking by the body of the people, so that the experience of the mass is behind a single voice" (68–69). Indeed, at one point, outlining the creative difficulties of early women novelists she explicitly laments that "when they came to set their thoughts on paper . . . they had no tradition behind them, or one so short and partial it was of little help" (79). And when she recounts her experience of reading a first novel by a new female talent, she reminds herself that "one must read it as if it were the last volume in a fairly long series . . . as the descendant of all those other women whose circumstances I have been glancing at" (84).

For all its similarity to Eliot and Bloom, Woolf's use of kinship and genealogical metaphors is, however, interestingly juxtaposed against an opposing pattern of images she associates with the hegemonic greed of the masculine tradition. *A Room of One's Own* begins with the demurral that she is not going to offer any kind of absolute, self-contained Truth about her subject, women and fiction; she says she will produce no "nugget of pure truth to wrap up between the pages of your notebooks and keep on the mantlepiece for ever" (3–4). Instead she proposes to "develop in your presence as fully and freely as I can the train of thought which led" to her conclusions (4). The polarization of images here—hard, condensed nugget *versus* flowing thought; unit of money saved from the past *versus* immediate personal presence—extends throughout her lectures, providing an undertext for her explicit critique of masculine traditions as monolithic, monumental prisons.

The first chapter on "Oxbridge," for example, repeatedly contrasts male and female versions of tradition. Her freedom of thought "sitting on the banks of a river" fishing for ideas (5) is initially set off against her confinement to the gravel path as she walks towards the university buildings (7). Picking up her initial image of a nugget, the "unending stream of gold and silver" (9)—the legacy of generations of men that built the stone monuments of academe—is contrasted with women's living legacy of children (22), just as the succession of gates closing behind her "with gentle finality" as she leaves the men's college (13) is contrasted with the dining room "swing doors" that "swung violently to and fro" after dinner at the women's college (18) and the hotel door that "sprang open at the touch of an invisible hand" when she returns that night (24).

The apparent jumble of ideas with which this first chapter ends is, in fact, carefully constructed so as to reinforce her distinctions between two possible kinds of tradition. Remembering how she had not been allowed to enter the university library she muses: "I thought how unpleasant it is to be locked out; and I thought how it is worse perhaps to be locked in" and then goes on to think of "the safety and prosperity of the one sex and the poverty and obscurity of the other and of the effect of tradition and of the lack of tradition upon the mind of a writer" (24). Like Eliot and Bloom then, Woolf recognizes that a sense of tradition is essential to the creative process, but she differentiates between the masculine tradition that locks men in and her and other female writers out, and the swinging doors of the less orthodox female tradition.

This differentiation is particularly obvious in Woolf's treatment of Milton in A Room of One's Own, another situation where her attitudes are the mirror image of Eliot's and Bloom's. Like her two fellow critics, Woolf sees Milton as a blocking figure, the colossus whose achievement breaks literary tradition in half. But whereas Eliot and Bloom see Milton as inhibiting the future of literature, Woolf sees him as cutting off access to an engendering past. As Gilbert and Gubar point out, Milton is for Woolf "the misogynist essence of . . . patriarchal poetry" (Madwoman 188). Milton appears three times in A Room of One's Own (at the beginning, middle, and end), and each time his specter is clearly evoked as part of the pattern of monumental edifice imagery Woolf consistently uses to characterize the masculine will to power.

Milton first comes to Woolf's mind as she is thinking about Charles Lamb, a male writer whom she clearly excludes from her list of masculinist pundits. Lamb's essays with "that wild flash of imagination, that lightning crack of genius in the middle of them which leaves them flawed and imperfect but starred with poetry" (7) are contrasted to the unchangeable stolidity of Milton's poetry. Woolf remembers that Lamb was shocked to discover that Milton had revised *Lycidas*: "To think of Milton changing the words in that poem seemed to him a sort of sacrilege" (7). The quasi-religious authority thus imputed to Milton, whose works seem to Lamb as though graven in stone, is then transferred to the masculine institution of the university. Proceeding toward the library that preserves the manuscript of *Lycidas*, Woolf is denied entrance by a figure "like a guardian angel barring the way with a flutter of black gown instead of white wings" who tells her that "ladies are only admitted to the library if accompanied by a Fellow of the College" (7–8).

This association of Milton with authority, religion, and edifice imagery is carried over to his next appearance in *A Room of One's Own*, at the end of the second chapter. Chapter one focused on the institution/edifice of the university and women's lack of access to education in its environs; chapter two is located in the British Museum, "another department of the factory" of London—one that has "swing doors" (26) that let women in, but is nonetheless filled with books whose titles bring to mind "innumerable clergymen mounting their platforms and pulpits" (27). Reading books by men about women in the British Museum Library reconfirms Woolf's thesis that the masculinist tradition of thinking locks men in as much as women out. Her discovery of the "instinct for possession, the rage for acquisition" (38), which drives men's lives in competition and to their deaths in war, is encapsulated at the end of the chapter by her encounter with a Miltonic piece of architecture, the Admiralty Arch: a "monument" like many other avenues "given up to trophies and cannon" that celebrates the masculine idea of glory (39). The arch, its surrounding buildings, and the statue of the Duke of Cambridge at its center represent the confines of masculine ideas, as contrasted with the wide sky representing the freedom to think granted to a woman of independent means. "Indeed my aunt's legacy unveiled the sky to me, and substituted for the large and imposing figure of a gentleman, which Milton recommended for my perpetual adoration, a view of the open sky" (89). Milton's appearance here seems gratuitous, except in so far as he is once again associated with a stone edifice glorifying male authority.

Woolf's last reference to Milton comes in her peroration; this is the injunction to "look past Milton's bogey," which Gilbert and Gubar discuss in *Madwoman* (188).[16] As they explain, this specter from the past is a "murderous phantom that, if it didn't actually kill 'Judith Shakespeare,' has helped keep her dead for hundreds of years" (188). Once again male traditions and female traditions are juxtaposed by Woolf, this time in a context that is her version of the Eliotic and Bloomian Apophrades or invasion of the dead by the living. The ghost of Milton is a "bogey," threatening to "shut out the view" of reality, trees, and sky (Woolf 118), but the ghost of Judith Shakespeare walks as an enabling presence. "This poet who never wrote a word and was buried at the crossroads still lives. She lives in you and me, and in many other women who are not here tonight, for they are washing up the dishes and putting the children to bed. But she lives; for great poets do not die; they are continuing presences; they need only the opportunity to walk among us in the flesh" (117).

For Eliot and Bloom, the relation of the individual to tradition is always tinged with the anxieties of a power relationship. The idea of tradition as a kind of interanimating organic unity is always on the verge of being hardened into a more rigid "idea of order." The threat of domination by tradition produces its necessary compensation in the form of their mutual hypothesis that the present can rewrite the past, the fear of invasion by history giving rise to the impulse to take the battle into the precursor's territory. Woolf's revision of them replaces, in Lipking's words, "authority" with "affiliation," turning war into "conversation" (Lipking 73), bringing the dead to life in the present instead of invading the past to nail down the corpses of potential vampires. From Woolf's perspective, Eliot and Bloom look like wandering Osirises who mourn the fragmented state of the literary corpus but do not acknowledge the existence of an Isis to pick up the pieces of the ruined edifice. Perhaps they are afraid she will find only thirteen pieces and, as in the past, reconstitute the body of her husband and brother without a phallus.

The Creative Process

The possibilities of using Eliot and Bloom to construct an alternative feminist poetics are also implied in the sexual paradoxes to be found in their metaphorical descriptions of the creative process. On the surface, both critics seek to perpetrate a myth of exclusively masculine engenderment. Like Milton they hold to a "patriarchal etiology that defines a solitary Father God as the only creator of all things" and set up this "cosmic author" as "the soul legitimate model for all earthly authors" (Gilbert and Gubar, *Madwoman* 188). However, if one looks closely, it becomes apparent that both men establish their definitions of poetic creativity on analogies and that both analogies are at a fundamental level sexually ambivalent.[17]

Eliot's catalyst image in "Tradition and the Individual Talent" is often quoted as the definitive description of the creative process for both his own criticism and that of his followers, the New Critics. The analogical image appears in two places in the essay.[18] First the catalyst is brought in to show how art may "approach the condition of science" in its "depersonalization." "I, therefore, invite you to consider, as a suggestive analogy, the action which takes place when a bit of finely filiated platinum is introduced into a chamber containing oxygen and sulphur dioxide" (*Essays* 7).

In its next appearance the image is much more complex, but is still designed to emphasize the impersonality with which the poet's mind engages in creative activity. "When the two gases previously mentioned are mixed in the presence of a filament of platinum, they form sulphurous acid. This combination takes place only if the platinum is present; nevertheless the newly formed acid contains no trace of platinum, and the platinum itself is apparently unaffected; has remained inert, neutral, and unchanged. The mind of the poet is the shred of platinum. It may partially or exclusively operate upon the experience of the man himself; but, the more perfect the artist, the more completely separate in him will be the man who suffers and the mind which creates; the more perfectly will the mind digest and transmute the passions which are its material" (*Essays* 7–8).

There is a crucial oscillation between the terms of this analogy. Is the poet's mind the womblike chamber in which the aesthetic reaction takes place, an enclosing space into which experience enters and inside which it is transformed? Or is the poet's mind the phallic filament ("finely filiated") that enters the yellow fog of reality and precipitates changes, causing the gas to become an acid but remaining masculinely unmoved, uncorroded by its contact with emotions? Is the process wholly involuntary, unconscious, and automatic, the mechanical creation of what Holloway calls a "tour de force linguistic protein molecule" (171)? Or does the poet consciously will and intend his choices?

Bloom's explanation of literary self-paternity is similarly ambivalent. For one thing, he manages to avoid throughout all of *The Anxiety of Influence* (except for one place, discussed below) any mention that it is usually women who give birth. Over and over again he says that the poet is engendering himself, being reborn—and always the process is exclusively male: "He must be self-begotten, he must engender himself upon the Muse his mother" (*Anxiety* 37). The poet is clearly the phallus in this passage, but where's the womb? If the male poet "gives birth to his own father" (*Anxiety* 26) doesn't that provide him with a female anatomy? The male poet becomes hermaphroditic, retaining no positive attribute of the female but only her negative inner space as a precondition of his own fertility.

Bloom's description of the parthenogenesis (paternogenesis?) by which the son creates the father is startlingly like Hélène Cixous's description of the way in which Western philosophy has always described the world in terms of hierarchical couples, dialectics in which one term—that associated with the female—is repeatedly elided. Citing a poem by Mallarmé as a "tragic dream, a father lamenting the mystery of paternity," Cixous explains how "in the extreme[,] the world of 'being' can function to the exclusion of the mother. No need for mother—provided that there is something of the maternal: and it is the father then who acts as—is—the mother." The situation she describes in Mallarmé's poem is exactly that of the young poet in Bloom; the mother is gone. "She does not exist, she may be nonexistent; but there must be something of her. Of woman, upon whom he no longer depends, he retains only this space, always virginal, matter subjected to the desire that he wishes to imprint" (Cixous, "Sorties," 92).[19]

There are two places in particular where the sexual ambiguity in Bloom's version of the creative process becomes even more noticeable. The first is where he quotes Isaiah, saying that the poet is like a woman in childbirth.

Like as a woman with child, that draweth near the time of her
delivery, is in pain and crieth out in her pangs; so have we been in thy
sight, O Lord.

We have been with child, we have been in pain, we have as it were
brought forth wind; we have not wrought any deliverance in the earth;
neither have the inhabitants of the world fallen.

The dead men shall live, together with my dead body shall they
arise. Awake and sing, ye that dwell in dust: for thy dew is as the dew
of herbs, and the earth shall cast out the dead. (*Anxiety* 73)

Here, in the voice of one of Bloom's own self-proclaimed precursors,
the trace of the female leaks through. In talking about the patrilin-
eage of Isaiah and Kierkegaard, Bloom admits the fear that the poet,
unlike the woman, will give birth only to wind. Bloom's wind has an
interesting resemblance to Eliot's sulphur dioxide: the "yellow fog"
that precedes the acid in his catalytic experiment, that is present in
"Prufrock" as the anesthetizing atmosphere enfolding the man unable to act on his emotions, that he refers to in "East Coker" III as
the "eructation of unhealthy souls."

A few pages later, Bloom seems to try to cover this trace,
this eructation, in his description of Error, the true "God of Poets"
(*Anxiety* 78). Bloom says that Error is a "bald gnome . . . who
lives at the back of a cave." Although the womblike cave again
remains, Bloom has evidently forgotten/misremembered Spenser's
Error whose threateningly androgynous anatomy is described as
being originally female.

> he saw the vgly monster plaine,
> Halfe like a serpent horribly displaide,
> But th'other halfe did woman's shape retaine,
> Most lothsome, filthie, foule, and full of vile disdaine.
>
> *The Faerie Qveene*, I, i, 14

An ironic reversal of "the figure of the youth as a virile poet," Bloom's
Error is bald and shrunken, an aging Prufrock who is quite the
opposite of Spenser's figure—definitively female in her fecundity.

> Of her there bred
> A thousand yong ones, which she dayly fed,
> Sucking vpon her poisonous dugs.
>
> *The Faerie Qveene*, I, i, 15

It is this *female* Error, whose "vomit full of bookes and papers was," who *really* can claim the demonic productivity Bloom's ephebes aspire to. It is surely an uncanny "return of the repressed" that Bloom's attempt to eliminate the female from the creative process produces such a correlative draining of masculinity. One wonders if there is a similar economy operating in Prufrock, where the inability to invoke the Presence of the woman except in synecdoches of dismembered body parts such as hands, eyes, arms, and fingers or the metonymy of pieces of clothing such as bracelets, shawls, and skirt hems is characteristic of an impotent persona half a century older than the twenty-three year-old poet.

Literature and Life

Both Eliot and Bloom are at least subliminally aware of the dangers of their own ambivalences, and both try to avoid it in similar ways—by an almost frightening rage for purity, which only barely disguises a fear and hatred of the female/feminine as traditionally associated with nature and with emotions. The two critics have fairly similar, contextual and antimimetic definitions of the autonomous nature of poetry. That is, both think that poetry is created out of poetry and not, strictly speaking, out of life. This defense of poetic autonomy is closely allied with ambivalence about the role of emotion in creating poetry and the role of nature as subject matter for inspiration.[20]

Throughout all of Eliot's work, both poetry and prose, there is a consistent intertangling of images and tropes associated with emotions, nature, and women. All of "Tradition and the Individual Talent" bespeaks the same desperate urge to run away from the "terror" of emotion that Eliot exhibits in "The Love Song of J. Alfred Prufrock."[21] His very use of the catalyst image is an effort to sterilize the emotions by making them scientifically impersonal, to burn the light brown hair off those porcelain arms. And then there is that moment—perhaps the most interesting one in the essay—when the cat comes slashing out of the bag: "But, of course, only those who have personality and emotions know what it means to want to escape these things" (*Essays* 10–11).

"Tradition and the Individual Talent" is typical of much of Eliot's criticism in simultaneously including and avoiding emotion.

Eliot's version of the creative process is basically expressive: poetry begins with emotions that the poet transforms into art. But somewhere along the way, he always finds it necessary to defuse emotions of that originating power, to make them safe and controllable in the objective context of art.[22]

That Eliot's rejection of emotion is a rejection of the female is the burden of "Prufrock" and a score of other early poems. As Gregory Jay points out, this rejection of women and emotions in Eliot's early poetry is also associated with a rejection of nature and the pleasures of the senses. "A boy's joy in his senses gives way to an almost morbid recoiling from sight, smell, hearing, taste, and touch. The things of this earth, including women, appear largely in their negation, while poetic and critical energy is invested in the countering orders of Eliot's cultural acquisitions" (27).

The replacement of the messiness of emotions, senses, nature, and women with the masculine control and neatness of the "idea of order" in tradition is especially clear in Jay's interpretation of "Gerontion." As he points out, in the typescript it was originally "Nature" not "History" that had "many cunning passages, contrived corridors" (22). And it is this "She" that deceives and empties out the questor in the poem, a "condensation of history and nature in the metaphor of woman" that places the blame for all debilitation on the illusory, betraying Other (Jay 23).

Perhaps the most shocking manifestation of this connection between emotions, poetry, and women is Eliot's response to Conrad Aiken's congratulations on the publication of Eliot's *Poems, 1909–1925*. As Aiken wrote in a letter to a friend, the reply to his congratulatory note was "a page torn out of the Midwives Gazette: instructions to those about to take exams for nurseing (*sic*) certificates. At the top, T. S. E. had underlined the words *Model Answers*. Under this was a column descriptive of various forms of vaginal discharge, normal and abnormal. Here the words *blood, mucous,* and *shreds of mucous* had been underlined with a pen, and lower down also the phrase *purulent offensive discharge*. Otherwise, no comment" (Aiken 109).

There would be some excuse for a scatological response from Eliot, for Aiken had written him from a hospital bed where he was recovering from a hemorrhoidectomy. But there is an inexplicable violence of disgust exhibited by Eliot about the subject of his own poetry, a virulent intensification of the sulphuric emetic identified with the creation of poetry in "Tradition and the Individual Talent," a sense that because poetry is made from emotions and is about women it must be a *"purulent offensive discharge."*

For Bloom, the rage for purity takes the form of what he quite early defined as the antinaturalism of Romantic poetry. Throughout Bloom's work there is a consistent opposition between nature, the body, and the senses (all traditionally and explicitly associated with the female) and the absolute imaginative autonomy he associates with the masculine strength of true poetic vision. *The Anxiety of Influence* begins with an epigraph from Wallace Stevens, calling for a new kind of criticism that would prove "that the theory / Of poetry is the theory of life" (4), but *life* for Bloom is exclusively spiritual and mental life, just as *humanism* for him often involves a transcendence and rejecting of the merely human body. The major point of *The Visionary Company: A Reading of English Romantic Poetry,* (1961; 1971) is that the Romantic poets are "not poets of Nature" (vii). And his reading of them follows an evaluative hierarchy based on the degree of trust exhibited in the autonomy of the imagination. Nature and her visual beauties are for Bloom as for his mentor Blake "Dirt upon my feet No part of Me" (Blake 555). In "The Visionary Cinema of Romantic Poetry" (1967) Bloom blames Eliot for being too wedded to nature and reality; he does not in Stevens's words "make the visible a little hard to see" (*Ringers* 38). The absolute imaginative autonomy of Romantic poetry includes also a "freedom from the tyranny of the bodily eye" (*Ringers* 38). In "The Internalization of the Quest Romance" (1968), Bloom's major position statement on Romanticism, he similarly maintains that the central choice of the Romantic imagination is between "either sustaining its own integrity or yielding to the illusory beauty of nature" (*Ringers* 16). These oppositions are built into a major symbolic structure in *The Anxiety of Influence*, where Bloom praises the "antithetical questors" the poets who pose themselves against nature, who are like the "young . . . pseudo-gnostics" who believe in "an essential purity that constituted their true selves and could not be touched by mere natural experience" (*Anxiety* 85).

As Margaret Homans makes clear in her introduction to *Women Writers and Poetic Identity*, Bloom is thus involved in a double denial of the female. First, by accepting the sexualized Romantic epistemology he denies her the role of creator: woman is the object of the internalized quest romance and therefore cannot be the subject who does the questing. Then, by exaggerating Eliot's post-Romantic sense of the autonomy of poetry he denies her in the role of other/external reality. The poet quests for a unity of self, not of self and other; the "poet-hero" is "not a seeker after nature but after his own mature powers" (Ringers 26). Bloom's focus on imaginative unity of selfhood elides the female from a quest whose "triumph" is the completion of "a dialectic of love by uniting the Imagination with its bride, a transformed, ongoing creation of the Imagination rather than a redeemed nature" (Ringers 28). For Bloom, the Romantic poet chooses between the "dark enchantment" of an illusory attraction to the feminine wiles of nature or the masculine daring of an imaginative autonomy that borders on solipsism (Ringers 31, 18).

Eliot and Bloom are major (if largely unconscious) coconspirators in what the French feminist Hélène Cixous calls "the logocentric project . . . to found (fund) phallocentrism, to insure for masculine order a rationale equal to history itself" ("Sorties" 93). Jay cites this drive to logocentrism as a major impetus for Eliot's poetry, a philosophical urge for order in which misogyny is not accidental but foundational. According to Jay: "Logocentrism translates differences within experience into a difference between opposing identities that are then arranged in a hierarchy. The Center exerts its authority through the exclusion of an Other whose trace can never be elided" (Jay 12n3).

Eliot's and Bloom's descriptions of the creative process can be seen as typical examples of the strategies of logocentrism, or more specifically phallogocentrism. Each creates an opposition between a valued Origin associated with masculinity and devalued supplement associated with femininity. They thus participate in the fairly common attempt to create a totally male myth of the engenderment of the word/world. They are the latest in a lineage of logocentric literary critics perpetrating a metaphorically defeminized version of the creative process that figuratively divests women from literary history both as participants in the battles of canon formation and as individual writers. But in the inevitable return of deconstructive processes, it is possible to recognize traces of the elided female Other circling back to reappear in their criticism.[23] Having perceived these traces, it then becomes possible for a feminist critic to use aspects of their critical theories to construct a version of poetic/literary history which includes and empowers the female.

NOTES

1. Historical anthologies from the Greeks to the present which are still in print but unrevised have equally few contributions by women. Walter Jackson Bate's *Criticism: The Major Texts* (Harcourt, 1952 1970) contains one essay by Virginia Woolf. Smith and Parks, *The Great Critics* (Norton, 1967) lists no women critics in its 787 pages or in its 133 page supplement. And, as Lipking points out, "the standard, large-scale anthology of *Critical Theory Since Plato* [Ed. Hazard Adams, 1971] does not find room for a single woman in its 1249 double-columned, small printed pages" (61).

2. See Appendix A, for a chart showing the sex of contributors to recent anthologies. The anthologies that maintain the most equal balance between the sexes are edited by Henry Louis Gates, Randolph Pope, and Susan Suleiman and Inge Crosman. It is instructive, though, to look at the specific contents of each volume. One would expect Gates's anthology on black literature to be especially sensitive to the situation of women in literary criticism, and it is. However, only one of the five essays by women is in his "Theory" section; the other four are in the "Practice" section, and all four are about novels; even the essay on Gwendolyn Brooks focuses primarily on her autobiographical first novel.

   The essays in the anthology edited by Pope are all examples of practical applications of metholodology, except for the first two essays about "Criticism of Criticism," which are authored by men. Of the other essays, those four that use theoretical constructs formulated by women are in the "Feminism" section, while the other essays by female critics all use constructs derived from previous, male critics.

   In many respects, Suleiman and Crosman's anthology most successfully circumvents stereotypes, the female-authored essays it contains being fairly evenly split between theoretical and practical perspectives. It is important, however, to note that both of the editors are women (the sex of editors tends to be crucially associated with how many other women appear in the anthology) and that the collection of essays is about reader-response criticism, a critical subfield usually allied with pedagogical concerns and therefore more open to women.

3. It is important, however, to distinguish essentialist explanations for

women's exclusion from theoretical criticism and lyric poetry from more sophisticated historical or hermeneutic explanations. As long as critics posit some innate, transcendent difference between male and female thought processes, they run the risk of reifying the cultural and historical norms of socialization processes into natural laws of biology. As Margaret Homans reminds us: "It is useful to describe the ways in which culture has defined woman, if it is remembered that these definitions are historical fictions, not necessary truths" (5). Both Homans (4) and Gilbert and Gubar ("Linguistics" 522) see French feminist theory as being particularly prone to this reification.

4. See Stephen H. Clark's essay later in this volume. Greg Jay also recognizes the sexual nature of the "disgust and fear" evident in Eliot's early work; see 26 and passim. Also see Lyndall Gordon, 23–28; 75–81. Gilbert and Gubar's most recent work contains a number of examples of male modernist misogyny; see "Tradition" and "Linguistics" and their forthcoming *No Man's Land*.

5. See Bloom's introduction to the book of critical essays on T. S. Eliot which he recently edited for a milder, more measured assessment of his aversion to Eliot.

6. A thorough discussion of Eliot's debt to Romanticism in his literary criticism occurs in George Bornstein, *Transformations of Romanticism in Yeats, Eliot, and Stevens*, 94–129. Frank Kermode's *The Romantic Image* and Murray Krieger's *New Apologists for Poetry* are classics on this topic. Also see C. K. Stead, *The New Poetic*, Chapter 6, for a particularly useful account of the Romantic origins of Eliot's ideas about creativity.

7. I got the idea for using Eliot and Bloom to differentiate ways that women can react to male precursors from reading Gilbert and Gubar's article on the ways women react to female precursors; see "Affiliation."

8. Greg Jay also notes this tendency, 4, 72.

9. I realize I may appear to be conflating two different historical breaks. For evidence that Eliot saw the decline of blank verse as an index to the split between feeling and thinking see my dissertation, 97 ff. The connection between the ability to feel and the language of drama is explained particularly clearly in " 'Rhetoric' and Poetic Drama," (*Essays*).

10. See Fite (56 ff.) for a fuller account of Bloom's attitude towards Milton.

11. Fite makes this same connection between Eliot, Frye, and Bloom (16).

12. Steven Polansky also quotes this passage in his account of Frye's influence on Bloom. Although Polansky's treatment of the relation between the two critics is the fullest in print, several other commentators have noticed the usually hidden obligation, most notably John Hollander

and David Kaiser. I believe my unpublished Ph.D. dissertation represents the only sustained attempt to extend Bloom's antithetical lineage back from Frye to Eliot and even unto Matthew Arnold.

13. In his early works Bloom repeatedly taunts Eliot for being wrong about Shelley and for being blind to his own Romantic roots. See *Shelley's Mythmaking*, 110, 165; *Visionary Company*, xvii, xxiii, 284, 463; *Ringers in the Tower*, 16, 32, 103, 114, 186, 229. After 1973, more of Bloom's references are aimed at discrediting "Tradition and the Individual Talent." He begins *The Anxiety of Influence*, for example, by ironically setting up Shelley as Eliot's precursor for the idea that "poets of all ages contributed to one great Poem perpetually in progress" (19). And in 1977 he nominated Eliot for the unpleasant honor of being "most over-rated" literary figure because "his verse is (mostly) weak; his prose is wholly tendentious"; see Kramer (also quoted by Jay 69n5).

14. See Polansky for an explication of Frye's treatment of this idea of metaleptic transumption in reference to Kierkegaard (238–39). Polansky's account provides a nice transition for my jump from Eliot to Bloom.

15. Bloom uses these two specific examples in his introduction to *T. S. Eliot*, 2.

16. Gilbert says the allusion to Milton has "no significant development" in *A Room of One's Own* (*Madwoman* 188); actually, the significance developed in my essay fits quite neatly into her entire argument, especially in the way that the image of the dark blocking angel connects with her identification of Milton with Bloom's Covering Cherub (*Madwoman* 188, 191).

17. For a discussion of the ambiguities involved in Frye's description of the creative process, see my dissertation, 307–11. The key passage in Frye is *Anatomy* 98, where he describes the poet as the midwife to the poem and the father of the poem as its form.

18. I realize that this image is polemical and programmatic and not at all typical of Eliot's later accounts of the poetic process; for a typical example of a later, gentler description see the conclusion to *The Use of Poetry*. Sheldon Leibman's article provides a good discussion of Eliot's later meditations on creativity.

19. I need to thank Sandra Gilbert for drawing my attention to this quotation in the somewhat different context of her article on father-daughter incest, "Life's Empty Pack" (365). As previous and subsequent notes show, this article (not to mention her and Susan Gubar's work in general) has been a major influence on my interpretation of Eliot and Bloom.

20. Sherry Ortner's essay "Is Female to Male as Nature Is to Culture?" is

a classic explication of this set of ratios. Cixous's previously quoted "Sorties" contains a complementary set of dichotomies.

21. James Miller's *T. S. Eliot's Personal Wasteland* contains an excellent discussion of the fear of emotion displayed in that poem and how it carries over into his criticism. See especially, Chapter 4, "Critical Theory: Escaping Personality—Exorcising Demons."

As Greg Jay points out, "renewed study of the personal dimension in Eliot's work" is one of the most significant ongoing revisions in Eliot scholarship. Jay's own work is a major contribution to this process, of which Lyndall Gordon's study of *Eliot's Early Years* is perhaps the outstanding example.

22. This, of course, applies most exactly to his doctrine of the "objective correlative," explicated in "Hamlet and His Problems" (*SE* 124–25).

23. See O'Hara (101–3) for a description of Eliot as a protodeconstructor. O'Hara sees Eliot's "enactment of paradoxical critical formulations" as "self-conscious," projecting on him a kind of Nietzschean irony of playful defensiveness. This view of Eliot is appealing in making him seem even more Modernist and more intelligent, but I think there is ample evidence that Eliot spent (as all of us do) a good deal of his time repressing things and lying to himself, so I am not sure O'Hara's confidence in Eliot's multiple self-awarenesses is always justifiable. At any rate, from a feminist perspective, Eliot as a deconstructor is just as aligned with the masculinist tradition in criticism.

APPENDIX

Breakdown of Recent (post 1977) Literary Criticism Anthologies According to Sex of Contributors (* = female editor)

Editors	Date	Male	Female	Total
*Elizabeth Abel *Writing and Sexual Difference*	1980	0	17	17
Jonathan Arac *The Yale Critics*	1983	11	0	11

G. Douglas Atkins &
  Michael Johnson
Reading and Writing
  DIFFERENTLY
	1985	9	4	13

Harold Bloom *Deconstruction and Criticism*	1979	4	0	4
Robert Con Davis *Literary Criticism: Modernism* *Through Post-Structuralism*	1986	28	6	34
*Shoshana Felman *The Question of Reading:* *Otherwise*	1977	9	4	13
*Elizabeth A. Flynn & *Patrocinio P. Schweickart *Gender and Reading*	1985	3	11	14
Henry Louis Gates *Black Literature and Literary* *Theory*	1984	9	5	14

Joseph Gibaldi
Introduction to Scholarship in
  Modern Languages and
  Literature
	1981	5	2	7

Josué V. Harari *Textual Strategies: Perspectives in* *Post-Structuralist Criticism*	1979	16	0	16
Paul Hernadi *Horizon of Criticism*	1982	24	1	25
— *What Is Criticism?*	1981	20	4	24

APPENDIX (continued)

Breakdown of Recent (post 1977) Literary Criticism Anthologies According to Sex of Contributors (* = female editor)

Editors	Date	Male	Female	Total
— *What Is Literature?*	1976	20	0	20
Gregory Jay *After Strange Texts: The Place of Theory in the Study of Literature*	1984	6	2	8
Charles Kaplan *Criticism: The Major Statements*	1985	29	1	30
Ira Konigsberg *American Criticism in the Post-Structuralist Age*	1981	8	2	10
Murray Krieger and L. S. Dembo *Directions for Criticism: Structuralism and Its Alternatives*	1977	6	0	6
Mark Krupnick *Displacement: Derrida and After*	1983	6	2	8
Randolph Pope *The Analysis of Literary Texts: Current Trends in Methodology*	1977	17	14	31
*Jane Routh & *Janet Wolf *The Sociology of Literature: Theoretical Approaches*	1977	8	4	12
*Elaine Showalter *The New Feminist Criticism*	1985	0	19	19
William Spanos *The Question of Textuality*	1978	24	1	25
John Sturrock *Structuralism and Since: From Lévi-Strauss to Derrida*	1979	4	0	4
*Susan Suleiman and 　*Inge Crosman *The Reader in the Text: Essays on Audience and Interpretation*	1982	12	14	26

APPENDIX (continued)

**Breakdown of Recent (post 1977) Literary Criticism Anthologies
According to Sex of Contributors (* = female editor)**

Editors	Date	Male	Female	Total

*Jane P. Tompkins
*Reader-Response Criticism: From
  Formalism to Post-
  Structuralism*
	1980	11	2	13

Tzvetan Todorov *Modern French Criticism*	1982	12	0	12
Mario Valdés & Owen Miller *Interpretation of Narrative*	1978	15	1	16
Robert Young *Untying the Text: A Post- Structuralist Reader*	1981	10	4	14

LEIGH GILMORE

The Gaze of the Other Woman: Beholding and Begetting in Dickinson, Moore, and Rich

Are analyses of sexuality and textuality that use an oedipal model inevitably bound to reproduce its scenario? Is there a model of sexuality within the oedipal tale that does not reinscribe the son's ambivalence toward the mother's body and make this feared and desired other the site of confrontation between an all-powerful father and a polymorphously anxious son? Is there a model of textuality that does not engender, in discourse, the family romance and, ultimately, maintain its hegemony? Even when an oedipal model is not explicitly applied, how escapable is its narrative in Western culture? The realization that Freud's "Oedipus" has become the master narrative of sexuality in Western culture, and thus reproduces the sexual and political ideology of patriarchy, may trouble us less than the notion that narrative has become complicit in structuring the Oedipus tale and its dissemination.

Modes of interpretation and analysis may be clearly linked to epistemology; yet, they are also intricated with narrative. That is, discussions of literature and literary history that make use of psychosocial insights that are derived from the Oedipus tale to describe real people, filtered through Freud's invention of psychoanalysis, variously resisted or extended by Jacques Lacan and others, and redirected to describe a massively displaced point of departure—literature—inherit not only the difficulty of reinterpreting sexuality as textuality, but also the narrative underlying that connection. For it entails the consequences of viewing the connection between sexuality and textuality (those mutually constitutive structures that engender and mark as "gendered" a writer) as two rewritings of the same narrative. Literature frequently emerges within psychoanalytic criticism as the proof of an ahistorical "self" (which possesses a sexual identity) and not, precisely, as a figure of the self (which would "exist" as a textual identity). In these interpretations, literary texts may be transformed into elegant instances of psychosocial dynamics. Thus, psychoanalytic studies of narrative or poetry embed another narrative level, by virtue of their theoretical orientations, in an already densely packed frame. The process of pressing psychosocial models evolved to describe "real women" into the service of literary studies is fraught with difficulty, and has been amply demonstrated by the legacy of Freudian and Lacanian theories about women's bodies and words. How, then, can feminist criticism make use of that strange bedfellow, the oedipal tale, without, however ambivalently, retelling and legitimizing its narrative?

In the writing of literary history, attempts to account for the specific and general features of identity formation and their place within generational continuity confront the oedipal narrative as an unavoidable model. Because Freud and Lacan offer familial narratives that appeal to critics discussing literary history, they loom large both as exemplary narrators and challenging fathers in this enterprise. In Freud and Lacan's retellings of the oedipal tale, the protagonists are clearly male; the conflict is staged over the mother's body; and the discourse that enables these theories is phallomorphic and phallogocentric. Freud and Lacan theorize a model of identity that assumes the male as normative human being and transgression as the privileged form of self-assertion. Facing this model, with varying degrees of resistance, the critic engages not only this narrative, but narrative as a mode of critical—that is, analytical—discourse: s/he tells the story of the relations between poems by raising them to the status of characters in the family romance. Strange alliances emerge from the use of particular narratives. Interpretations as different as Harold Bloom's theory of poetry and Sandra Gilbert and Susan Gubar's revision of the dynamics of influence recreate the narrative teleology engendered by the family romance.[1]

Bloom's theory of poetic influence shares the agonistic element that characterizes Freud's theory of identity and gender formation; thus, Bloom's theory of textuality accordingly echoes Freud's theory of sexuality. Gilbert and Gubar argue that Bloom is right about Freud, on one hand, and right about male literary history, on the other, but go on to examine the consequences of those totalizing structures for women writers. While Gilbert and Gubar's deft tip of the hat to Bloom is wittily subversive in that it credits him with a rather more limited authority than he may desire, and suggests that subversion characterizes the female creative response as they describe it, Gilbert and Gubar's theory resides in the attic of a house of Freud and Bloom's making. Thus, theories of sexuality and textuality become complicit in the plots that structure their insights. The elements of the oedipal drama possess axiologically potent charges and the blindnesses generated within this narrative economy shape the values and visions of interpretation.[2] Yet this tale has proved so irresistible, its retelling has become more than a heuristic, if less than a rite of passage.

For poets and critics working, with degrees of self-consciousness, within an oedipal epistemology, the body of the mother functions as the topos of legitimation. Other sites and scenes remain *terra incognita*. Driven by a narrative teleology that unites written plots and their "real life" counterparts in a patriarchal family model, women have been offered limited roles and scenes to play. Feminist critics confront the rhetorical and epistemological baggage that models of literary tradition share with psychosexual stereotypes and conventions when we attempt to rewrite female literary tradition as the oedipal family romance. For when we focus on women writers, we find differences opening within literary history; we find a poetics that resists patriarchal and heterosexist assumptions projected through the oedipal tale onto women's literary affiliations. While feminist and nonfeminist critics continue to find ways to retell the story of literary inheritance as an oedipal narrative, I would like to examine what Emily Dickinson's "I Think I Was Enchanted," Marianne Moore's "Marriage," and Adrienne Rich's "Transcendental Etude" reveal about poetic engendering, inspiration, and the limits of narrative.[3]

How might this tale change, and how might it cease to be a tale, if we examine the poetics of beholding and begetting enacted in these poems? If the conceptual space is textuality, which we can take to be the dense interrelations of poems assembled within varying interpretive frames, and if arrangements of the elements crowding that space represent literary tradition, how might a line of poetic influence drawn through Dickinson, Moore, and Rich define a project without the parameters of the totalizing oedipal narrative? For these poets, the practice of grouping together historical contemporaries, or, more precisely, grouping them with only their male contemporaries, has proven singularly unhelpful: they still seem to have come out of nowhere. Such a "nowhere" is created by theories and practices that locate them as anomalies rather than originals who demand we revise the context that marginalizes them. It is even tempting to metaphorize the nowhere from which they emerge as the maternal body; yet, the use of such a metaphor further risks reproducing the maternal body *qua* "nowhere" as the topos of legitimation. Such troping privileges the mother in a way these poems do not. Focusing on the figure of the mother here blocks out the sight of the other woman. Because in contradistinction to what the fathers may theorize, Dickinson, Moore and Rich aren't looking at men at all: they're looking at the other woman.

The other woman in these poems functions variously as an enabling force, a symbol offering access to the Symbolic realm, and, potentially, a lover. This multiplicity is consonant with descriptions of the muse in women's poetry as a dense and varied embodiment of mother, lover, and creative force. When the speakers encounter a precursor/muse, the look they share does not produce lack; rather, it resists the economy of the same, as Freud and Lacan prescribe it, that would reinscribe beholding in a dynamic of dominance and submission. I draw together these powerful poets and exemplary critics to reflect on the relation between vision and desire, the masculine self-identification of seeing and being, and the poetics of beholding and begetting.

The significance of the gaze follows from the centrality attributed to the oedipal phase, which establishes the primacy of the phallus and constructs a version of subjectivity based on the mastery that derives from phallic privilege. According to Jacques Lacan, the moment a child recognizes his (*sic*) image in the mirror marks a crucial stage in the construction of the ego (Lacan, 1977, 1–7). Lacan enlists the visual dimension in a grand project: the child enters language at the same time he can manipulate his image in the looking glass. His recognition of the mirror image as "me" and the mother as "not-me" signifies the differentiation of self and other, and the establishment of ego boundaries to fit this world. During the mirror stage, the child's fragmented body image begins to coalesce and form an identity organized around the coherent bodies it perceives. The process of identification with others who are also selves depends on alienation from the maternal body. Introduction to language coincides with the child's "new body" and produces another alienation, this time in language, a signifying system that circumscribes and limits the individual who must be "spoken by it." Gone are the fluid experience of the immediate Imaginary and the unrepresentable Real. They are hereafter mediated by the Symbolic order that enables their mastery. Above the mirror, which gives access to self and symbol, Lacan might post the sign, "The Law of the Father." For the little girl, "excluded by the nature of things which is the nature of words" (*Séminaire XX*, 68), the sign may as well read, "Abandon hope all ye who enter here."

Women's exile from the symbolic rests in part on Lacan's assertion that seeing and understanding are simultaneous and identical; that is, simply seeing an image unproblematically reproduces its meaning. The image's nature in the real, the imaginary, and the symbolic possesses an essential unity. No interpretation is necessary; the sign is instantly legible. Lacan's lack of analysis and reliance on nature dramatize the operative limits of his discourse: The gendering of the little boy depends on his unity with the image in the mirror; this assures his unproblematic induction into the Law of the Father. The primacy of vision and the male's privileged relation to the visible are based for Freud and Lacan on *the* thing worth seeing: the phallus. Lacan comments revealingly: "the symbolic use of which is possible because it can be seen, because it is erect; of what cannot be seen, of what is hidden, there is no possible symbolic use" (quoted in Heath, 1971, 54).

Lacan's remarks on Bernini's *St. Teresa* and female pleasure exemplify this tendency: "[Y]ou only have to go and look at the Bernini statue in Rome to understand immediately she's coming, no doubt about it" (quoted in Heath, 1971, 51). The statue, *qua* woman, is adequate to itself: perfectly legible, unambiguous in meaning. The passage is striking in its certainty, "no doubt about it." Lacan assumes the relation being seeing and knowing as if the woman's body can only stage the obvious, as if it must both betray and offer up its pleasure to the male spectator/interpreter. Lacan's abandonment of theory in the face of the sexual abandon he reads in the statue indicates he is reproducing an ideology he has not fully inspected.

His reliance on nature reveals the extent to which he is gripped by the demands of (its) vision.

The unseeability of the female genitals assures the woman's lack of prestige in the symbolic order. She is envisaged as the castrating woman; her genitality totalizes her symbolic function. For Freud, this sight and site of fear and knowledge are linked to another's gaze: "probably no male human being is spared the fright of castration at the sight of a female genital" ("Fetishism," *SE*, XXI, 154). Such fear and desire mingle in a remarkable way, for as Laura Mulvey has claimed, "The paradox of phallocentrism in all its manifestations is that it depends on the image of the castrated woman to give order and meaning to its world" (6). When the question of difference is unproblematically sorted by the simple test of sight into the categories, "have" and "have not"; and when seeing and knowing, the visual (sight) and the topographical (site), are collapsed in the symbolic dimension; we seem headed toward a massively resistant tautology —"what you see is what you get"—that suppresses the troubling questions of difference.

Both Lacan and Freud require the little girl's "realization" of her place in this order, of her inferiority perforce, in a way that continues to elide the difference between seeing and knowing. She sees the little boy's penis, instantly acknowledges its superiority to her own—invisible—genitals, interprets her sexuality as lack, and is on her way to "becoming" a normal woman. The subordination of the female depends on theorizing her inferiority as self-generated: she must actively subordinate herself in order to develop normally. The visual dimension activates her "becoming"; her incipient normality depends on the simultaneity of vision and knowledge. The activity of her vision is unsettling when compared with the little boy's passivity. He neither insists nor coerces, he simply displays. Were we to believe Freud and Lacan, the little girl's natural reaction is produced by the axiomatic superiority of what dangles before her. Yet her own gaze is clearly imposed, *ex post facto,* by a sexual ideology that cannot allow her not to reach this conclusion and demands she acquiesce to its imperatives. Yet, what may a woman see of herself or other women in conditions of self-effacement and estrangement? What identity must she construct where the rules of sexual identity and aesthetic reception, indeed of the hermeneutic act itself, are mapped onto a phallomorphic order?

Although hermeneutics and psychosocial development may seem an improbable couple, both depend on acts of reading to arrive at "truth" in a way that subordinates the process to a conclusion that must seem self-evident, existing prior to and independent of the reading that produced it. Hermeneutics, traditionally, drives through acts of reading toward meaning in such a way that reading, ultimately, recedes before the truth. Psychoanalysis, one tendency of which is to describe transhistorical features of identity, employs interpretation to the same ends. For example, Freud discusses female subjects as a means toward an end: a conclusion—no matter how complicated, conflicted, and undecidable—about female sexuality where real subjects fade into their symbolic function. Freud's use of the hermeneutic process replaces women with Woman, particular truths with the Truth. The conclusion presents, in discourse, the appearance of stability. A little girl does not, for example, recall the acts of reading that produced her "inferiority." Insofar as she was a skillful interpreter, her process of interpretation dissolves into its conclusion.

Feminist revisions of the oedipal tale retrace Freud's steps back through the father-son encounter to the undifferentiated mother-child bliss of the preoedipal stage. Here, the mother remains the first lover for the daughter who never loses or fully replaces her attachment to the mother (Chodorow, 1978, 127), and the mother cathects her daughter as a narcissistic extension of herself. The son, who is a more clearly differentiated other, lacks the fluid ego boundaries that characterize female bonding, and constructs more rigid self-other distinctions. Many feminist literary critics are compelled by this model, for it offers a congenial way to conceptualize the female poet's relation to precursors and muses as a female network of affiliation, collaboration, and reciprocity. American feminists situate their subjects historically in order to argue for the social construction of gender; however, interpreting the human psyche and its relation to culture remains a hermeneutic enterprise insofar as it postulates a transcendental function for understanding.[4] Although when French feminists and American psychosociologists reread femininity, they are more attentive to the multiplicity of women's experience, their work remains aligned with hermeneutics because they strive to describe the meaning of female experience and identity. This commingling of psychoanalysis with the powerful narrative structure

dramatizes the necessity and the consequences of trying to speak/ write oneself into a tradition that excludes women poets. Cress has devoted her energy to a patriarchal poetic men's club that cannot admit her. When Cress attempts to write herself into the poetic tradition, represented in this encounter by "Dr. Williams," her depths are denied; she becomes "some surface crust of myself" that nothing can penetrate and from which nothing can issue. This impenetrability signals a fatal rupture of identity, "a blockage, exiling myself from myself." The silence of the male and his refusal to hold her gaze acts as a divisive force that Cress internalizes as an opaque surface incapable of reflecting her self: her surface has "congealed" into undesired, ambiguously protective armor. If Cress looks to the man as gatekeeper, she will find no sympathy, no possibility of identification or engagement. Indeed, beyond the gate he is identical with the city itself.

In *A Room of One's Own*, Virginia Woolf describes two forms the exile of women writers takes. The "I"-as-outsider describes an externally prohibitive version of exile: "he was a Beadle; I was a woman. This was the turf; there was the path" (Woolf, 1929, 6). The second version suggests the internalization of exile where the "I"-as-mirror "possess[es] the magic and delicious power of reflecting the figure of man at twice its natural size" (Woolf, 34). Commenting on both exiles, Woolf concludes the former is less deeply damaging: ". . . I thought how unpleasant it is to be locked out; and I thought how it is worse perhaps to be locked in" (Woolf, 24). In *Paterson*, Cress is reduced to this looking-glass function. She briefly reflects the passage of those for whom the city's maze of poetic influence is comparatively clearly mapped. The male poet looks at her and sees nothing; that is, nothing other than a magnified version of himself. She looks at him and sees, simply and devastatingly, nothing. He will not hold her gaze and the dynamic of beholding and begetting is destroyed in this refusal.

Wandering in the wilderness of poetic exile, Cress has looked to the father/mentor for inclusion and shelter and has, in turn, lost the self formed through a belief in such a community. Her request, *qua* young poet, for guidance is not rejected out of hand in the poem. In fact, another set of letters brackets hers with a significant difference; for the second epistle writer, A. G., is no exile, but a full-fledged prophet on the horizon. A. G., exuberantly confident and filled with "good-natured" competition, swaps shop talk with the father/poet. There is no personal peril in the exchange, only the joyous possibility of camaraderie. A. G. earns his place by demonstrating intimacy with the "City": "Also I have been walking the streets and discovering the bars—especially around the great Mill and River streets. Do you know this part of Paterson? I have seen so many things . . . I wonder if you have seen River Street most of all, because that is really at the heart of what is to be known" (Williams, 1963, 194). Their shared, secret knowledge compounds Cress's exclusion. The (af)filiation of father and son at the oedipal/textual crossroads is made possible by the master discourse—the oedipal narrative—that inscribes the city and the roles its residents play out.

Insofar as they are denied an active role in the city, women are identified with Nature in the poem. As such the Woman/Nature construct functions as both the condition and boundary of the story inscribed in *Paterson*: she is the threatening and desired wilderness that the Man/City must both conquer and defend himself against. Interpretations advanced by recent feminist theory allow us to raise the stakes and claim that Paterson stands in for Western metaphysics specifically in this function: When A. G. looks at Dr. Williams, the gaze is not deflected; rather, the mutual regard offers an occasion for identification. The exile imposed by the empty gaze between Cress and Williams reenacts the exemplary and cautionary tale of the woman poet in the city of patriarchal poetry. She lacks knowledge of a female poetic tradition, which might valorize her efforts. Instead, she finds at the entrance to the labyrinth of language the sign I had Lacan post earlier, "The Name of the Father," which, for Cress, has similar implications as "Abandon hope."

The oedipal scene of male transgression and bonding is so deeply inscribed in *Paterson* that Cress cannot steer herself out of its ruts. She vanishes into silence. Indeed, in retelling her story as a narrative of failed identification, I reproduce the family romance, which comes to seem embedded in my argument even before I begin to shape it: the oedipal tale invades reading and writing. However, in the poems by Dickinson, Moore, and Rich, a different gaze compels the poet and enables her to move *in writing* against this narrative and to produce, instead, a world in poetry without the familiar symbols and scripts. I recognize this scene as different, as *without* narrative, in part because it tells so unfamiliar a tale in which meaning is delimited by a visionary rather than a visual dimension; one in which beholding engenders female poetry. Such an economy of influence is driven by dynamics of desire that do not reproduce the violence of the male gaze, nor do they necessitate the anxiety of influence described by Harold Bloom. A poetics of enchantment and identification emerges from the gaze of the other woman. The encounters in all three poems occur in a field of reciprocity where the Romantic agon of the family romance give way to scenes of female romance, scenes which cannot speak in Oedipus and in Freud.

Emily Dickinson's "I think I was enchanted" (#593) describes an encounter between a "sombre Girl," the young poet herself, and a "Foreign Lady," whom critics have assumed to be Elizabeth Barrett Browning. The poem presumably marks Dickinson's reading of Browning's *Sonnets from the Portuguese* and can also be read as a quest poem, of sorts; one in which the poet courts the muse represented here by the Foreign Lady. Dickinson significantly alters the patriarchal version of this tale by setting the scene of psychic and poetic individuation within the context of romantic intrigue. Both muse and poet are female, and their interaction resists the dominance and submission that would result from compulsorily heterosexualizing their relationship. Creativity is not an alien force to be seized or seduced from a feared and desired other; transgression is neither privileged nor eroticized in the exchange. An oedipal configuration would recast the encounter according to the necessities of its plot and displace, or ignore, the function of a female precursor in the formation of the "Girl's" identity as a poet.

The Lady functions first as a precursor, but quickly combines the aspect of lover and muse as her poetry enchants the "sombre Girl." Dickinson metonymically shifts from the natural to the textual body—"I read that Foreign Lady"—to set up the crucial move in the first sentence. What follows "The Dark" is suspended by a dash that *could* lead to any number of conventions about the dark continent of femininity and the similarly mysterious and vaguely hostile forces of creativity. Yet, this dark "felt beautiful," a phrase that is suspended almost like a gasp between dashes. It is significant that the dark neither engulfs nor coerces the young poet; rather, she is "enchanted." The recognition and admission of pleasure then produces a stanza that dramatizes the upheaval of this encounter and the sensual nature of the confusion.

Dickinson interrogates the association of femininity and darkness by recasting them in a "Lunacy of Light." The poem inverts the hierarchy implicit in the binary opposition, dark/light, in order to burst its limitations. The natural order ("whether it was noon at night") and divine order (Or only Heaven—at Noon") are equally capable of confusion, disguise, and transformation. The poet, enraptured by the scene, cannot "tell," so complex is the question of seeing when light can be lunatic. Does the enchantment stall ominously with this declaration—"I had not the power to tell"? The pun on "tell" is potentially dangerous for a poet. Has she been struck silent by the precursor's power? Will she regain a voice? Dickinson keeps our eyes on sight in order to dazzle us in the nearly hallucinatory stanza.

We are treated to a display of transformations: bees become butterflies that become swans. The relation between seeing and knowing is moved away from the "natural" proofs on which Lacan relies. Language has the capacity to effect changes that are impossible in the natural world. And the Lady's realm, in contradistinction to what Lacan or Williams would prescribe, is, emphatically, not simply nature, but the nature of poetry. Poetry employs nature as a metaphor, here, in a way that makes the scene of the Girl's initiation clear: she is being shown the wonders of poetic nature as an equal in the symbolic realm. Sight recedes before sound, "Titanic Opera," as words are joyfully overheard and interpreted. The Girl's interaction with the scene prompts her "Conversion of the Mind" and consummates her newly gained relation to language and the mother/muse/lover. The poem shifts to a present tense in which the powerful speaker embraces the "strong poet" and the "Divine Insanity" she represents.

The figure of reading the Lady returns as the young poet now has access to "Tomes of solid Witchcraft." The connection between seeing her and reading her draws together the figures of "Lady" and "Tomes" as keys to enchantment. The Lady offers pleasure in a way that is strikingly different from how Lacan reads St. Teresa's ecstatic display. The spectacle in Dickinson's poem is mutual: beholding the Lady enables the Girl to engender herself as poet and to accomplish the transition from Girl to Lady where neither must be negated. Such inclusion offers an antidote to any relapse of "normal" vision. The sense of inoculation reveals the danger of such a vision. For

Cress, to look for inclusion in a poetic order composed entirely of men, necessitated her exclusion and silence; Dickinson's "Girl" possesses a talisman against this fate. The tomes suggest why the dark and "Divine Insanity" are so liberating. While the enchanter may be remote physically—"Magicians be asleep"—her power to charm remains potent. Dickinson may still read her "Magic" and catalyze the marvelous transformations again. The Girl's induction to poetic language is marked by an erotic engagement with a precursor who functions as a way into language.

The multiple transformations of identity in a poem where bees can become butterflies register a fluidity of boundaries we don't associate with the natural world. The poem is concerned with transformations that are made possible by the nature of poetry. Thus studies that describe real women remain of provisional use to the discussion of this poem if only because we are led away from rules of nature to the play of language. Still, we may recognize Chodorow's insights about female identity as powerfully more in tune with the strains of this "Titanic Opera" than any of Freud's warnings about the Girl's dangerous narcissism and "immature" choice of sexual preference. The fusion of precursor/lover/fellow poet the poem depicts, for example, is consistent with feminist psychosocial readings of female development. The mother remains the daughter's first lover. The Girl never rejects the mother as the primary love object; rather, she adds a libidinal attachment to the father to the preexisting attachment to the mother without negating it. Identities emerge here in order to fuse, not to fight. Yet, the bonding occurs in language where the poet can choose to recognize a particular mother/lover/muse and cast a spell that draws the enchantment into a field of reciprocity.

Is the body in question, we may ask, a natural or textual one? The bodies overlap in the poem, figuratively, because both the Lady and her tomes are capable of being read. In nature, Chodorow argues, an unsubstitutable experience (being a woman) is bound up with truth (female identity); a particular content (flesh) is productive of meaning (word). Hélène Cixous finesses this point when she writes, "It is impossible to *define* a feminine practice of writing, and this is an impossibility that will remain, for this practice can never be theorized, enclosed, coded—which doesn't mean that it doesn't exist" (Cixous, 1975). The impossibility of definition may remain, but that

impossibility seems designed to ward off the killing stasis of enclosure. Cixous avoids penning women out of or in codes that would
fix them at any of the levels "feminine practice of writing" implies;
that is, with regard either to gender or genre expectations imposed
by the structure of definition. The contours remain open to change;
yet, such a practice exists in a way that pulls together and distinguishes literary relationships of influence from their "real-life"
counterparts. The exchange Dickinson imagines features characteristics Chodorow describes as specifically female, but Dickinson's
arena and the shiftiness and fluidity she commands are specifically
poetic.

We must also question the extent to which Chodorow enables
us to see the homoeroticism of the gaze. The fluidity of the exchange
between sombre Girl and Foreign Lady and the erotics of the gaze
that powers Dickinson's poem appear in other poems by women. If
we see the female relationship in "I Think I Was Enchanted" mainly
as a figure for the mother-daughter relationship we would consider-
ably chasten the energies of a poem that more fully suggests the
attraction of lovers.

Marianne Moore joins Dickinson in looking at another woman;
one who is at first distant, older, more experienced in craft, but
becomes a figure for the poet herself as well as a powerfully attrac-
tive sexual presence who is multiply available to the poet's beholding. Dickinson never represents the powerful female's sexuality as
heterosexual, and in "Marriage," Moore so critiques the institution
she anatomizes, that heterosexual desire reads as a failed project for
generating much in the way of poetry or anything else. When we ask,
"What does looking with the poet at the other woman enable us to
see?" we could begin by focusing on what *not* attending to the gaze
of the other woman obscures in Moore's poetry.

Moore has been married to the tradition of elite modernism.
Her male contemporaries regarded her highly, and her critics point
with demonstrable consensus to the same virtues her peers praised:
modesty, restraint, decorum, chastity, morality, humility, and tech-
nical precision. Not exactly the grand hurrah we might expect for
the poet whom Williams, speaking for Eliot, Pound, Stevens, et al.,
heralded as "our saint." It is not simply because "chastity" and "morality" have slipped in critical value that we feel the ambivalence of
this praise. These terms build toward a tautology grounded, again, in

an ideologically loaded vision of nature: Moore writes this way because she is a woman; her verse exhibits feminine virtues; it could do
no other. Eliot sums up this conflation of poetic and cultural values,
and elides Nature and poetic nature, in his review of "Marriage" in
The Dial: "There are several reasons (buried in this essay) why Miss
Moore's poetry is almost completely ignored in England, beside the
simple reason that it is too good, 'in this age of hard striving,' to be
appreciated anywhere.

"And there is one final and 'magnificent' compliment: Miss
Moore's poetry is as feminine as Christina Rosetti's, one never for-
gets that it is written by a woman; but with both one never thinks of
this particularly as anything but a positive virtue" (Eliot, 1923, 597).

Eliot tempts the reader to excavate the buried reasons and, perhaps, indicates where to start digging. Those reasons are buried just
beneath the "magnificent"—even Eliot places it in quotes—compliment of femininity. The compliment is meted out with damning
equivocation: Eliot has nowhere else, to my knowledge, written in
praise of femininity. For Eliot, to be reminded so unavoidably of the
poet would violate his theory of the impersonality of poetry; that
is, a poet has a medium to express, not a personality. We might ask,
"Is the medium, then, feminine, or is femininity an aspect of the
poet's personality?" If Eliot were intimating that the medium itself,
language, is feminine, he would stand as a surprising precursor in
the debate surrounding the possibility of a female common language.
However, Eliot mainly suggests that female poets always express
their gender and that it is only with Rosetti and Moore that one
doesn't read this disclosure "particularly" as anything but a positive
value. "Generally," then, femininity and its exposure in verse are
negative. What the positive value of femininity might be is buried
deeper, in this essay at least, than I can uncover. Eliot must have
shared the sense with other critics of Moore that the comment is
self-evident, and the consequence of such an assumption is the im-
position of cultural stereotypes about femininity, specifically female
nature, on women's poetry.

By placing Moore within a male modernist tradition that controls praise and blame with the same signifier, "feminine," we lock
her into an interpretive context that tames her poetic power and
obscures the enabling gaze of the other woman in her work. This
isolation is a recurrent feature of the attempt to retell the story of

poetic tradition within the oedipal drama. The woman poet does not only negotiate the persistent tension between her own poetic aspiration and perceived historical and economic restraints, but must also struggle to revise these limitations as enabling strategies. Against the visionary and visual dimensions that result from reading the same narrative everywhere, Dickinson, Moore, and Rich revise cultural constraints as powerful poetry.

Revision, as Adrienne Rich describes it, is "the act of looking back, of seeing with fresh eyes, of entering the text from a new critical direction—[it] is for women more than a chapter in cultural history: it is an act of survival" ("When," 1979, 35). Moore revises a powerful master narrative by offering the figure of Eve, the first woman, as a writer. Moore's encounter with this figure reflects on the institution of marriage and finds the key to resisting its imperatives demands a corresponding revision of the biblical relationship between divine and human language. She begins by restoring to Eve, the first exile from the symbolic, some of her luster. Eve is, proportionally, as powerful in this poem as she is powerless (or debased) in interpretations deriving from the *Genesis* account of her role in the fall. While Eve is capable of empowering the poet who gazes at her, those gains are measured against Adam's dwindling force. The poem is more concerned with the instability of that crucial union than its monolithic representation, and that interest is reflected at several levels in the poem.

If we look in "Marriage" for the conventions of heterosexual union, we find no "I do," no consummation, and the only proposal —Adam's " 'why not be alone together?' "—seems to come after Eve has asked for the first divorce—" '*I* should like to be alone.' " The poem shifts the institution of holy matrimony into the arena of exchange: "The institution / Perhaps one should say enterprise." The language of economics—enterprise, obligation, steel/steal, goldenness, spoils, criminal—reveals the situation is post-Edenic despite the presence of Adam and Eve. Marriage, in its fallen state, must now be negotiated, or avoided. The metonymic displacement where "institution" becomes "enterprise" and "religion" gives way to "psychology" grows still shiftier by the mobility of pronouns from *one* to *I* to *we*. In spite of all the linguistic transit, though, there is no immediate other in the scene—the speaker is musing alone, equivocating, playing with names in a way that reinscribes her in the Edenic scene.

The speaker's gaze is drawn to Eve who gives her a "start." The pun reveals the speaker's surprise and begins her process of looking at Eve. The equivocal, "I have seen her when" implies a former knowledge of Eve's grandeur and suggests that even if Eve's image has been tarnished over time, the mesmerization of the poet's beholding restores her strength. Eve's relation to language in this poem is significantly different from her access to language prescribed both by the biblical account of Adamic language and by Lacan's theory of language. In *Genesis*, Adam talks directly with God. Language is immediate and fully present. Adam names the world according to a natural and inevitable correspondence between signifier and signified. By the time Eve arrives, all the work (naming) has been completed and she, presumably, is the first person to experience the relationship between signifier and signified as arbitrary.

In Moore's vision, however, Eve embraces and flourishes in the multiplicity of language. Like Moore, no potential poetic material exceeds her grasp. So flexible is her access to human language, so accomplished and delighted is Eve in the diversity of communication that she is "able to write simultaneously / in three languages— / English, German and French— / and talk in the meantime; / equally positive in demanding a commotion / and in stipulating quiet[.]" Eve speaks and writes circles around Adam, who becomes increasingly tamed in the poem, and dazzles the beholder. When Eve speaks, Moore slants the *I*, so that even though Adam and Eve share the same pronoun, Eve's identity signifies an emphatic difference.

The scene recedes into what some critics describe as an ironic reinscription of psychology that threatens to drown all in a poisonous wash of consciousness. But "the strange experience of beauty" whose "existence is too much" refers to the poet's encounter with a powerful female precursor and she is as overwhelmed by the encounter as was Dickinson's sombre girl. The violence in the scene results from the speaker's gaze being torn from the lover/mother/muse. Before we lose sight of Eve altogether, the speaker commands: "See her, see her in this common world." The world that the poet and Eve inhabit is their common female one of language and experience. If Eve is the "central flaw" in both Eden and the common world, she commands a powerful force by holding the center. While Adam has only "ways out but no way in," she is already contained in the center. Constitutively flawed as both may be, she still controls the way in.

Adam's beauty, although figured in one line as a "crouching mythological monster," is containable in miniature. He fits into Moore's ornamental menagerie in a way the powerful Eve never could. She is an anomalous figure in Moore's work. Adam's force diminishes in the poem as the figure of Eve dominates the institution of marriage and the symbolic realm of language. His action and mobility are reduced through language that reveals his lack of agency: "forgetting . . . plagued . . . dares not . . .unnerved . . .dazzled . . . impelled"—until he "stumbles over marriage" and is "unfathered by a woman." Once the male is "unfathered," that is, denied immediate access both to the Father and to his privileged relation to language, he falls into a world of women. He experiences the same exile from the fluid reciprocity of language and identity that defined Cress's experience.

The issue of psychic and poetic individuation raised by Dickinson's poem is echoed here. About Adam, Moore writes, "he loves himself so much, / he can permit himself / no rival in that love." About Eve, "She loves herself so much, / she cannot see herself enough." This mirror stage is not contained in the oedipal tale. The narcissism of the gaze of the other woman exists in a dynamic characterized by the unmediated identity associated with the mother's breast. The friction of individuation in the relationship between self and other is figured more as romance than rivalry. The speaker in the poem is being pulled away from Eve, away from narcissism, toward a proper bonding with a heterosexual Other (Adam) that Eve has already rejected. But the poet beholds an Other who is not merely a reflection of herself, nor an alien and indifferent precursor. Rather, she beholds Eve who gives her the "start" to beget poetry. The danger implicit in Dickinson's experience of dazzling, which in its first moment prevents sight and speech, is addressed in "Marriage" by the command to "See her." The gaze between Eve and the speaker describes an appreciative looking on that is earned by refusing to drown in what patriarchy would consider the dangerous pool of female narcissism. If this danger is analogous to the potential for silence before the Foreign Lady, then Dickinson and Moore's revision of this gaze removes the scene from the plot that would demand this response.

This gaze, to distance it further from the oedipal scene, is a figure for the body's gesture of looking and is transcribed not as an emotion recollected in tranquility, but in the sensual complexity of being caught in the act. The women do not transgress against each other or the maternal body, but against a narrative that would prohibit their potential enchantment. As a figure, the gaze of the other woman is nonnarrative and does not, as such, reproduce a paradigm of beholding and begetting that would function invariantly across a female poetic tradition. Rather, the scene of this encounter functions as a matrix of poetic engendering and marks a site of female-directed desire in which the poet finds another woman and her self fused in the activity of writing, of begetting language. The power Dickinson, Moore, and Rich discover in this gaze resides in its potential to create a scene in language where the poet may know herself as a woman writing by seeing herself caught in the act of witnessing another woman (writing). Representation as action mimes what it represents and enacts what it reports. By doubling the image and bringing two women together in a poem, this scene constructs the possibility that literary history may offer the woman writer something other than silence.

In "Transcendental Etude," Rich describes the clear-eyed, level, and mutual gaze between women as capable of generating "a whole new poetry." The poem closes *The Dream of a Common Language* (1978), a volume that makes explicit many of the concerns that fueled Dickinson and Moore's poetry. Rich recognizes that women have been prohibited from looking to each other, and from learning of traditions and origins, and have therefore been severed from connections that would heal this forced separation. Women, she claims, need to know each other in order to re-member their history. Her insight reflects with particular clarity on the woman poet whose ability to engender poetry is circumscribed within a discourse that allows her only to be the site/sight for patriarchal poetry. The gaze of the other woman, however, is so radical, so powerful as to be capable of begetting nothing less than "a whole new poetry." The poem breaks from an italicized lyric of female love to declare: ". . . two women, eye to eye / measuring each other's spirit, each other's / limitless desire, / a whole new poetry beginning here." No longer beholden to reproducing the oedipal narrative that makes such contact virtually unthinkable, the poet beholds the power of desire made manifest enough to measure as "limitless." Such is the transition capable of breaking the hold of the oedipal narrative and redirecting our gaze to other scenes.

Yet the gaze in this poem differs from those in Dickinson and Moore. Ironically, Rich's "two women, eye to eye" is perhaps the most chaste image of the three. Absent is the dazzling, the start, the swoon that begets the poet's birth into "a whole new poetry." The concerns are the same, but Rich's solitary, brooding speaker's language, though she encounters another woman, remains consistent throughout the poem. In this case, biography and a psychosexual interpretation are of the least use to us in their strictest application: Rich is the only poet of the three to present herself self-consciously as a lesbian. For Dickinson and, to a lesser extent, for Moore, the homoerotics of the work remain most explicit as a part of their poetics. Rich's lesbianism, however, powerfully permeates her career and ties together what we know of the poet and what we know of her poems. What we know of the poet's life may cause us to expect a certain narrative if we remain within an oedipal frame that compels sexuality and textuality to tell the same story.

The gaze of the other woman bears a burden in this poem signified as early as the title. "Transcendental Etude" contains the possibility of reverie as well as the demand of work, of "study." It is self-conscious in the manner of a sketch that may thus be seen to offer a prototype of the new transcendence. This gaze is more circumspect in its presentation of the sexually suspect "swoon." We might well expect this from a poem that claims: "we have to take ourselves more seriously or die."

The "start" in this poem occurs as "my car startling young deer in meadows—one / gave a hoarse intake of breath and all / four fawns sprang after her / into the dark maples." This is a perilous moment of beauty; the car's menace anticipates the "hit-and-run hunters, glorying / in a weekend's destructive power." The poem separates no space from the violence of the world. Even "all this sweetness, / this green world," though persistent in its power to charm and soothe, masks the despair of human life and is contaminated by appropriation: "sentimentalized, photographed, / advertised to death." Nature here can always die despite its fecundity, and instead of seeking transcendence in nature, Rich—no Emerson or Thoreau, she—apprehends how the profusion of beauty descends originally and ultimately to "rockshelves that underlie all life."

The material that will yield transcendence is "natural history," specifically, women's lives. And although one's own life might seem the most available subject of study, women have been denied theirs and denied the knowledge of this denial: "But in fact we were always like this, / rootless, dismembered: knowing it makes the difference." Women must tell tales outside the oedipal, tales which no one has spoken or heard. When the speaker observes a woman musing alone, there is empathy but no fusion. "The woman who sits watching, listening, / eyes moving in the darkness / is rehearsing in her body, hearing-out in her blood / a score touched off in her perhaps / by some words, a few chords, from the stage: / a tale only she can tell." And again, at the end of the poem, a woman "quietly walk[s] away," begins to compose something, then decomposes into nature: "becoming now the shard of broken glass / slicing light in a corner, dangerous / to flesh, now the plentiful, soft leaf / that wrapped round the throbbing finger . . . / now the stone foundation, rockshelf further / forming underneath everything that grows."

Both observations bracket the encounter that generates "a whole new poetry," and remain outside the dynamics of beholding and begetting in a way that begins to show how various possibilities of the female gaze may exist once one begins to write and read them.

The stanza that inscribes the female gaze and begins *"Homesick for myself, for her"* repeats the earlier alienation whereby the speaker is both herself and the other woman, and neither of them. Where the "homesickness for a woman" is the homesickness "for ourselves" or for the speaker's self, the encounter is sealed within self-referentiality. There seems to be no outside to this closed circle of longing. Rich's "two women" are undistinguished, substitutable: *"I am the lover and the loved."* Yet, it is this gaze that most completely breaks from the oedipal narrative of desire and transgression, of "falling" in love, of engendering poetry from an encounter with a muse, and prompts, in Dickinson's phrase, "Conversion of the Mind." For the closed circle is declared infinitely rich in its capacity to generate something new, something we do not recognize, a look that does not inspire lack, a poetic landscape without a Sphinx or an Oedipus. We will need "Tomes of solid Witchcraft" to find our way.

NOTES

1. Harold Bloom, *A Map of Misreading* (New York: Oxford University Press, 1975). *The Anxiety of Influence* (New York: Oxford University Press, 1973). Sandra Gilbert and Susan Gubar, *The Madwoman in the Attic* (New Haven: Yale University Press, 1979).

2. See Paul de Man, *Blindness and Insight* (Minneapolis: University of Minnesota Press, 1971) for a full discussion, in a different context, of this problem.

3. Emily Dickinson, #593, in *The Complete Poems of Emily Dickinson,* ed. Thomas H. Johnson (Boston: Little, Brown, 1960 edition); Marianne Moore, "Marriage," in *The Complete Poems of Marianne Moore* (New York: Penguin, 1981 edition); Adrienne Rich, "Transcendental Etude," in *The Dream of a Common Language* (New York: Norton, 1978). While I owe all the members of Sandra M. Gilbert's seminar on "American Sexual Poetics" at The School of Criticism and Theory, 1984, tremendous gratitude for their insight and suggestions, I owe particular thanks to Marilee Lindemann whose reading of this poem influenced my thoughts on a female literary tradition. All errors are, of course, my own.

4. See, for example, Nancy Chodorow, Dorothy Dinnerstein, and Carol Gilligan.

PART TWO

Crossing Lines/Extending Boundaries

MARILEE LINDEMANN

"This Woman Can Cross Any Line": Power and Authority in Contemporary Women's Fiction

I

Alive. This music rocks
me. I drive the interstate,
watch the faces come and go on either
side. I am free to be sung to;
I am free to sing. This woman
can cross any line.

Joy Harjo, "Alive"[1]

Feminist critics have been dancing in the minefields and frol-icking in the wilderness of critical theory for some time now,[2] singing merrily all the while of the virtues of a genuinely cross-cultural approach to women's writing. Practically speaking, however, our feminist dancing shoes and hiking boots have been relegated to the back of the closet, while most of us continue to pad quietly around the house in a pair of comfortable old patriarchal slippers. Theo-retical claims and parenthetical apologies aside, most mainstream feminist criticism still posits the literature of "heterosexual, white, middle-class, English-speaking women"[3] as some sort of "norm" for literary study. We have not yet made an honest, vigorous test of our assumption that, despite the acknowledged differences of class, race, nationality, history, or sexual preference, "women's culture forms a collective experience within the cultural whole, an experience that binds women together over time and space."[4]

There are several reasons for the reticence of feminist critics to put their practical moneys where their theoretical mouths have been for so long. One, of course, is that, despite any claim of solidarity and cultural pluralism, the political movement to which feminist literary criticism is so inextricably linked *has* been a movement dominated by "heterosexual, white, middle-class, English-speaking women." Further, the effort to institutionalize women's studies has no doubt contributed to the tendency of feminist critics to shy away from the less "legitimate" literatures of black, lesbian, native American, and even WASP-American women. Despite the revisionary zeal and brilliance of their efforts, the quest for professional validation has generally confined the focus of American feminist critics to redefining the canons of literature that have long been safely entrenched in the halls of academe—that is, primarily nineteenth- and twentieth-century British literature.[5]

Finally, however, and perhaps to their credit, feminist critics have feared to tread too boldly across the delicate but profoundly real lines that separate women writers in American society. Clearly, the path to pluralism is mined with serious risks as well as exciting possibilities. Politically, if we acknowledge that the act of criticism is neither innocent nor value free, we must acknowledge that the "heterosexual, white, middle-class, English-speaking" literary critic is painfully vulnerable to charges of intrusion, invasion, and cultural imperialism of a most pernicious sort. We avoid what we do not know partly out of embarrassment or fear of the unfamiliar, but partly also out of respect for the need of any oppressed group to retain its own autonomy and identity. We keep our questions of gender out of nonwhite, nonmiddle-class struggles for cultural existence because, we seem to confess in all of those apologetic footnotes, our femaleness does not compensate for our whiteness—our access, our complicity, our guilt.

At some point, however, even the most heartfelt apologies and confessions cease to be adequate substitutes for the real leaps across cultural bounds that will be necessary in order to prove our claims of a powerful and coherent female identity. Politically and pedagogically, I believe feminists have reached this point. In this essay, therefore, I would like to take some initial steps in this direction by exploring contemporary women's fiction as a unique and exciting ground upon which we are enabled and in fact compelled to "cross any line" of race or class, first as readers and ultimately as critics. By focusing on narrative strategies and metaphors in works by authors of various backgrounds, I hope to locate and describe a pattern by which a number of women writers seek to gain access to linguistic power and cultural authority. In each of these writers, such authority is unquestionably female, and in each case the reader (regardless of gender or race/class identity) is implicated in those strategies in ways that both politicize and spiritualize the act of reading—since what distinguishes these writers is their insistence that reading itself functions as an initiation into the specifically female[6] processes of knowing and telling that the novels describe. Thus, the real radical potential of these texts is the extraliterary force they acquire in the mind of the reader, who becomes equally empowered, converted out of a victimized consciousness and into the regenerative powers of either sexuality or textuality. Like the narrator in one of the works I will discuss, Gayl Jones's *Corregidora*, we as readers incur an obligation to "make generations," to bear children or bear witness: to face the Corregidoras in our selves and in our pasts, to gather the evidence, to pass on the tale, to wait, to survive, to *know*. So as critics, of course, to consider these works is to participate directly in these same political, psychic, and epistemological processes, since even the most "academic" interpretation is precisely the retelling and passing on that such stories require. For this daring yet delicate task, the feminist critic would do well to kick off her house slippers, polish up her hiking boots, and test out the toes of her dancing shoes. Crossing lines can be a risky business.

II

There is no such thing as a solitary polar explorer, fine as the conception is.
　　　　Annie Dillard, "An Expedition to the Pole"[7]

With the wit, aplomb, and deep literary self-consciousness that characterize her at her best, Annie Dillard's contention that "There is no such thing as a solitary polar explorer" epigrammatically dismisses rugged individualism, that amorphous yet profoundly powerful notion so central to both the ethos and the mythos of America. Dillard's charming menagerie of characters—careering into one another and sliding giddily off their ice floes, losing themselves in the gazes of weasels and young daughters, continually breaking into song and dance before the God they seem unable to avoid—compels us to rethink deeply held masculinist assumptions about the relationship of an American self to social, political, and physical landscapes.[8] Annette Kolodny has already traced the history of these assumptions in American life and letters and explored the dangerous consequences of the mentalities of individualism and conquest.[9] Elizabeth Abel has argued that an alternative pattern for understanding women writers may lie in recent findings by object-relations psychologists, primarily in Nancy Chodorow's feminist reformulation of the Oedipus complex, and she has begun to consider the implications of women's "mode of relational self-definition"[10] for burgeoning feminist theories of literary influence and experience.

In what follows, I will perforce ignore—though I certainly do not wish to *deny*—the possibility that male writers from culturally marginalized groups also write out of a sensibility radically different from those of the authors who have populated American fictions of quest and con-quest with "solitary polar explorer[s]" from Natty Bumppo to Rambo and the hungry new teen idols of video-rock. Clearly, the works of writers such as Jean Toomer, N. Scott Momaday, and, from a Latin American context, Gabriel García Márquez provide ample and formidable evidence that Emersonian Self-Reliance is not the universal assumption of male writers.[11] If, however, we accept Abel's reading of Chodorow[12] and consider as well the multiple oppressions faced by female members of already oppressed groups,[13] then, I believe, the feminist urge toward a cross-cultural canon of women's literature is justified. The relative fluidity of female identity, Dillard's masterful blending of psychic slipperiness and narrative authority—such factors are clearly related, and they indicate to me that Abel's examination of female friendships, though illuminating, leaves many stones unturned in the rich territory of contemporary fiction by women. Through an examination of three representative texts—particularly of Leslie Marmon Silko's *Ceremony*, as well as of Gayl Jones's *Corregidora* and Marilynne Robinson's *Housekeeping*—I will trace the lineaments of the much broader quest toward female power and authority to which I have already alluded. Henceforth I will refer to this quest as the "tropographic" impulse in women's writing—from the Greek *tropos* (turn, way, manner, style), *topos* (place, locality), and *graphos* (written, writing). Generally, then, the phrase describes the desire of many women writers to chart out alternative worlds in figurative language: not the masculine Worlds Elsewhere of style and pristine selfhood, but female Worlds Within-and-Out, in which the boundaries of the self and the form of the novel are equally fluid, and in which we are all—women and men, readers and writers—encouraged to leap off our ice floes and enter into the invigorating Arctic waters of *un*solitary polar exploration.

The first expedition to what Dillard has termed the "Pole of Relative Inaccessibility"—"that point of spirit furthest from every accessible point of spirit in all directions"[14]—that I will consider is set, alas, not in the Arctic but in a drought-ridden section of western New Mexico. Nevertheless, Leslie Marmon Silko's *Ceremony* stands as a beautifully crafted and often terrifying example of the power of psychic and narrative fluidity in contemporary women's writing. At its simplest level the novel recounts the struggle of Tayo, an Indian half-breed and World War II veteran, to readjust to Indian society within a white world—and, more importantly, to rediscover the ancient healing powers of the ceremony in the context of a world gone seemingly mad with the destructive force discovered in the uranium mines of his homeland. As myth, the story resonates with the warrior/hunter's quest for wholeness and home as well as with the struggle of an ancient tribe whose dabblings in magic have resulted in drought and separation from the offended earth.[15] Politically, it is a plea to all peoples to realize that "all human beings [are] one clan again . . . united by a circle of death that devoured people in cities twelve thousand miles away."[16] Artistically, it is a brilliant integration—in form and substance—of the native American and postmodernist literary traditions, shifting radically in time, space, and even genre to render the chaos of Tayo's journey out of war and fragmentation and yet framed and fortified by the mythic impetus toward convergence, toward a unity ultimately more powerful than the nuclear circle of death.

For Silko, this faith is firmly grounded in narrativity itself—in the curative and creative powers language derives from its role in sacred stories, ceremonies, and rituals.[17] In the poetic epigraph to the novel, Silko explicitly defines these powers as female and pledges

her allegiance to them by aligning the role of the narrator with that
of Thought-Woman, a central figure of organic, creative energy in
native American mythologies:

> Thought-Woman, the spider,
>   named things and
>   as she named them
>   they appeared.
>
> She is sitting in her room
>   thinking of a story now
>
> I'm telling you the story
>   she is thinking. (1)

"I'm telling you the story / she is thinking": This is Silko's only
overt declaration of narrative presence, and yet the quiet force of
this voice echoes throughout the novel, both in the myth-poems
that comment on and enlarge Tayo's story and in the plot that operates at its realistic level. For the male protagonist, the only hope
for recuperation lies in the possibility of recovering this alienated
female power, a power from which Tayo is increasingly separated
—initially, by the early death of his mother and, ultimately, by his
seduction into the white man's offer of a glorious love/death af-
fair with America the Great White Woman. "Anyone can fight for
America," an army recruiter tells Tayo and his cousin Rocky in an
early flashback, "even you boys. In a time of need, anyone can fight
for *her*. . . . *Now I know you boys love America as much as we do*,
but this is your big chance to show it!" (66, emphasis added). But,
of course, this America is finally revealed as the objectified bitch
goddess of the white man, who gives and withholds her favors according to the whims of a tyrannical female will. For the Indians,
these favors—"the cold beer and the blond cunt" (43)—last only as
long as the war does, and when they return home their bitterness
and self-hatred are projected onto the starved and starving female
landscape: "Look what is here for us," remarks Emo, the Indian irrevocably drawn into the circle of death, "Look. Here's the Indians'
mother earth! Old dried-up thing!" (25).

Shattered from transpersonal, tribal selfhood into the powerlessness of the merely personal, the Indians fall victim to the tale
of "witchery" that lies at the center of the novel, Silko's myth of
an evil set into motion by the story of a people who grow away

from the earth, who "see no life / When they look / they see only objects." Consequently, "They fear / They fear the world. / They destroy what they fear. / They fear themselves" (142). Caught in the cycle of grief and fear, Tayo himself is vulnerable to the plan "the destroyers" (200) had laid for him, to playing out the pathetic story of "a drunk Indian war veteran" (265) or of "Indian people who are only marking time and waiting for the end" (243), uselessly despising or, worse, believing in the white man's codes and cures of individualism —since, as the doctors in the veteran's hospital explained, "he had to think only of himself, and not about the others, [and] he would never get well as long as he used words like 'we' and 'us'" (132). Even at his worst, however, Tayo realizes the falseness of the "cure" into self-consciousness, knowing that "medicine didn't work that way, because the world didn't work that way. His sickness was part of something larger, and his cure would be found only in something great and inclusive of everything" (132).

Tayo's success in finding his cure ultimately lies in his ability to face and to fuse the insistent echoes of the female narrative voice that add such a powerful, controlled undercurrent to the apparent chaos of his story: in the Laguna words he is "frantic" to understand in the novel's opening nightmare scene "because he thought [they] were his mother's" (5); in his aunt's well-meaning struggle first to save, then to explain the "Little Sister" lost to alcoholism and sexual abuse—because in losing her, Auntie knew, the people "were losing part of themselves. The older sister had to act for the people, to get this young girl back" (71). Still more powerful, however, is the voice of Tayo's blind grandmother, whose quiet telling of "the long ago, time immemorial stories" is not drowned out either by the science teacher who "explained what superstition was, and then held the science textbook up for the class to see the true source of explanations" (99) or by the horrors of the war.[18]

Finally, then, what Tayo learns is that the power of witchery should be countered not by the destructiveness of the warrior, but by the corrective, collective, and female vision of the storyteller, by acquiring the ability of the male speaker in the novel's poetic frame—to rub one's belly and know that, through story, this too "is moving," that "there is life here / for the people" (2). From this perspective, Tayo is able to "read" his "world made of stories" (100) not as a reeling chaos, but as a creative flux ("no boundaries, only transitions through all distances and time" [258]) ultimately stabilized by a knowable if—as Dillard would have it—"relatively inaccessible" source. Thus, Tayo's task in the climactic scene of witchery that unfolds before him near the end of the novel—in the parodically ritualized torture of his friend Harley—is to witness it, to know that the "whirling darkness" of witchery will "come back on itself" (274), and to return to his people to offer them the story, because, "the ear for the story and eye for the pattern were theirs; the feeling was theirs: we came out of this land and we are hers" (267).

From the initial, "*I'm* telling *you* the story / she is thinking," Silko is careful to involve readers directly in the spiritual/imaginative processes of *Ceremony*, to extend to us the same set of visions and possibilities she offers Tayo. Like the quiet assurance and prodding of Betonie's prayers during Tayo's ceremony ("I will bring you through my hoop, / I will bring you back. / Following my footprints / walk home / Following my footprints / Come home, happily . . ." [150]), the repetitive, recapitulative style of the narrative both demands and guides our attention, urging us toward the "point of convergence" (257) upon which myth insists. For Tayo, this point lies in the recognition of "the way all the stories fit together—the old stories, the war stories, their stories—to become the story that was still being told" (258). For the reader, this point functions both within the novel and in the world beyond it. Our first task is to come to terms with the protagonist in his varied and shifting contexts—in the plot of the Indian war veteran as well as in the myths of the Sun Man's quest to free the rain clouds and the journey of fly and hummingbird to ask forgiveness of the tribal mother. But by patterning the novel so closely after healing songs and rituals (it begins and ends, for example, with the traditional offering to the sun) and by insisting in the final myth-poem that any "victory" over witchery is only temporary ("It is dead for now. / It is dead for now. / It is dead for now. / It is dead for now." [274]), Silko has forced us into the ongoing process of the ceremony. In the end, the half-breed, the orphan, the war veteran finds his way home—to the belly of his tribe, to a land where the clouds are at last heavy with rain and the people are anxious for his story. And if we are good readers, Silko implies, we must wonder if the same thing could be said of our selves and our own roles in the "story that [is] still being told."

Although Silko most consciously and explicitly articulates the tropographic impulse by the terms of an identified mythopoetic tradition, the pattern of *Ceremony* is clearly evident in the works of a host of other contemporary women writers. Among poets, for example, one thinks of the endless journeys and explorations that constitute Carolyn Forché's effort to "gather the tribes," to re-assemble a sense of female language and origins: *"That from which these things are born / That by which they live / That to which they return at death / Try to know that."*[19]

For Adrienne Rich, the urge "to know that" is the "homesickness for a woman" that can only find release in the "whole new poetry" of a fluid, sexual / mythical selfhood, of "two women, eye to eye / measuring each other's spirit, each other's / limitless desire."[20] Among novelists, Alice Walker, as "author and medium" of *The Color Purple*, draws readers into the seemingly intense privacy of Celie's correspondence with God—trusting us immediately, but guiding us irrevocably away from our own images of the "old white man" in the sky and toward Shug Avery's exuberantly female sense of "being part of everything," of feeling God's presence as intimately and sweetly as one feels the hand of a lover "rubbing high up on [one's] thigh."[21] And in Toni Morrison's *Sula*, the stripped down qualities of style and structure, combined with the intricacies of metaphor, force readers into a creative engagement with the story that inevitably implicates us in its ending: both in the relief and affirmation behind Nel's acknowledgment that she and Sula "was girls together" and in the infinitely variable sense of selfhood(s) implied in her "circles and circles of sorrow."[22]

But in Gayl Jones's *Corregidora*, the desire to know and to speak the female self explodes in a context of such brutal violence that the reader aches for, yet can barely believe in, the possibility of any other world. Like *Ceremony*, it is a story of literal and figurative recovery: When we first meet Ursa Corregidora, she has, at twenty-five, undergone a hysterectomy after being pushed down the stairs by her maniacally jealous husband, Mutt Thomas. The first-person narrator carries in her own name (which she refuses to relinquish in marriage) the horrifying legacy of "old man Corregidora, the Portuguese slave breeder and whore monger," who "fucked his own whores

and fathered his own breed."[23] Ursa's great-grandmother and grandmother were each Corregidora's slave and mistress, and each bore
a daughter by him. Three generations later, the name—his, theirs,
Ursa's—bears powerful maternal and narrative demands: "U. C.," as
Ursa is called early in the novel, functions both as a question intended to test or guide the reader/listener's perceptions (Do *you* see?
I want *you* to *see*.) and as an imperative toward a knowledge that is
neither comfortable nor pleasant (*You* will *see*. I can make *you* see.).
Indeed, many of the key actions of the novel are essentially visual
and even voyeuristic—as when Ursa walks in on her second husband
in bed with another woman (99–100), or when Ursa's mother catches
her father watching her grandmother powder her breasts (148), or
in the flashback to a younger Ursa, who witnesses her best friend
having sex with a boy in the grass (159). "All you like to do is watch,"
an embittered May Alice later asserts to the still virgin Ursa after
she has had a child (167).

Ursa is also, however, a compulsive listener, and her listening often has profound consequences—as, for example, when she
overhears her friend Catherine ("Cat") Lawson taunting the fourteen-
year-old girl Jeffy in bed, realizes the nature of their relationship,
and flees in fear and repulsion from the woman whose friendship
and fried chicken had helped nourish her back to health after her
stay in the hospital. Ursa's listening has its origins deep in her past
and in the past of her grandmothers, in their faith that evidence preserved and passed on will ultimately condemn the slave breeders in
that moment "when the ground and the sky open up to ask them
that question that's going to be ask" (45). Their voices, relentless
and mesmerizing, transfix Ursa as a child, haunt her as a woman,
and establish both the considerable force of this narrative and the
reader's peculiar position in it:

> Great Gram sat in the rocker. I was on her lap. She told the same
> story over and over again. She had her hands around my waist, and I
> had my back to her. While she talked, I'd stare down at her hands. She
> would fold them and then unfold them. She didn't need her hands
> around me to keep me in her lap, and sometimes I'd see the sweat in
> her palms. She was the darkest woman in the house, the coffee-bean
> woman. Her hands had lines all over them. It was as if the words
> were helping her, as if the words repeated again and again could be

a substitute for memory. As if it were only the words that kept her anger. (10)

As in *Ceremony*, the reader is situated carefully in the narrative by a female figure associated with age, wisdom, and authority. The tautness of the language, the brutality of the worlds described, the sense of impending, inevitable judgment—all combine to hold us in the story precisely as Ursa is held by Great Gram: one has the strange yet certain sense that, "She didn't need her hands around me to keep me in her lap."

Ursa's true task, however, and the task of this formally disjointed novel, is to go beyond the perhaps too simple expiation afforded by the grandmothers' endless repetitions—to reach past mere words to the deeper "explanation behind the words," to express the more meaningful "soot crying out of my eyes" (74)—because, as Ursa ultimately realizes, "Everything said in the beginning must be said better than in the beginning" (60). Here, Jones's vehicle for the tropographic impulse is Ursa's career as a blues singer, through which the last of the Corregidora women can make the necessary claims of kinship with her past as well as achieve a degree of separation from it. Throughout the novel, Ursa's singing voice and her identity are explicitly linked—from Cat Lawson's assertion that, after her injury, Ursa's voice is better because "it tells what you've been through" (49), to Mutt's acknowledgment twenty-two years later that what he'd needed to know all along was "that you've still got your voice, that you're still Ursa" (210). Like Silko's Thought-Woman breathing life into the tribal stories, Jones's blues singer is emblematic of a female creative power that must be—fiercely, lovingly—nourished and protected: "*I am Ursa Corregidora. I have tears for eyes. I was made to touch my past at an early age. I found it on my mother's tiddies. In her milk. Let no one pollute my music. I will dig out their temples. I will pluck out their eyes*" (87–88).

Her singing voice is, like the narrative voice, an unsettling combination of pain and power, "a hard kind of voice," as the owner of the Spider (a nightclub in which Ursa performs) explains, ". . . like calloused hands. Strong and hard but gentle underneath. Strong but gentle too. The kind of voice that can hurt you. . . . Hurt you and make you still want to listen" (110). Ursa's songs are more than a mere substitute for her lost ability to make biological generations; they are a profound transformation of the linear passing on of history and "conscious" ("They can burn the papers but they can't burn conscious, Ursa" [24]) into a larger, circular notion of time and human consciousness in which there is space for the "private memory" (104) Ursa craves from her mother and for herself, as well as for the collective memories to which she feels so obligated. As she puts it, "I wanted a song that would touch me, touch my life *and* theirs. A Portuguese song, but not a Portuguese song. A new world song. A song branded with the new world" (59).

The calculated ambiguity of Ursa's "new world song"—is it, one wonders, a song *from* the new world? *About* it? *Toward* it perhaps?—creates a tension that bristles powerfully throughout *Corregidora* and is caught in a shockingly logical moment of equipoise at the novel's end. The constant shifts in narrative perspective and Ursa's insistence on a consciousness capable of reconciling opposites (since hate and desire are "two humps on the same camel" [102]) perhaps prepare us for her reunion with Mutt, but they do little to prepare us for that "split second of hate and love" in which Ursa realizes the true nature of her inheritance as a Corregidora woman: the power to take a man in oral sex to "a moment that stops just before sexlessness, a moment that stops just before it breaks the skin: 'I could kill you' " (184). Ultimately, however, Ursa's new world is a place strikingly similar to Tayo's, a world in which opposing forces are held in a safe yet delicate balance. If, in *Corregidora*, the balance established between men and women is chiefly one of terror, it is a terror nonetheless mitigated by tenderness, by Ursa's refusal to use the power she discovers. The discovery alone is enough to carry her beyond victimization and away from twenty-two years of emotional numbness, to insist finally that "I don't want a kind of man that'll hurt me neither" (185). The painful irony, of course, is that Ursa's demand is in some sense too little and too late, since Mutt had long ago exercised his power to destroy her sexually by pushing her down the stairs. But if the experience of the novel teaches the greater powers of seeing, of bearing witness, then Mutt too must be credited for some degree of recognition—of past cruelties and the present need for tenderness—in the rich and sparingly worded conclusion: "He held me tight" (185).

On the surface, there would seem to be some perversity in any effort to link Marilynne Robinson's *Housekeeping* to works such as *Ceremony* and *Corregidora*, novels in which quests for female narrative power are coupled with or couched within broad and often brutal racial struggles for cultural survival. Robinson's lush and dazzling lyricism might appear to be simply an example of the whimsical flights of fancy that seem possible in the lily-white, virtually all-female world described in the novel. But since I began with a premise and a promise of cross-culturalism, I would like to conclude with the example of an author who explores such a world with a set of concerns and strategies that clearly connect her to those whose artistic territories are fraught with more overtly violent racial or sexual tensions. Besides, when a novelist plunges her story to the bottom of an icy lake when we are a scant three pages in, dare we skid too lightly across its surfaces and dismiss it as mere "fancy"?

From beginning to end, the hushed tone of the narrative voice in *Housekeeping* is a net tossed over the readers' eyes, a net that at times protects us and at others deceives us in this watery journey through the female imagination. "My name is Ruth," the narrator announces in the first sentence[24]—with a soft but disarming directness that deeply submerges the tensions at work in the passage that follows, disguising with Dickinsonian subtlety that this is a profoundly subversive story of a female tribe happily gathered on the margins of the dominant culture. The passage continues: "I grew up with my younger sister, Lucille, under the care of my grandmother, Mrs. Sylvia Foster, and when she died, of her sisters-in-law, Misses Lily and Nona Foster, and when they fled, of her daughter, Mrs. Sylvia Fisher. Through all these generations of elders we lived in one house, my grandmother's house, built for her by her husband, Edmund Foster, an employee of the railroad, who escaped this world years before I entered it" (3).

Hovering just below the benign, even ladylike narrative surface of this opening, which goes on to relate the grandfather's fondness for travel literature and painting mountains, are the discomfiting "facts" of *Housekeeping*: that, like *Ceremony* and *Corregidora*, it is an unapologetic story of female power in the face of cultural orphanage, dispossession, and namelessness, a mythology of the transients, drifters, and outlaws who know and care for one another right beneath our noses, with or without our knowledge—or consent. But by the time we reach the end of the novel and realize that this sweet, trustworthy narrator—whose strange whirlings into metaphor we tolerate simply because they *sound* so pretty—has stumbled across a railroad bridge in the dead of night with that crazy Sylvie. . . . Well, by then, of course, it is too late: We have been duped into liking her, despite—or perhaps, we even speculate, because of—her fondness for metaphor and her "increasingly erratic behavior" (213).

The cumulative effect of all this delightful metaphorizing—which might make a picnic of the resurrection (96–97) or a Delphic oracle of a "scattering of leaves and paper" (85)—is gradually to un-moor us from the psychic certainty of our own calm surfaces, to ease us down "into the darker world, where other sounds would pour into our ears until we seemed to find songs in them, and the sight of the water would invade our eyes, and the taste of the water would invade our bowels and unstring our bones, and we would know the seasons and customs of the place as if there were no others" (150). Indeed, the narrative itself seems to be suspended in some watery medium—most likely amniotic fluids—not merely because of Ruthie's pre-occupations with her mother's unexplained d(r)ive into the lake, but also because of the tendency of the images to "swim and flow" (162) so easily, so organically into one another: as when the simple act of tasting a cup of water evolves quietly into the image of a God who "is known to have walked upon water, but He was not born to drown." The image of His life melts inevitably into the awareness of His death and then to the human need to recreate His presence—and those of all the wanderers and the perished—in memory (193–95).

On the one hand, the tropography of Robinson's novel appears to be a poetics of feminine conservatism—a naive nostalgia for the grandmother's "serenely orderly and ordinary life" (25) or for the prenatal bliss of "walk[ing] forever through reachless oblivion" (214). Working against this, however, is Ruthie's insistence, that "Perhaps memory is the seat not only of prophecy but of miracle as well" (196)—the miracle being the promise that the integrity possible in the mind will ultimately be realized in the world. The true house to be kept is thus the house of the imagination, which obliterates the distinctions between past losses and future possibilities by according them equal degrees of mental "reality": "For need can blossom into all the compensation it requires. To crave and to have are as like as a thing and its shadow. . . . And here again is a foreshadowing—the world will be made whole" (152).

"The world will be made whole": The old women making their songs out of sorrow, the woods full of stories of perished settlers, the people in bus stations with their elaborate lies designed to disguise their loneliness—all of these sorrows might converge in and be erased by our power to ". . . imagine that [if] Noah's wife, when she was old, found somewhere a remnant of the Deluge, she might have walked into it till her widow's dress floated above her head and loosened her plaited hair. And she would have left it to her sons to tell the tedious tale of generations. She was a nameless woman, and so at home among all those who were never found and never missed, who were uncommemorated, whose deaths were not remarked, nor their begettings" (172).

For the reader, this "nameless woman" is a puzzle that, when solved, functions as the novel's central, totalizing metaphor, the link that defines Robinson's chain of housekeepers and homewreckers. Here, Noah's wife throws open the shutters at the apex of the Flood, an action that recalls the boundary-free nature of Sylvie's housekeeping: her belief in "stern solvents, and most of all in air," her willingness to open the house to "wasps and bats and barn swallows," and her fondness for dining in the dark (84–86). Elsewhere, gazing out "on the tenth or fifteenth night of rain," Noah's wife's sense of loss underscores and enlarges Ruthie's own sense of orphanage, related in her story of the young girl in the orchard who realizes that "the world was gone, the orchard was gone, her mother and grandmother and aunts were gone" (203–4). Her widow's dress connects her to Ruthie's grandmother, and her unspectacular walk into the water links her, of course, to Ruthie's mother.

Noah's wife functions most crucially, however, in establishing Robinson's concept of narrativity in her refusal to tell the sons' "tedious tale of generations." Clearly, *Housekeeping* is a tale of generations, but it is an exuberantly and almost exclusively female saga. As narrator of this revisionary myth, the nameless woman becomes, like Ursa Corregidora, the bearer of all the names and all the meanings of the past, as well as a map forward to future possibilities. As an amalgam of Ruthie, Sylvie, Helen, and the grandmother, Noah's wife undercuts the stability of any narrative "I," the accuracy of any "eye" —even as she taps into the potentially greater power of multiple

selves and shifting perspectives. For the reader, she is both an important link to the mythic past of Judeo-Christian culture and a quiet
condemnation of that culture's failure to tell the whole story.[25] But
most importantly, she is an invitation to be claimed by the lake—to
pick one's way carefully across a railroad bridge in the dead of night
and realize that the laws of the water are likewise those of the mind:
for both are receptacles that contain as well as forces that transform objects/reality. Like Woolf's Judith Shakespeare, Noah's wife is
a paradigmatic figure of the female artist whose sources of creativity
lie in the domestic and the ordinary. Unlike her tragic predecessor,
however, Robinson's nameless woman finds an outlet for her imaginative energies and is rescued from obscurity, giving herself a name
—several in fact—and passing on the triumphant knowledge that
what is "lost to all sense . . . [has] not perished, not perished" (160).

III

> My heart is moved by all I cannot save:
> so much has been destroyed
> I have to cast my lot with those
> who age after age, perversely,
> with no extraordinary power,
> reconstitute the world.
>   Adrienne Rich, "Natural Resources"[26]

As feminists and critics, whether we imaginatively compare
our tasks to hopping freight trains, singing the blues, or encoun-
tering mythical witches in the critical desert, we must acknowledge that our goals are, like those of the authors I have considered
here, ultimately and profoundly similar. By reconstituting their various worlds in terms that valorize and celebrate female power, these
writers do not offer merely the naive "separatist fantasies of radical
feminist visionaries"[27]; rather, they force us to confront the dangers
of the half-world we inhabit, even as they establish the contours of
an alternative territory in which the brutalities of nuclear power,
sexual violence, and human separation might not seem so hopelessly
necessary. Further, they give practical proof to feminist theories of
a coherent female identity that cuts across lines of race and class,
since each of these writers demonstrates a fundamental concern with
the dispossession of women as a cultural group and significantly
subverts the form and language of the novel in order to re-claim

and re-create the powers of a female selfhood lost or buried beneath layers of patriarchal culture. Instead of victims, vamps, and fawning "heroines," they have given us singers, swimmers, bridge-crossers, map-makers, storytellers—"Thought-Women," in short, who have discovered and tread fearlessly across—or dive blissfully into—the fluid depths of the female psyche. If this fluidity carries with it a unique capacity for bonding—for merging, for empathy, for the joy and the terror of being "girls together"—we must pause to consider seriously what we have entered into in the act of reading these texts. Ultimately, of course, the reader must realize that our relationship to the narrator precisely replicates the central power relationships portrayed in the novels themselves. Like Tayo and Ruthie struggling to come to terms with the symbolic and literal losses of their mothers and Ursa's bitter quest to overcome the loss of her biological ability to be a mother, we as readers are finally obliged to hear in the narrative voice echoes of our own lost powers, to see in its vision glimpses of the sources, the possibilities, and the stronger selves from which we seem so separated. Over and over again, these narrators assure us that the world can and will "be made whole." Having been spun so masterfully into their songs and ceremonies, dunked so thoroughly in their Arctic waters, and lifted so gently aboard their passing freight trains, what choice do we have but to try to make it so?

NOTES

I am indebted to Toni Morrison, who convinced me that this paper could be written, and to the organizers of the Graduate English Symposium at Rutgers University, where I was able to air and share these ideas in April 1984. E. Ann Kaplan's insightful comments on this occasion were invaluable signposts on the road to revision, and I am grateful for her careful attention.

1. Joy Harjo, *She Had Some Horses* (New York: Thunder's Mouth Press, 1983) 55–56.
2. Annette Kolodny, "Dancing through the Minefield: Some Observations on the Theory, Practice, and Politics of a Feminist Literary Criticism," *Feminist Studies* 6 (1980): 1–25. Elaine Showalter, "Feminist Criticism in the Wilderness," *Writing and Sexual Difference*, ed. Elizabeth Abel (Chicago: University of Chicago Press, 1982) 9–36.
3. Judith Kegan Gardiner, "On Female Identity and Writing by Women," *Writing and Sexual Difference*, 183, n. 11.
4. Showalter, "Feminist Criticism," 27.

5. A quick survey of some of the major texts to come out of the feminist critical movement demonstrates the occupational bias toward British literature: Ellen Moers's *Literary Women* (Garden City: Doubleday & Co., Inc., 1976) offers perhaps the most extensive comparative survey of the Anglo-American tradition, but the American side of the hyphen pulls up short in her study of "the great writers." Elaine Showalter's *A Literature of Their Own* (Princeton: Princeton University Press, 1977), Sandra M. Gilbert and Susan Gubar's *The Madwoman in the Attic* (New Haven and London: Yale University Press, 1979), and Nina Auerbach's *Woman and the Demon* (Cambridge and London: Harvard University Press, 1982) all focus their considerable energies and talents on Victorian England. Recently, of course, several exciting new studies have begun to rectify this imbalance, though thus far the greatest emphasis is still on white women in mid-nineteenth century America. See, for example: Nina Baym, *Woman's Fiction* (Ithaca: Cornell University Press, 1978); Ann Douglas, *The Feminization of American Culture* (New York: Random House, 1977); Mary Kelley, *Private Woman, Public Stage* (New York: Oxford University Press, 1984); Annette Kolodny, *The Land Before Her* (Chapel Hill: University of North Carolina Press, 1984); and Jane Tompkins, *Sensational Designs* (New York: Oxford University Press, 1985).

6. To avoid charges of essentialism, I should point out that, here and throughout this paper, I use the word *female* to describe an identity constructed by cultural and political forces—not biological ones. Although I refer to the effort of these writers to "re-claim and re-create the powers of a female self-hood lost or buried beneath layers of patriarchal culture" (120–21), I mean nevertheless that the "selves" recovered in this excavation process are more intellectual than physiological, more femi*nist*, perhaps, than femi*nine*.

7. Annie Dillard, *Teaching a Stone to Talk: Expeditions and Encounters* (New York: Harper & Row, 1982), 27.

8. For evidence of this bias among (male) critics of the American persuasion, see, again, some of the classic critical texts: Richard Poirier, *A World Elsewhere* (New York: Oxford University Press, 1966); D. H. Lawrence, *Studies in Classic American Literature* (1923; New York: Penguin Books, 1977); Leslie Fiedler, *Love and Death in the American Novel* (1960; New York: Stein and Day, 1975); F. O. Matthiessen, *American Renaissance* (New York: Oxford University Press, 1941). For an insightful analysis of how this bias has informed the canon of American literature, see Nina Baym's "Melodramas of Beset Manhood: How Theories of American Fiction Exclude Women Writers," *American Quarterly* 33 (1981): 123–39.

9. Annette Kolodny, *The Lay of the Land*. Chapel Hill: University of North Carolina Press, 1975.

10. Elizabeth Abel, "(E)Merging Identities: The Dynamics of Female Friendship in Contemporary Fiction by Women," *Signs* 6:3 (1981): 413–35. Nancy Chodorow, *The Reproduction of Mothering: Psychoanalysis and the Sociology of Gender* (Berkeley: University of California Press, 1978).

11. For a presentation of some of this evidence, see Vernon E. Lattin, "The Quest for Mythic Vision in Contemporary Native American and Chicano Fiction," *American Literature* 50:4 (1979): 625–40.

12. I refer particularly to Abel's conclusions about the possibilities of Chodorow's theories for psychological formulations of female literary relationships: "Women writers since Austen and Dickinson have felt a particular bond with one another, and twentieth-century women writers are explicit about their concern with formulating and conserving a tradition. This concern with collectivity mediates the desire for originality and places women writers in a different historical as well as psychological situation from their male contemporaries. As the dynamics of female friendship differ from those of the male, the dynamics of female literary influence also diverge and deserve a theory of influence attuned to female psychology and to women's dual position in literary history" (434).

13. For a variety of perspective on these multiple oppressions, see Cherríe Moraga and Gloria Anzaldúa, eds., *This Bridge Called My Back* (Watertown, Mass.: Persephone, 1981).

14. Dillard, *Teaching a Stone to Talk*, 19.

15. For a much more thorough discussion of the mythological underpinnings of *Ceremony* than I can offer here, see Kathleen Sands, ed., "A Special Symposium Issue on Leslie Marmon Silko's *Ceremony*," *American Indian Quarterly* 5:1 (1979).

16. Leslie Marmon Silko, *Ceremony* (New York: Signet Books, 1977) 258. Future references will be made parenthetically within the essay.

17. Paula Gunn Allen similarly discusses the place of language in native American cultures in "The Sacred Hoop: A Contemporary Perspective," in *The Sacred Hoop: Recovering the Feminine in American Indian Traditions* (Boston: Beacon Press, 1986) 54–75.

18. Of equal importance here is that the men who act as Tayo's spiritual guides in his journey are defined in large part by the rightness of their sexual/mythical relation to a female creative source. Most significant is his uncle Josiah, who is involved with the Mexican woman Night Swan/Tse-pi'na ("the woman veiled in clouds" [91]). She guides Josiah to the spotted cattle that serve such an important symbolic function

in his nephew's quest, and she in fact initiates Tayo into the powers and processes of the ceremony in a sexual encounter (102–5).

19. Carolyn Forché, "Burning the Tomato Worms," *Gathering the Tribes* (New Haven and London: Yale University Press, 1976) 4.

20. Adrienne Rich, "Transcendental Etude," *The Dream of a Common Language: Poems 1974–1977* (New York: W. W. Norton & Co., 1977) 75–76.

21. Alice Walker, *The Color Purple* (New York: Washington Square Press, 1982), 178.

22. Toni Morrison, *Sula* (New York: Alfred A. Knopf, Inc., 1973), 149.

23. Gayl Jones, *Corregidora* (New York: Bantam Books, 1976), 8. Future references will be made parenthetically within the essay.

24. Marilynne Robinson, *Housekeeping* (New York: Farrar, Straus & Giroux, Inc., 1981), 3. Future references will be made parenthetically within the essay.

25. For additional studies of women writers and revisionary mythology, see Susan Gubar, "Mother, Maiden, and the Marriage of Death: Women Writers and an Ancient Myth," *Women's Studies* 6 (1979): 301–15, and Alicia Ostriker, "Thieves of Language: Women Poets and Revisionist Mythology," *Stealing the Language* (Boston: Beacon Press, 1986) 210–38.

26. Rich, "Natural Resources," *The Dream of a Common Language*, 67.

27. Showalter, "Feminist Criticism," 14.

LAURA NIESEN De ABRUÑA

The "Incredible Indigo Sea" within Anglo-American Fiction

I began to feel I loved the land and to know that I would never forget it. There I would go for long walks alone. It's strange growing up in a very beautiful place and seeing that it is beautiful. It was alive, I was sure of it. Behind the bright colours the softness, the hills like clouds and the clouds like fantastic hills. There was something austere, sad, lost, all these things.

Jean Rhys, *Smile Please*

I

The Caribbean[1]—the "incredible indigo sea," as William Faulkner calls it[2]—maintains, beneath the high tide of Anglo-American fiction, a passionate but submerged interest in issues of identity and difference, of self and other, and of early childhood. Any list of Caribbean characters in British or American fiction reveals women whose high energy is sublimated in secondary roles[3]: Bertha Antoinetta Mason in Charlotte Brontë's *Jane Eyre* (1847), Cora Munro in James Fenimore Cooper's *Last of the Mohicans* (1826), Eulalia Bon in William Faulkner's *Absalom, Absalom!* (1936), and Bertha Antoinette Mason in Jean Rhys's *Wide Sargasso Sea* (1966). In the two British novels, *Jane Eyre* and *Wide Sargasso Sea*, the women are a mirror image of one another.[4]

This essay examines the intersection of racism and sexism within an imperialistic context, a nexus evident in each of these texts. As Tzvetan Todorov has pointed out, racism is "the display of contempt and aggressiveness toward other people on account of physical differences (other than those of sex) between them and oneself" (171). This definition is particularly useful in looking at the novels presenting West Indian women because a simple extension of the definition to include differences of sex shows the common basis of racism and sexism in intolerance of difference. And since sex and race are the two most obvious and irreducible signs of difference, the intersection of both in West Indian women renders them extremely vulnerable to sexual racism.

But what is the context in which the attitudes toward the intersection of gender and race occur? All of these novels, with the exception of *Wide Sargasso Sea*, are written by writers who are not themselves West Indian. And, as Gayatri Spivak points out, it is impossible to read modern English literature without establishing the "fact" that imperialism was considered a crucial part of the "cultural representation of England to the English" (243). The role of literature in the production of acceptable cultural representations was taken for granted by the author and the contemporary readers of *Jane Eyre*. Insofar as North American novelists reproduce sexist and racist representations of West Indians, they are imitating the "mother" country and contributing to the longevity of stereotypes about Caribbean peoples. This is the case in *Last of the Mohicans* and *Absalom, Absalom!*. While I start this essay by examining the West Indian woman in a classic nineteenth-century British text, *Jane Eyre*, and continue by showing similar attitudes in those nineteenth- and twentieth-century North American texts, I shall end with another British novelist, Jean Rhys. The significant difference here is that although Rhys is white, she is the only West Indian in this group, and she has, significantly, reinscribed *Jane Eyre* within *Wide Sargasso Sea*.

There is a problem in looking to a white woman writer as the most promising of all these novelists. As Abdul R. JanMohamed has stated in a recent article, the comprehension of the "Otherness" found in the African-Caribbean woman is possible only "if the self can somehow negate or at least severely bracket the values, assumptions, and ideology of his culture" (65). Although Rhys cannot claim fully to understand the "Otherness" of most West Indian women, because most are African-Caribbean rather than white Creole, she does seem able to return to Bertha Mason the dignity taken away by Brontë. In Rhys's fiction, we also see a successful "syncretism" between the white Creole woman Antoinette and the black Creole woman Tia. JanMohamed would argue that such an attempt is almost impossible. Comprehension of the "Other," he says, "entails in practice the virtually impossible task of negating one's very being, precisely because one's culture is what formed that being" (65).

This social determinism denies the possibility of attaining a critical perspective on one's own culture; it is also not an accurate description of Jean Rhys's fiction. JanMohamed claims that colonialist literature attempting to explore the racial "Other" is only another form of ethnocentrism: "Such literature is essentially specular: instead of seeing the native as a bridge toward syncretic possibility, it uses him as a mirror that reflects the colonialist's self-image" (65). Yet, in *Wide Sargasso Sea*, Jean Rhys defies this pessimism. As I shall show, Antoinette does negat͏ʰᵉ self in sacrificing that self and thus transcends the values, assumptions, and ideology of her culture. She demonstrates that syncretism is possible between white Creole women and African-Caribbean women if the women can "bracket" the sexism, racism, and imperialism that are thrust upon them.

Because the two British novels *Jane Eyre* and *Wide Sargasso Sea* are mirror images of one another, I shall begin and end my argument with two of the most important Caribbean women in Anglo-American fiction, one of whom only hints at syncretism, while the other fully explores this possibility. Both of these novels concentrate on the distortions in identity experienced by women in patriarchal cultures. Jane Eyre struggles to maintain an identity separate from Mr. Rochester's; and Bertha Antoinetta Mason struggles to preserve her sense of personality from insanity. Nancy Chodorow has used psychoanalytic object-relations theory to explain how sex, gender, and family organization determine a sense of personality in women —and men—in Western cultures (7). Chodorow argues that early development of both males and females depends on the quality of bonding between the mother and the child. Whereas their early relationship is characterized by a close, symbiotic relationship, the child gradually comes to perceive the mother as separate. In fact, the child develops a sense of self only by realizing that it is separate from the mother. This sense of self is what I shall term an *identity*. Chodorow argues that female identity formation is a different process from male identity formation. Young females experience themselves as less separate from their mothers than young boys and tend to define themselves in relation to others (93). Young boys, on the other hand, move more quickly to a fixed self-concept that identifies with the father figure, although they are left with anxieties surrounding issues of masculinity and autonomy that seem to affect their later relationships with women. A young girl's self-concept is more dependent

on the mother-daughter bond; and a woman's ability to merge with
the mother while preserving a sense of individual existence and importance is crucial to a stable personality.[5] The mother-son bonding,
on the other hand, while equally intense at the early periods, is less
likely to extend itself in oversymbiosis and narcissistic overidenti-
fication on the mother's part. Consequently, the son has an easier
time establishing a sense of a separate ego but a more difficult time
in developing relational interaction.

Both Brontë and Rhys present women in the process of finding,
in Jane's case, and losing, in Antoinette's case, an individual identity.
In the novels by these women writers, then, there is a greater emphasis on the women characters' struggles to define themselves as "subjects"—separate from others; whereas in the novels by Cooper and
Faulkner, the women are more often seen as "objects"—the already
defined "Other" who is a passive victim of various economic, social,
sexual, or racial strategies. Chodorow's theory suggests that such a
difference is the result of the women writers' heightened sensitivity
to the struggle of young women in developing a self-concept.

Despite the tendency of the male writers to repress the West
Indian woman as subject in their texts, we still have a tradition of
vital women characters spanning two centuries, into and beyond
the 1960s. Why, then, has our literature resolutely repressed the energy of the Caribbean, whether Creole or African-Caribbean, and
elbowed her out of major social roles, or even critical inquiry?[6] The
question is doubly important because, as Ronnie Scharfman argues,
psychological oppression does not always lead to loss of identity and
victimization among the West Indian women presented in Caribbean literature (Scharfman 88–89). In comparing a French Antil-
lean novel, *Pluie et Vent sur Télumée Miracle* (Simone Schwarz-
Bart) with Jean Rhys's *Wide Sargasso Sea*, Scharfman finds a loss
of personality in Antoinette and a strengthening of personality in
Télumée. Antoinette fails in all of her personal relationships, and
descends into madness. But the French novel celebrates the success
of Télumée, whose ego survives a disastrous romantic relationship
because she feels herself part of an African-Caribbean community
and is nurtured through a strong bonding with the women in her
family. Antoinette's major problem is that her mother rejected her
and refused to acknowledge her as a separate person. This, combined
with the pressures of imperialism and sexism, pushed her into in-

sanity. Télumée is nurtured by her grandmother, who affords her the identity that is usually offered by the biological mother, and is able to establish strong ego boundaries so that she does not experience diffusion when her sexual relationships end.

However, the case is very different for the West Indian women in the Anglo-American novels that recreate the English cultural assumptions of imperialism. These women live at the margins of societies populated by men who are not only not Caribbean, but invariably—whether husband, lover, or friend—white and Anglo-Saxon. The males in several of these novels, most notably *Jane Eyre*'s Mr. Rochester, prefer to love and to be loved by Victorian "dolls"— short, "slim," passionless, blonde women. Yet these men marry or cohabit with dark-haired women of average stature: Bertha Mason is a Jamaican Creole, black-haired and olive-complected, and as large as her husband; Cora Munro is dark, passionate, and African-Caribbean; Eulalia Bon is of mixed French, Spanish, and black blood; and Rhys's Bertha Antoinette Mason, who seems to be a Creole, appears "not English or European either" to her husband (67). In a letter to Diana Athill, Jean Rhys says she intended Antoinette to be "dark" and mysterious, "with some French or Spanish blood, perhaps with the seeds of madness, at any rate hysteria."[7] Race, as well as gender, is of course at issue here since all of these women suffer from intolerance of difference. In each case, the woman is experienced as doubly "Other" because she has physical and sexual characteristics that mark her as different from the more powerful male. Whatever is "foreign" causes uneasiness.[8] Yet, when the woman is "dark" and Caribbean (her partner's coloring is irrelevant)—either by complexion (i.e., black or brown hair and eyes), or nationality (Spanish or French), or race (African-Caribbean)—she is even more easily targeted and identified with the "Other"—whatever differs from the dominant group and is therefore foreign, alien, and "bad."

The pairing of the dark-featured woman with a feared lack of control, of letting go, or sexual passion, is a classic misogynist gesture in European literature. In fact, there is an entire critical literature on the preference of male writers for light over dark "maidens."[9] In North American literature as well there is a tradition of the dark-dangerous woman contrasted with the pale-sexless woman ideal, who is less threatening. Again, racism and sexism intersect. When light and dark women are paired in the same novel, they can represent two sides of the human psyche, although they are rarely regarded in the same way.

We find these fears associated with "dark" women in a novel written by a woman. Sandra Gilbert and Susan Gubar argue in *The Madwoman in the Attic* that "dark" Bertha Mason functions symbolically as the "fair" Jane Eyre's "double." Bertha projects Jane's repressed sexuality and anger about her dependent position in society (*Madwoman* 360). Even though Brontë attempts, at least unconsciously, to heal the psychic split between Jane's two selves through her identification and sympathy with Bertha, the "dark" woman remains the animal part of the self that must be punished through immolation.

Brontë was never really able to demonstrate the syncretic possibility of a relationship between Jane and Bertha. Moreover, whatever identification takes place between Jane and Bertha is so suppressed as to be missed by most readers; their functions as "doubles" was not discovered until Gilbert and Gubar pointed this out. Such identification may have been an impossibility in a culture—or cultures—obsessed with the project of cultural imperialism in the West Indies.

The presentation of "dark" women as the dangerously sexual and racial "Other" is exactly what we do find in the North American novels written by authors who have converted the British imperialistic project to their parallel, "pioneer" conquest and subjugation of their new world. I shall look at some objects of these attitudes and argue that the Caribbean women in these novels are presented as experiencing very similar emotions. All of them (whether they are white Creoles, black Creoles, or of mixed ancestry) are perceived as the "racial" and sexual "Other" in their imperialistic-patriarchal society. This society experiences uneasiness about the culture it is exploiting, and this uneasiness unconsciously becomes a part of the fiction.

II

An early British example of such victimization is the disastrous marriage of Edward Fairfax Rochester and Bertha Antoinetta Mason in Charlotte Brontë's *Jane Eyre* (1847). The woman is the daughter of Jonas Mason, a merchant, and Antoinetta Mason, a Creole, both of whom were living in Jamaica when Rochester was sent there by his father and his elder brother Rowland (276). Rochester is manipulated by his father, who refuses to leave him any portion of the estate, and arranges, behind Edward's back, to have Mr. Mason give over his daughter and a fortune of thirty thousand pounds in marriage to his son. Edward is taken in by this farce, marries Bertha, and only later suffers from severe marital incompatibility. Even more disturbing is the discovery of his mother-in-law's fate as an irretrievably alcoholic woman incarcerated in an asylum (291).

Rochester's cold-blooded marriage was not unusual when great fortunes were made in sugar cane, and the revenues made the West Indies England's prized possession. Creole and African-Caribbean daughters of wealthy planters inherited large fortunes that would be transferred by law, through marriage, to their husbands unless a pre-nuptial arrangement protected them. In a letter to Francis Wyndham, Jean Rhys claims that many women like Bertha were taken back to England and, once used, discarded like sallow, shopsoiled dolls: "The West Indies was (were?) rich in those days *for* those days and there was no 'married woman's property act.' The girls (very tiresome no doubt) would soon once in kind England be *Address Unknown*. So gossip. So a legend."[10]

By the time Rochester would have visited Jamaica, the island where he met Bertha, its economy was on the decline. In 1838, the Emancipation Act abolished slavery in Jamaica, bringing an economic crisis for the plantation owners because they lost their right to free labor (Dash 202). To make matters worse for the planters, in 1846 the British government withdrew its protection of Jamaica's sugar market, then in competition with Cuba and Brazil (Dash 202). All the sources of power became muddled. According to Cheryl Dash, the Creoles' position was difficult and ambivalent: "Very few whites chose to remain and live on the estates and those who did were consequently ostracized and felt to be not quite as good as the 'real British' were."[11]

In Brontë's *Jane Eyre*, the Mason family might have felt serious financial constraints that tempted them to hold back "secrets": Bertha's mother in the asylum, her alcoholism, her son's mental retardation (he is called a "dumb idiot," *Jane Eyre* 291). They were eager to bring Rochester into the family—even at the cost of thirty

thousand pounds. Both sides asked few questions. As Rochester remarks, "Her family wished to secure me, because I was of good race;
and so did she" (290).[12]

Although candor was withheld on both sides, Rochester is
embittered by what should have been obvious: he regrets that his
wife is not a childlike porcelain doll, but a dark-haired, tall, olive-
complected woman. He feels that such betrayal releases him from
his marital vows in order to marry Jane Eyre, who is more "English."
Added to attempted bigamy is his evaluation of Bertha's mental
breakdown as a kind of inherited curse: "Bertha Mason is mad; and
she came of a mad family; idiots and maniacs through three generations!" (277). We suspect that the dark complexion of the "Creole's"
family and her gender are more repugnant to Rochester than the
family's problems. As a result, Bertha is presented as the product of
a three-generation ancestral curse.

Surprisingly, and despite his curious middle name, Edward Fairfax Rochester is olive-complected, "swarthy" (172), and himself dark
(272). He comes to hate his equally "dark" wife, finding her "in-
temperate and unchaste" (291), without offering much evidence for
the former and none for the latter. Yet he confesses to a list of
"mistresses" such as Céline Varens, Giacinta, and Clara (296). After
Richard, Bertha's brother, thwarts Rochester's plans to marry Jane,
he seeks self-justification by telling Jane about his Caribbean experiences. He clearly disliked Jamaica on emotional and irrational
grounds, and attempted to displace his discomfort and uneasiness
onto the "demon" Bertha. A negative prejudice is clear in his descriptions. The night especially is transformed into a hell, with a
bottomless pit inhabited by the devil-Bertha:

> It was a *fiery* West Indian night; one of the description that frequently
> precede the *hurricanes* of those climates. Being unable to sleep in bed,
> I got up and opened the window. The air was like *sulphur-streams*—
> I could find no refreshment anywhere. Mosquitoes came buzzing in
> and hummed *sullenly* round the room; the sea, which I could hear
> from thence, *rumbled* dull like an *earthquake—black clouds* were
> casting up over it; the moon was setting in the waves broad and *red*,
> like a *hot cannon-ball—she* threw her last *bloody glance* over a world
> quivering with the *ferment of tempest*. I was *physically influenced* by
> the atmosphere and scene, and my ears were filled with the *curses* the
> *maniac* still shrieked out. (293 emphasis added)

This is a self-confessed projection of the landscape of Jamaica as hell.[13] It runs with sulphur streams, red-hot cannon balls, and a Lucifer incarnate who makes Rochester literally ill. Nature itself is thrown into disorder by this place. The land suffers earthquakes and hurricanes; the air is cursed with sullen black clouds; and bloody glances fall from the moon.

The tirade is simply a description of Rochester's state of mind. Bertha is a convenient scapegoat for his hatred of his father since she is now financially dependent on him and emotionally unstable. Apparently, Rochester hates the tropics and the women inhabitants; and for a time he hates all women. "Last January . . . sourly disposed against all men, and especially all *woman*kind (for I began to regard the notion of an intellectual, faithful, loving woman as a mere dream), recalled by business, I came back to England" (297). His feelings about England, on the other hand, are completely positive. They represent security, hope, purity, and life—everything he believes is debased in Jamaica. Directly following the Jamaica passage is a glowing portrait of home that posits a British elysium to the Jamaican hell. "The *sweet* wind from Europe was still whispering in the *refreshed* leaves, and the Atlantic was thundering in *glorious liberty*; my heart, dried up and scorched for a long time, *swelled* to the tone, and filled with *living blood*—my being longed for *renewal*—my soul thirsted for a *pure* draught. I saw *hope revive* and felt *regeneration* possible" (293 emphasis added).

Rochester's homeland is a place of hope and life whereas the foreign place is a hell of despair. Rochester confuses fear and insecurity for reasoned motivation, so that his self-justification does not seem to him to be a rationalization. He hates Bertha because she is alcoholic, insane, and brutalized. He has turned her into an animal, a brutalized Caliban whom he has manipulated and rejected. But he also hates her because his father and the Masons manipulated him, and his culture shock must be displaced. The genuine question becomes: Is Rochester, who "puts aside" a wife because "her tastes were obnoxious" to him (291), not partly responsible for the effects of this rejection? At the very least we might expect compassion—not hatred, even though that is never the case with the powerful man and his Caliban.

Instead, Rochester dehumanizes Bertha and treats her as if she were a caged animal who must remain in the upstairs bedroom.

Gayatri Spivak has cited many examples of Bertha's dehumanization to animal status in *Jane Eyre*. Spivak sees this degradation as a product of the nineteenth-century British belief in "imperialism as social mission" (247). Through Bertha Mason, Brontë blurs the boundary between human and animal, thus representing the opportunity or even "duty" of the imperialist to civilize the "not-yet-human Other" (247). After the wedding is broken up by Richard Mason, Rochester attempts to justify himself by showing them the "embruted" (278) woman whom he has rejected to "seek sympathy with something at least human" (278). Jane herself calls Bertha a "clothed hyena" (279) and seems to agree with Rochester's attitudes. Such feelings are evident in the well-known passage, which Spivak also quotes, describing the visit of the wedding guests to Bertha's chamber. "In the deep shade, at the farther end of the room, a figure ran backwards and forwards. What it was, whether beast or human being, one could not, at first sight, tell: it grovelled, seemingly, on all fours; it snatched and growled like some strange wild animal: but it was covered with clothing, and a quantity of dark, grizzled hair, wild as a mane, hid its head and face" (278). In the case presented here the dehumanization is more than self-imposed disintegration. Bertha is unquestionably turned into an animal, even by Jane, who in some respects is sympathetic to her. In *Jane Eyre*, insanity results from the internalization of "racism" and sexism directed at West Indians, since the breakdown of a "dark" foreign woman occurs directly after a relationship with a powerful male.[14]

III

In North America, too, the literary presentation of West Indians, especially women, has been egregious and perverse. The new world's literary tradition prolongs the exploitation of the Caribbean woman, at least as presented in fiction. American authors turn the West Indies into a mythic wilderness ready for a new generation of shrewd Puritans to pummel and pluck it. As early as 1826, James Fenimore Cooper's *Last of the Mohicans* examines prejudice, especially as directed toward native Americans. Even the novel's epigraph, the words of the suitor, the Prince of Morocco, from *The Merchant of Venice* (II.ii. 1–2), reflects Cooper's emphasis on xenophobia or what we have called racism. The "dark" prince asks "Mislike me not for my complexion, / The shadowed livery of the burnished sun." Yet, the novel sacrifices a young West Indian woman. Because she is Caribbean, Cora Munro is prevented by death, the novel's *deus ex machina*, from marriage to the Mohican Indian, Uncas. Intermingling of races always threatens to occur in this novel but is always thwarted by death. Earlier, Cora's father was distraught that Duncan Heyward, a white southerner, was interested in his elder daughter Cora. Ironically, Heyward loves Munro's younger daughter Alice, whose mother was English. Alice is the "fair one" (23) while Cora is "dark" and "dark-eyed" (25).

When Heyward asks to marry one of his daughters, Munro assumes he means Cora. He feels obligated to explain her heritage to Heyward, and in doing so reveals many experiences similar to Mr. Rochester's. Like Rochester, Munro feels deprived of the wealth commensurate with his class. His poverty forces him to break off with his fiancée, and serve in the navy, eventually reaching the West Indies: "I had seen many regions, and had shed much blood in different lands, before duty called me to the islands of the West Indies" (187). Munro marries an African-Caribbean woman in the West Indies and, unlike Rochester, is able to control feelings of alienation; the couple has a daughter, Cora. Since he is Scottish, Munro believes that island slavery is England's fault, and that he held no reservations about his wife, who also made him a wealthy man.

But now that his wife is dead and he lives in the United States, Munro apologizes for his daughter's heritage. A defensive tone, a need to justify himself, creeps into his conversation with Heyward. Munro's apologia for Cora, which is unnecessary for his English daughter, reveals unconsciously held assumptions. Edward Rochester, in his justification, tells Jane about the "Creole's" mother whom he suspects is alien and dangerous. Notice that in Munro's speech the same emphasis falls on the mother as transmitting "unfortunate" social class.

> There [the West Indies] it was my lot to form a connection with one who in time became my wife, and the mother of Cora. She was the daughter of a gentleman of those isles, by a lady whose misfortune it was, if you will," said the old man, proudly, "to be descended, remotely, from that unfortunate class who are so basely enslaved to administer to the wants of a luxurious people. Aye, sir, that is a curse entailed on Scotland by her unnatural union with a foreign and trading

people. But could I find a man among them who would dare to reflect on my child, he should feel the weight of a father's anger! (187–88)

His emphasis on "fortune," and "misfortune," and "unfortunate" clashes with his posture as defender of his daughter. He is like Huck Finn whose decision to "go to hell" rather than accept Jim's slavery is dependent on the belief that what he has done, or intends to do, defies his sense of society's proper order. Although Munro says he accepts his daughter, he has really been very much a part of what Spivak calls the social mission of imperialism. He does not mistake the reactions of his fellow North Americans. Had Duncan been interested in Cora, he would now have second thoughts. He is conscious of a prejudiced feeling as "deeply rooted as if it had been ingrafted in his nature" (188), and his eyes fall to the floor in embarrassment. Munro is incensed that Heyward then speaks of Alice rather than Cora. Ironically, Munro does not realize that he has also contributed to the "unfortunate" position of Caribbean women like his wife and daughter. As a military officer, he cannot dissociate himself from the king of England or his "foreign and trading people" since Munro's duty in the West Indies certainly involved enforcement of British control and came as a reward after he had "shed much blood in different Lands" (187), presumably at the direction of the same king.

In twentieth-century North American literature the belief in the West Indies as a place for exploitation does not fade but gains force. Speaking even casually of the Caribbean, North American novels characterize it, without irony, as the new world's safety valve. Jamaica, for example, gives the poor, ambitious, and shrewd, that is, unscrupulous, white male an opportunity to "get rich quickly." This mythologizing process continues into the 1920s when Jay Gatsby, the center of F. Scott Fitzgerald's *Great Gatsby* (1925), goes to the West Indies in his first money-making venture. The Caribbean marks a turning point in James Gatz's career, a shedding of his old name and a rebirth as Jay Gatsby. Dan Cody, Gatsby's mentor, is a "pioneer debauchee" in the tradition of the pirates. He raids and rapes the earth, particularly by extracting metals—copper in Montana, silver in Nevada, and gold in the Yukon.

To young Gatz, Dan Cody's yacht represented everything that was worthwhile. The pioneer-piratical spirit of plundering other places—new places outside the Middle West, appealed vastly to him. The meeting linked James Gatz with the spirit of money grabbing: "And when the *Tuolumne* left for the West Indies and the Barbary Coast Gatsby left too" (126–27). Exploitative, nonproductive extraction of the earth's resources is part of Cody's business ethics. Even his boat, the *Tuolumne*, is named for a town made famous during the early California gold rush. That era is also associated with the West Indies, when sugar cane started after the mining projects had exhausted the metal deposits. Both of these places, the West and the West Indies, are related by family to the Barbary Coast, the haunt of legendary and historical pirates.

The most blatantly destructive attitudes toward the West Indies in North American literature are held by the protagonist of William Faulkner's *Absalom, Absalom!* (1936). Sutpen, a poor, southern, and white West Virginian, has a tremendous imagination and a grotesque sense of self-creation through courage, cleverness, and unscrupulousness. As a "successful," or at least wealthy Mississippi planter, Sutpen tells his friend Colonel Compson that a "boy symbol" (261) was created the moment that he was rejected at the "big house" and ordered, by a black servant, to go to the back door. Instead of despising the class and slave-based society, the boy resolves to gain its weapons and become powerful within it.

Sutpen went to the West Indies because by that time, the 1820s, it was rumored to be a place to make quick fortunes with slave labor. As an oversized gradeschooler, Sutpen hears his teacher recount the Caribbean myth through a text. "What I learned was that there was a place called the West Indies to which poor men went in ships and became rich, it didn't matter how, so long as that man was clever and courageous" (242). No one knows why Sutpen chose Haiti, but Faulkner knew that it was the poorest country in the Western Hemisphere, and the place where slaves had revolted to gain their freedom earlier than on other islands. When Sutpen arrives the uprisings were still occurring. Overseer for a French planter, Sutpen saves the plantation when the slaves burn all of the cane fields and assault the house during an eight-day seige. The planter, his daughter, and Sutpen hold on until the ammunition runs out and he walks out to calm the slaves through his sheer ability to endure their machete cuts. Next morning the drums have stopped; Sutpen is engaged to the daughter, Eulalia Bon.

He is involved, unwillingly, in the same type of intermarriage as Colonel Munro. Sutpen finds that his mother-in-law, whom he thought "Spanish," was also part African-Caribbean. A man imitating the 1820s southern aristocracy could not admit this marriage to his design. After the child Charles Bon is born, Sutpen calls on his design and calmly explains the racial impediment to wife and father-in-law, who probably did not understand these imported attitudes toward equality and caste. On his side, Sutpen, like Rochester, believes the family deceitful because they hid "secrets." On the other side, Eulalia and the planter would not have thought mixed heritage a divisive issue, or even an important subject in a prenuptial agreement.

Faulkner is opening the major focus of the book—the immorality and self-destructiveness of the southern plantation system—to indict not only the United States, but all of the Americas. The problems of slavery and racism were Haiti's problems, as well as the curse of any place in the Americas where the sheen of the conquistadores' gold came from the blood of the slaves. Faulkner indicates that the history of Haiti's slave-based, sugar cane economy that brought injustice and violence should have been an early 1820s lesson for North American plantation owners. To Faulkner, the West Indies is a metaphor of a major disaster of the Americas: ". . . a theater for violence and injustice and bloodshed, and all the satanic lusts of human greed and cruelty, for the last despairing fury of all the pariah-interdict and all the doomed—a little island set in a smiling and fury-lurked and incredible indigo sea" (250). The phrase "all the pariah interdict" opens the focus even further to include any victim of discrimination in any place. Specifically, we are asked to consider the similar situation that will occur in the South: "The South would realize that it was now paying the price for having erected its economic edifice not on the rock of stern morality but on the shifting sands of opportunism and moral brigandage" (260).

Sutpen "puts his wife aside" as if he were a biblical patriarch especially selected by God for another marriage. But Eulalia Bon cannot be placated by a monetary settlement, nor can her son Charles. Twenty-eight years after Sutpen leaves Haiti, Charles is Henry Sutpen's intimate friend and the fiancé of Henry's sister Judith. Whether Charles's actions were motivated by revenge is unclear; but painfully clear is Sutpen's second refusal to acknowledge his first son and his grim decision that Henry must kill Charles to prevent—not incest —but miscegenation.

Because Bon himself seems to disapprove of mixed marriages, he carries a fatal self-hatred within himself, an infection spread from exposure to southern Americans like his father. Like Edward Rochester, but without his xenophobia, Bon would commit bigamy in marrying Judith since he has a "contractual arrangement" with an "octoroon mistress." Like his father, Bon is willing to "put his wife aside" and dooms himself to repeat his father's injustice: Bon prefers Judith, an American Jane Eyre accepted by the culture, over his first "dark" wife.

In *Absalom, Absalom!*, as often happens in Faulkner's novels, misfortune plagues three southern generations, until the House of Sutpen is destroyed by the ancient curses of bigotry and slavery. One disaster follows another through four generations. Henry kills Bon when they return to Sutpen's Hundred after the Civil War and spends his life running in fear of retribution until coming home to die. During the war the plantation is ruined; later Judith dies nursing Sutpen and Eulalia's grandson. Bon's son, Charles Etienne De Saint Velery Bon, suffers immense confusion about his identity; he attempts to resolve the problem by marrying a dark-skinned woman, and is periodically beaten by others who perceive him to be white. His son experiences a symbolic change of name to "Jim Bond," which downgrades him from good (bon) to enslaved (bound). Suffering the double bond of racism and Sutpen's initial rejection, Bond is alienated from the family; and by the novel's end his whereabouts are unknown.

In contrast to Brontë, Faulkner uses his narrators to present Sutpen's rapacity in the West Indies with irony; his injustice brings his own failure and degradation. The reach extends furthest in Faulkner since he always places the issue of Haiti and the West Indies in a large moral context as a battleground of blood, greed, and death. Faulkner's imagined evocation of Haitian history is wonderfully concrete, sensitive, as well as the most memorable in North American fiction. The narrative voice moves beyond the breadth of the characters' understanding without overt moralizing. Haiti is:

> . . . a little lost island in a latitude which would require ten thousand years of equatorial heritage to bear its climate, a soil manured with black blood from the two hundred years of oppression and exploita-

tion until it sprang with an incredible paradox of peaceful greenery and crimson flowers and sugar cane sapling size and three times the height of a man and a little bulkier of course but valuable pound for pound almost with silver ore, as if nature held a balance and kept a book and offered a recompense for the torn limbs and outraged hearts even if man did not . . .—the planting of men too; unsleeping blood that had vanished into the earth they trod still cried out for vengeance. (250–51)

Faulkner is aware of the paradox of oppression and a greenery punctuated with crimson flowers—the bloody red hibiscus. The island's physical beauty is the scene of spiritual unrest, cruelty, and the need for vengeance. A primal bloodshedding incurring fratricidal guilt that will not easily vanish, even after the end of slavery, is this passage's greatest insight. And yet, even in Faulkner's passage there are some negative overtones. The African-Caribbeans are pictured as passive during hundreds of years of oppression when in reality the resistance to slavery and brutality was fierce. In attempting to suggest that African blood spilled on the earth led to further violence, Faulkner chooses the verb *manured* to describe this process and thereby negates his intentions and reveals some of his own ambivalent attitudes. Thus, even Faulkner's generally sympathetic attempt to convey the experience of African-Caribbeans is tainted by the Anglo-American tradition of cultural imperialism. Both the West Indian men and the women in Faulkner's novels remain victims.

IV

In the last and most recent novel to be examined, Jean Rhys's *Wide Sargasso Sea* (1966), we return to the victimization we first saw in *Jane Eyre* (1847). Rhys tells the story of the "creolized" West Indian women—those who have some European or American heritage but have made the islands home and subsequently forgotten any direct link with "unreal" England, France, Spain, or America. Rhys's *Wide Sargasso Sea* (1966), *Voyage in the Dark* (1934), and the short story collections in *The Left Bank* (1927) and *Tigers Are Better Looking* (1927; rpt. 1968) are the best explorations of the creolized group, whose confusion in identity after the colonial era is rarely recognized.

Unlike the male novelists—Cooper, Fitzgerald, and Faulkner —whose Caribbean women remain victims, Rhys attempts to redeem West Indian women through a recreation of the childhood, adolescence, and marriage of *Jane Eyre*'s Bertha Antoinetta Mason. Unlike Charlotte Brontë, who dehumanizes Bertha and thrusts her into a cage, Rhys reinscribes Bertha in her text and gives her back the humanity stripped by the nineteenth-century context. In addition, Rhys is interested in Antoinette's psychological dignity and sets about explaining and understanding her descent into insanity as a result of a personality diffusion caused by her mother's indifference to her. Rhys implies that her insanity is partly the result of living in a colonized environment; but she is also interested in the difficulties of creating an identity that is flexible, yet secure enough to survive the marriage to Rochester. Rhys investigates the mother-daughter bond between Annette and Antoinette and shows the destruction caused by the mother's refusal to acknowledge the importance of her daughter. A careful look at *Wide Sargasso Sea* shows that the destructive relationship between Antoinette and her mother Annette is at fault for much of Antoinette's precarious sense of herself.

As a young woman in Dominica, Rhys read her father's copy of *Jane Eyre*. Interested and disturbed by Brontë's "madwoman," Rhys incubated a fictional vindication of the abused West Indian for most of her adult years and then for the twenty years she took writing *Wide Sargasso Sea*. As Rhys explained to Francis Wyndham, this was her most deeply felt novel: "But *I*, reading it [*Jane Eyre*] later, and often, was vexed at her portrait of the 'paper tiger' lunatic, the all wrong creole scenes, and above all the real cruelty of Mr. Rochester."[15]

Rhys intended to create a past for Bertha Mason as a West Indian woman rather than a lunatic. Taking us back more than one hundred years, Rhys recreates the atmosphere of Antoinette's childhood in the 1830s, only a few years after the Emancipation Act of 1833 had freed the slaves in Jamaica. Her father is dead, and her mother, Annette Cosway, is self-absorbed and "pretty like pretty self" (17). Antoinette clings to her African-Caribbean duenna Christophine and friend Tia, whose warmth, superstition, and animism she shares. Tia and Antoinette separate after a fight over money— three pennies—and an exchange of insults. Antoinette calls Tia a "cheating nigger" (24); Tia is able to defend herself and add spite, calling Antoinette a "white nigger" (24).

When a group of enraged islanders burns the house, the family escapes only because their parrot catches fire—a bad omen. Seeing Tia in the crowd, Antoinette runs to her, despite their fight. Tia is the only reminder of Antoinette's former life, so she tries to find a reflection of her identity in Tia's eyes. But the violence has gone too far and ruins their desires.

> As I ran, I thought, I will live with Tia and I will be like her. Not to leave Coulibri. Not to go. Not. When I was close I saw the jagged stone in her hand but I did not see her throw it. I did not feel it either, only something wet, running down my face. I looked at her and I saw her face crumple up as she began to cry. We stared at each other, blood on my face, tears on hers. It was as if I saw myself. Like in a looking glass. (45)

But the two young women do not meet again. That evening Annette's son Pierre dies. She loses her mind and is placed under the "care" of a man who rapes her periodically while Mr. Mason is away on "business." Antoinette spends most of her time at her convent school wishing she were dead, or thinking about death.

When Antoinette is seventeen Mr. Mason invites Rochester to the island to meet her, and here the story merges with *Jane Eyre*. Rhys grants some sympathy to Rochester as overwhelmed by his new environment, but he soon develops into the bigoted Rochester of *Jane Eyre*. He is even more disconcerted by their move to the French-speaking and wilder island of Dominica. Because the jungle is too lush for his sensibility, he projects his bewilderment onto his wife and resents her as too flamboyant.

In a new twist to the story, Rochester is captivated by the island's beauty within a few days, in spite of his insecurity; and Antoinette becomes a symbol of that too. Just as he envies the jungle, he also envies her liveliness, freedom, and open sexuality. But resentment of his father and fear of potential island violence are involved in his attitude toward her. He believes she has a "hidden secret," which he does not realize is her female sexuality, that will reveal the place to him. Particularly mysterious is the bathing pool. "It was a beautiful place—wild, untouched, above all untouched, with an alien, disturbing, secret loveliness. And it kept its secret. I'd find myself thinking, 'What I see is nothing—I want what it *hides*–that is not nothing'" (87). The description applies to the beautiful and disturbing qualities of both the woman—especially her hidden womb—and the place itself. And for Rhys, violence was always part of the West Indian "magic" under which Creoles and visitors fell. Rochester, she believes, was "magicked" by the place and the woman but was too weak to preserve either.[16] Antoinette is a symbol of the island's elusiveness and its danger; he is unconsciously preparing to reject both the island and the woman.

Rochester is clearly emotionally involved with Antoinette but also fiercely jealous, repressed, and unable to match her liveliness and sensuality. Antoinette is a "dark" beauty whom Rhys intended to be, like the Brontë's Bertha, part Spanish or French. Because she is a "dark" West Indian woman, Antoinette is an easier target for Rochester's venom. He regards her "breeding" suspiciously and, shocked by the island's intermingling of races, wonders about Antoinette's heritage: "She never blinks at all it seems to me. Long, sad, dark alien eyes. Creole of pure English descent she may be, but they are not English or European either" (67). Noticing Rhys's preference for dark-skinned characters in her novels, Helen Nebecker argues that Antoinette is a mulatto: "Antoinette, herself, is, by heritage, creole, though by implication of mixed blood" (Nebecker 139). Either way, Rochester's attitude is racist because he is scapegoating a woman whose "darkness" facilitates a rejection of what he perceives as physically different.[17]

Rochester throws Antoinette's fragile emotional stability into utter confusion once he believes the stories told about her and her mother. He withdraws, refusing to call her "Antoinette," but using "Bertha" and "Marionetta" (puppet) as substitutes—attempts to dehumanize her and turn her into the not-quite-human "other" that he can manipulate. Antoinette had believed her husband to be the one escape from her obsession with death, but now Christophine accuses him of driving his wife insane: "Everybody know that you marry her for her money and take it all. And then you want to break her up, because you jealous of her" (152). Rochester in fact will treat her abominably, label her insane, and lock her in an attic; but he is not indifferent to her. Despite himself, he is drawn to her with a fiercely destructive force that propels him as much as her. When Christophine suggests that Antoinette might marry someone else, he feels "a pang of rage and jealousy" (159). He will not allow her to forget him or to love anyone else: "Vain, silly creature. Made for loving? Yes, but she'll have no lover, for I don't want her and she'll see no other" (165). In Brontë's account, we accept Rochester's version of the story even though the author does not present many of Rochester's inner thoughts. In *Wide Sargasso Sea* Rhys attempts to go more deeply into Rochester's mind to explain the genesis of his hatred for Antoinette. Yet we finally dislike him much more than we did after reading *Jane Eyre*; and we realize that Antoinette is not congenitally insane but, like her mother, driven insane.

We finally have very little sympathy for Rochester, who turns into a monster. He hates his father and brother, the climate, his wife's sexuality, the landscape, Antoinette's friendships with African-Caribbean women, and her acceptance of African folk traditions. Leaving the island, he feels sexual disgust for his wife and a curious attraction for the island, for which Antoinette is now symbol: "She had left me thirsty and all my life would be thirst and longing for what I had lost before I found it" (172). Strong sexual disgust, created by not only the sexual difference but also the perceived racial difference is crucial in defining Rochester's reaction to Antoinette. Again, the intersection of sexual and racial difference provokes aggression and contempt. By the time Antoinette reaches England, her personality has shattered and she is ready for her keeper, Grace Poole. Had Antoinette developed a strong sense of identity in Jamaica, she might have survived psychically. But the cruelty Rochester carries, unconsciously, is part of the island's vicimization and has destroyed any sense of herself or of security from her family.

Christophine's advice to Antoinette is to become self-reliant: "Get up, girl, and dress yourself. Woman must have spunks to live in this wicked world" (101); but "spunks" are not engendered by Antoinette's past experience, which was a continual rejection by her neighbors, the former slaves, and her mother.

Part of Antoinette is already dead because her mother found a daughter tiresome and preferred her son Pierre. Ironically, she and Antoinette are related by imagery suggesting physical and emotional similarity. The daughter inherits the mother's frown that "might have been cut with a knife," her sitting posture (head bent), her alcoholism, and her hysteria. The mother fatefully refuses to admit a connection with the female child. "She pushed me away, not roughly but calmly, coldly, without a word, as if she had decided once and for all that I was useless to her. . . . 'Oh, let me alone,' she would say, 'let me alone,' and after I knew that she talked aloud to herself I was a little afraid of her" (20).

The mother's inability to help the daughter form a sense of worth, as Chodorow has taught us, is a complex doom for Antoinette.[18] Any problems in the process of mother-daughter bonding lead to distortion in the daughter's self-concept: "In all of these cases, the mother does not recognize or denies the existence of the daughter as a separate person, and the daughter herself then comes not to recognize, or to have difficulty recognizing, herself as a separate person" (103). The daughter will feel unrecognized and "empty of herself," therefore experiencing boundary confusion in relation to her ego. When Annette denies attachment and symbiosis, Antoinette's diffusion is assured.

In Part Three of the novel, which Antoinette narrates in part, she tries to remember something she "must do." Then she dreams of the night their house at Coulibri burnt and experiences a reconciliation with the self she had been seeking since that night, when her life changed and Tia deserted her.

> The wind caught my hair and it streamed out like wings. It might bear me up, I thought, if I jumped to those hard stones. But when I looked over the edge I saw the pool at Coulibri. Tia was there. She beckoned to me and when I hesitated, she laughed. I heard her say, You frightened? And I heard the man's voice, Bertha! Bertha! All this I saw and heard in a fraction of a second. And the sky so red. Someone screamed and I thought, *why did I scream!* I called "Tia" and jumped and woke. (190)

This is the novel's end and its climax because it predicts action beyond the novel's time frame: "Now at last I know why I was brought here and what I have to do. There must have been a draught for the flame flickered and I thought it was out. But I shielded it with my hand and it burned up again to light me along the dark passage" (190). Antoinette will recreate the events of her dream. She sees herself and Tia as belonging to the same group. Given the choice between Rochester, who is calling her, and Tia, who is re-calling her to their intense friendship, Antoinette achieves a new confidence, jumps, and wakes. Given her imprisonment, her legal helplessness and confusion, torching Rochester's baronial cage is the one act of liberation and assertion she could have chosen, and does choose, to achieve what Christophine calls the "spunks" to battle for herself. Unlike Brontë's Bertha who turns, in rage, to biting Richard and attacking Rochester, Rhys's Bertha realizes her revenge in a human way that surprises her captors and reasserts her presence, even though it costs her life.

Identity is a pressing issue in recent fiction such as *Wide Sargasso Sea* because it affects both the male and female literary characters from the Caribbean. In the culture itself, integrity and dignity have been continually assaulted by exploitation and racism. In the fiction, women characters act, perhaps at the unconscious level, as metaphor for the failure of the imperialistic powers to admit full humanity to the islanders, especially those who live in the "mother" country.[19] Do the vengeance cited by William Faulkner and the "cruelty" of Rhys's Rochester negate the possibility of syncretism in Anglo-American literary creations? The answer is certainly no because we find in Rhys's Antoinette and, retroactively, in Brontë's Bertha, an assertion beyond death, a refusal to be ground down and out of literary consciousness. The problem studied here is literary; and so is the solution of one text (Rhys's) talking to another (Brontë's) and, through this conversation of daughter with literary foremother, redeeming the humanity of the "dark" Caribbean woman.

Rhys reinscribes the "dark" Caribbean women in her text and restores her dignity, giving Bertha back to herself and to us, the readers. More importantly still, Rhys manages to create the syncretism between Tia and Antoinette, two women characters, which some critics have claimed is impossible. Despite the rejection of her mother, Antoinette is able to compensate for this intimacy by reestablishing a bond with her childhood friend Tia. *Wide Sargasso Sea*—because it is written by a West Indian woman who understood on a deep level the nexus of racism, sexism, and imperialism in the West Indies—succeeds in "bracketing" the ideology, values, and beliefs of colonialist literature. Antoinette is able to negate herself in her final moment to merge herself with Tia. It is significant that such syncretism takes place between two women characters who find in one another's eyes a mirror—the reflexive and affirming intimacy they have found nowhere else.[20]

NOTES

1. In this essay, the term *West Indian* is meant to be synonymous with *Caribbean*. This essay must also select a few islands from the Caribbean or West Indies. Specifically, I shall refer to Dominica, Haiti, and

Jamaica; generally, however, the essay's focus is on certain experiences that are common to those people, especially women, who emigrate from a Caribbean island to England or the United States. Although I can induce no definitive conclusions from these examples, they do point to two hypotheses—that Anglo-American fiction takes a negative attitude toward the Caribbean woman; and that the link between an imperialistic power's exploitation of a colony and the degradation of colonials is implicit in Anglo-American fiction. If this is the case, much more should be said about the hidden assumptions in literary presentation.

2. William Faulkner, *Absalom, Absalom!* (New York: Modern Library, 1936), 250. The phrase "incredible indigo sea" refers specifically to Haiti, where Thomas Sutpen married his first wife, Eulalia Bon.

3. My evidence here cannot include every Caribbean woman in British and American literature, but only a selected group of fictional characters familiar to North American readers.

4. Jean Rhys, Ella Gwendolen Rees Williams, was born in Roseau, Dominica, in 1890. Throughout her life she claimed to identify with both the English and African-Caribbean cultures. Her parents were Welsh and Jean herself left the island in 1907, to return only once, during the 1930s, before her death on May 14, 1979. Because Rhys spent most of her life in England, Cornwall, and Devonshire, I place her among the British writers rather than the native Caribbean writers. See Jean Rhys, *Smile Please: An Unfinished Autobiography* (Berkeley: Creative Arts, 1979).

5. Since its publication in 1978, Nancy Chodorow's *Reproduction of Mothering* (Berkeley: University of California Press, 1978) has become the standard reference in feminist psychoanalytic object-relations theory about ego formation and gender differences in psychological development. See Part II: "The Psychoanalytic Story," Chapter 5: "Gender Differences in the Preoedipal Period," 92–110, for specific information. A brief but cogent summary of Chodorow's theories is presented in Judith Kegan Gardiner's article, "On Female Identity and Writing by Women," *Writing and Sexual Difference*, ed. Elizabeth Abel (Chicago: University of Chicago Press, 1980), 177–91.

6. There is much confusion about the word *Creole*. The term has referred to many groups of people, including the European settlers in the West Indies (or Caribbean), the African emigrants in the West Indies, and the French population in Louisiana.

   As a general term, *Creole* can refer to most people living in the West Indies. The *Oxford English Dictionary* offers this definition: "In the West Indies and other parts of America, Maurituis, etc.: *orig.* A

person born and naturalized in the country, but of European (usually
Spanish or French) or of African Negro race: the name having no connotation of colour, and in its reference to origin being distinguished
on the one hand from born in Europe (or Africa), and on the other hand
from aboriginal." (See *The Compact Edition of The Oxford English
Dictionary*. Vol. 1. A–O. Oxford: Oxford University Press, 1971), 1163.

   Modern usage often implies a white man or woman, sometimes
distinguished as "creole white": "a descendant of European settlers,
born and naturalized in those colonies or regions, and more or less
modified in type by climate and surroundings." (*Oxford English Dictionary* 1163). In this paper "Creole" indicates "white Creole" while
"African-Caribbean" means "black Creole."

7. Jean Rhys, "To Diana Athill," Sunday 20th [1966], *The Letters of Jean
   Rhys*, eds. Francis Wyndham and Diana Melly (New York: Viking,
   1984), 297.

8. See also the dialog between the Caribbean woman Anna Morgan, from
   Jean Rhys's *Voyage in the Dark* (1934), and her English stepmother,
   Hester, whose xenophobia draws her into hatred of Anna's friendship
   with their black cook Francine. While they are living in Dominica,
   Hester's fear and discomfort open up a well of racist thinking. She says
   to Anna: "I tried to teach you to talk like a lady and behave like a lady
   and not like a nigger and of course I couldn't do it" (*Voyage* 65).

9. For a detailed discussion of the pale woman-dark woman contrast, see
   Claire Rosenfeld, "The Shadow Within: The Conscious and Unconscious Use of the Double," in *Stories of the Double*, ed. Albert Guer-
   ard (Philadelphia: Lippincott, 1967). Examples of novels that contrast
   the "dark" and "light" woman are Herman Melville's *Pierre*, James
   Fenimore Cooper's *Last of the Mohicans*, and Nathaniel Hawthorne's
   Blithedale Romance.

10. Jean Rhys, "To Francis Wyndham," Thursday [1964], *The Letters of
    Jean Rhys*, eds. Francis Wyndham and Diana Melly (New York: Viking,
    1984), 271.

11. Cheryl Dash, "Jean Rhys," *West Indian Literature*, ed. Bruce King
    (London: Macmillan, 1979), 202–3. In Jean Rhys's story "The Day
    They Burned the Books," the narrator voices the Creoles' resentment
    of their position. Disliked by most islanders because their ancestors
    were slaveowners, they are also snubbed by the British who consider
    them provincial. "I was tired of learning and reciting poems in praise
    of daffodils and my relations with the few 'real' English boys and girls I
    had met were awkward. I had discovered that if I called myself English
    they would snub me haughtily: 'You're not English; you're a horrid
    colonial.'" [See Jean Rhys, "The Day They Burned the Books," *Tigers
    Are Better Looking* (London: Andre Deutsch, 1968), 42–43.]

12. In the context of the mid-nineteenth century, the word *race*, when used without an article, indicates family or social rather than racial background. The *Oxford English Dictionary* gives as primary defini-tion: "Denoting the stock, family, class, chiefly in phr. *of* (*noble*, etc.) *race*. (*The Compact Edition of the Oxford English Dictionary*. vol. II. P–Z. Oxford: Oxford University Press, 1971), 87.

13. Rochester draws this conclusion himself: " 'This life,' said I at last, 'is hell: This is the air—those are the sounds of the bottomless pit!' " (293).

14. In an early short story, "Mixing Cocktails," Jean Rhys's narrator specu-lates on this type of prejudice. She ascribes it to a human desire to bring everyone to the same level. "So soon does one learn the bitter les-son that humanity is never content just to differ from you and let it go at that. Never. They must interfere, actively and grimly between your thoughts and yourself—with the passionate wish to level up every-thing and everybody." [See Jean Rhys, "Mixing Cocktails," *The Left Bank: Sketches and Studies of Present-Day Bohemian Paris* (London: Cape, 1927), 89].

15. Jean Rhys, "To Francis Wyndham," April 14th [1964], *The Letters of Jean Rhys*, eds. Francis Wyndham and Diana Melly (New York: Viking, 1984), 262. Rhys made a similar statement in 1968. "The mad wife in *Jane Eyre* always interested me. I was convinced that Charlotte Brontë must have had something against the West Indies, and I was angry about it. Otherwise, why did she take a West Indian for that horrible lunatic, for that really dreadful creature? I hadn't really formulated the idea of vindicating the mad woman in a novel but when I was rediscovered I was encouraged to do so." [See Jean Rhys, "Fated to Be Sad," Interview with Hannah Carter, *The Guardian*, 8 August 1968, 5.]

16. In a letter to Diana Athill, Rhys claims that Rochester is infatuated with Dominica. "I have tried to show this man being magicked by the place which is (or was) a lovely, lost *and magic* place, but, if you understand, a *violent* place. (Perhaps there is violence in *all* magic and *all* beauty—but there—very strong) magicked by the girl—the two are mixed up perhaps to bewildered English gent, Mr. R., certain that she's hiding something from him." [See Jean Rhys, "To Diana Athill, April 28th [1964], *The Letters of Jean Rhys*, eds. Francis Wyndham and Diana Melly (New York: Viking, 1984) 269.]

17. Rhys creates a more violent version of this situation in the short story "The Day They Burned the Books." Mr. Sawyer, an Englishman, settles in the Caribbean and comes to hate everything about it. He marries a "coloured" woman and when drunk abuses her verbally, and some-times physically as well, pulling her hair out one night at a dinner party and yelling: "You damned, long-eyed, gloomy half-caste, you

don't smell right." See Jean Rhys, "The Day They Burned the Books," *Tigers Are Better Looking* (London: Andre Deutsch, 1968), 41. Notice the similarity in the responses of Mr. Sawyer and Mr. Rochester, who cannot stand to look at the "long" eyes of these women. They cannot live in harmonious relations with women whom they perceive as alien.

18. Scharfman uses philosophical and psychoanalytic theories of mirroring to explain this dysfunction. "In Jean Rhys' novel, the lack of such a mirroring bond—the mother's refusal or inability to allow her small daughter to perceive her reflection in a loving gaze—is at the source of Antoinette's fatal quest for identity" (Scharfman 90). For this argument, Scharfman draws on Jacques Lacan's discussion of the alienated image of him or herself that the infant perceives in the mirror. See Jacques Lacan, "The Mirror Stage as Formative of the Function of the I," *Écrits: A Selection*, 1966, trans. Alan Sheridan (New York: Norton, 1977), 1–7. The crucial importance of positive mother-daughter bonding to a child's ego is the focus in Nancy Chodorow, *The Reproduction of Mothering: Psychoanalysis and the Sociology of Gender* (Berkeley: University of California Press, 1978).

19. Scharfman sees this relationship in stronger terms. The women such as Annette Cosway Mason are raped, which is a symbol of the island's rape. Speaking of Rochester and Antoinette's marriage, Scharfman claims that "The failure of their relationship functions as a metaphor for the failure of the colonial experience. Having raped what is left of the islands, the imperial power does not forgive them for wanting any part of the debts incurred" (103–4). The problem with this metaphor is that Annette, Antoinette's mother, is raped by former slaves, not the former slaveowners. The players in this insidious game should be differentiated more clearly.

20. I would like to thank my colleagues Janet Haugaard (University of Puerto Rico at San Juan) and Stephen Clark (Cambridge University) for their suggestions on the first and second drafts of this paper.

Feminine Voices in Exile

I

The beginning of the twentieth century opened doors for women writers in the Hispanic literary world. With the emergence in Latin America of the Hispanic Modernist movement (1880–1910), Hispanic women began to play a significant role in literary history, first, mainly as readers, then as literary producers, as writers. Although the liberation of Hispanic women writers occurred later than that of their sisters in England and the United States, this generation of Hispanic women writers, like their English-speaking cousins, was empowered by preceding generations of women writing in their language. Virginia Woolf's description of the historical advance of women writers in England needs only slight adaptation to fit the situation of Hispanic women writers who traced their literary lineage back to such exceptional foremothers as Santa Teresa (Spain) and Sor Juana de la Cruz (Mexico) in the sixteenth and seventeenth centuries: "The 17th century produced more remarkable women than the 16th. The 18th than the 17th, and the 19th than all three put together." In sheer numbers alone the "advance in intellectual power . . . [was] not only sensible but immense."[1]

The Hispanic Modernist movement was more than an aesthetic and elitist attempt on the part of writers, especially poets, to escape through art the coarse reality of the bourgeois world. Hispanic Modernist writers were reacting to the social ferment caused by capitalist expansion, but their reaction led them to rebel against rather than to seek refuge in the great literature of their cultural past. For the first time, Latin American writers felt the full influence of European literature unfiltered by the literature of hegemonic Spain. Isolated from the rest of Europe, Spain was suffering the loss of its last colonies, and Spanish writers were obsessively analyzing the painful history of their homeland. Perhaps for this reason, Spanish Modernism was inspired by, but never achieved the greatness of, Latin American Modernism.

Once Hispanic writers had been politicians, presidents of their countries, professors, and military leaders; now casualties of the process of modernization, Hispanic writers were marginalized specialists. Within their isolated specialization, they sought to recreate language and literature.[2] Through their use of bold metaphors and images that appeal to the senses, through their imaginative recreation of myths and use of musical effects, through their exploitation of symbolism and Parnasism,[3] and through their incorporation of other arts into their poetry, plays, and fiction, these writers revitalized Spanish poetry and prose.

Modernist works attracted many women readers who responded to their use of myths that exalted woman as the origin and end of everything, as the silent recipient of the eternal secret (the sphynx), and as the muse of the male poet. As Modernist Muse, woman did not and could not speak herself. Captured in poetry as the "eternal feminine," as a beautiful or hideous object that attracted the poet since she gave life and death, woman became a self only at the moment she possessed or was possessed by the poet. In this regard it is enlightening to read "Mía" ("Mine," 1896), one of the most beautiful poems of Rubén Darío, the best known representative of Spanish American Modernism: "Mine: that's your name. / Is there more harmony? / Mine: light of day; / Mine: roses, flames" (Mía: así te llamas. / ¿Qué más armonía? / Mía: luz del día; / Mía: rosas, llamas") (569). In "Mía" and in other poems by male Hispanic Modernists, woman becomes harmony, beauty, passion, only through her relationship with the male poet. Significantly, before Mía "melted her sex" "with the strong sex" of the poet, she was "pale," nonexistent, not yet a being. She was a "chrysalis" (569).

Although the concept of woman offered by Modernist poetry is very negative and stereotypical, the beauty of its images and the evocative power of its language made some women desire objectification by male poets. A group of women writers at the beginning of the nineteenth century shielded themselves by using the mask of the male writer, confirming the "eternal feminine" created by male poets. These women writers did not challenge the oedipal paradigm expressed in male poetry (Gilbert and Gubar 5). Later, at the beginning of the twentieth century, when some Latin American women writers dropped the male mask to find their own authentic literary voices, they were denied literary acceptability. Refused status and intellectually ostracized by the literary establishment of their day, these women exiles continue to be published and to be read widely. The reevaluation of their significance to Hispanic literary history must be a concern of Hispanic feminists.

However, the outlook for feminist critics of Hispanic women authors is not bright. For critics, especially women critics, whose work is to analyze literary works as well as to influence literary producers, have been censored when they have tried to study literary works written from a feminine perspective and focused on women's issues and experiences. With the exception of *Femme* in Mexico, some isolated groups in Latin America, and several American Hispanists in the United States, the majority of women critics of Hispanic literature do not dare to write literary criticism as women. To feel *jouissance* and to write about it and under its spell is fine for women who create literature, but it is terribly risky for women who analyze that literature. To write literary criticism, or less presumptuous yet, to apply and adapt feminist criticism to Hispanic literary works is therefore to enter an academic "ghetto" with no exit. It is necessary to read and study Hispanic women poets, such as the women I examine in this essay, because they map the way for feminist critics to follow in the perilous journey to self-knowledge and feminism. They show us how to take the risks necessary to identify and to advance women's literary interests and creativity.

II

In this essay I will analyze the works of two Spanish American post-Modernist writers, Delmira Agustini (Uruguay, 1887–1914) and Alfonsina Storni (Argentina, 1892–1938). Both writers were recognized by their male colleagues and critics, as well as the public in general, though male critics praised their poetry for its supposed virility, failing to recognize and to applaud the struggle of both women to find their authentic poetic voices. Alberto Zum Felde, an influential student of Agustini's work, writes:

Thoroughly feminine in her sensitivity, feminine to the darkest roots
of her self. . . . Delmira Agustini's poetry is, at the same time, of a
matchless mental virility, perhaps with the exception of the sublime
Santa Teresa's. The word virility seems, in this case, strong and paradoxical: but, indeed, there is not another word in our limited language
of definitions, to express her faculty of mental abstractions, and that
energy of her expressions that sometimes she has, all of what is proper
of the male mentality; because the two ways of intellectual abstraction, the metaphysical and the mathematical, are male characteristics.
(Zum Felde, *Delmira Agustini* 27–28)

Did this prestigious critic use the words *virile* and *virility* to indicate that Agustini's poetry has superior quality? Is her poetry as
good as that of male writers? Or, did Zum Felde discover that Agustini's language, images, tropes, eroticism belonged to male language,
to the male's symbolic discourse? Therefore, was Agustini another
woman poet who could not escape from the dominant/dominating
discourse? Or, finally and even more important, was Agustini an an-
drogyne, a linguistic/poetic hermaphrodite? Zum Felde ended the
paragraph I have just quoted with the following sentence: "A modern endocrinologist would tell us immediately that it is a problem
of glands."

Agustini did not write like the Other in phallogocentric culture
(Felman 2–10). She indirectly subverted the position given to women
by male poets by assuming a "literary phallus." She was schizo-
phrenic: a man/woman. In her own life, she was conventionally
"feminine" (e.g., a beautiful young woman, she was very obedient to
her mother's orders and wishes and she liked to be called "La Nena,"
"Baby").[4] But, oh scandal, she was also sexually unconventional!

The overprotected Delmira, who received no formal education
that would fit her to leave the security of her childhood home,
who had no friends, who was always accompanied by her dominant
mother María Murfeldt Triaca de Agustini, surprised and shocked
the social and intellectual circles of her time with the maturity, sensitivity, and eroticism of her poetry. She also surprised her public
with her marriage to a good but mediocre man, Enrique Job Reyes,
astonishing it later by divorcing him and maintaining a secret relationship with him until July 1914, when he murdered her in his
bedroom. Furthermore, this apparently naive girl of genius kept a
passionate and open correspondence with prominent male writers

(Rubén Darío, Manuel Ugarte, Alberto Zum Felde). In her letters, especially those she wrote to Darío and Ugarte, she showed herself to be tormented by the conflict between her inner life and the stagnant norms of Uruguayan society at the beginning of the twentieth century.

Delmira Agustini is a paradox as is the country where she lived and worked. In Marxist or materialist terms Agustini's life and poetry mirror the dissociation in Uruguay between a new industrial base and an infrastructure that was not ready for it; between a liberal legal system and a reality that was very far from achieving liberal goals. Uruguay appeared to be a liberal and progressive country. Its legal system could only be compared with those of the most advanced European countries of the day. Nevertheless, everyday life in Uruguay was grounded in a tradition that was both sexist and provincial.

With regard to "women" as a class, it could be said that women obtained important legal advances (though these advances were obtained for them by men). In 1907, the Parliament accepted the divorce law; in 1913, Batlle y Ordoñez, one of the great Uruguayan statesmen, founded the University for Women. But women in a provincial town like Montevideo, despite its airs of a cosmopolitan capital, agreed to stay in the roles tradition had assigned them. Ironically, men's concessions on women's behalf bound women even more securely to the status quo by eliminating the possibility of their achieving class consciousness and the motivation to fight for their rights.

Although there might have been material causes for the contradications that we find in Agustini, in Zum Felde's romantic but disparaging terms, Agustini's eroticism and poetical power were the result of a state of inspiration that transformed her into a different and genderless being. Her eroticism and sexuality, according to Zum Felde, became transcendental and her poetry, early interrupted by her death, was in a process of becoming mystical (Zum Felde, *Proceso*). The critic who admired the beauty and intelligence of Agustini struggled to recapture the mythical "woman" in this poet who was evidently doing something new, something "virile," or, better yet, something so "feminine" that the Uruguayan critic was frightened. However, in the opinion of another critic, Arturo Sergio Visca, who studied and published Agustini's intimate letters, there is no gap

between the poet and the woman. Her poetic eroticism is real and
intense. Agustini succeeded through literature in unveiling this real
self. I tend to agree in part with Visca. But I cannot accept the
view that Agustini's poetry is a mere literalization of her actual
experiences.

As I shall show, Agustini's poetry is universal because it incar-
nates the desires, fears, the *jouissance* of women.[5] Trying to discover
a real lover or lovers under her tropes is to fix her in one of the categories that Western male or phallogocentric culture has designed for
women: the madam, the prostitute. When on December 26, 1913,
Agustini's poem "Serpentina" ("Serpentine") appeared in the magazine *Fray Mocho*, N. Manino, a person unknown to Agustini, but one
who read her works and saw her picture in the magazine, responded
to the poem and its author in these terms:

> "Serpentine" made me forget my decision [to escape from Agustini's
> attraction] and I answered [he wrote an erotic sonnet "To Delmira
> Agustini"] excited by the passion in which your flesh breathes in the
> unbosoming, that I understand, because I am also, lascivious . . . let's
> vibrate together since our bodies and our souls like vestals feed that
> fire! Oh! Delmira, how voluptuous would be our struggle of pleasure,
> of sensuality. . . . I closed my eyes and I shivered dreaming of two em-
> braced serpents, twisting themselves drunk with eroticism, in order
> to fall exhausted by a spasm . . . during an intermission! (Visca 73)

Who was Manino? Who was that passionate reader who needed
to respond to Agustini's poem with another poem? Who was the
man who understood Agustini's metaphor as a solicitation for a real
lover? The same questions must have been formulated by Agustini,
who, upon reading Manino's poem, wrote to him. Although Agustini's letter has not been preserved, Manino answered that letter on
February 16, 1914, saying that he was not someone known to Agustini who was hiding his real name and personality under an assumed
name. He insisted that he was a reader excited by the "fire" of her
poetry. The true identity of Manino remains unknown. I prefer to
believe his assertion that he was merely a reader and admirer, representative of the general reader who did not know how to react to
a poem in which a woman ceased being a man's dream and became
her own dream, her own creation, and dared to desire for herself.[6]

A woman who wrote and dared to write "If I dream my body in this way, my mind is like this: / a long, long, body of a serpent, / vibrating eternal, voluptuously!" ("Si así sueño mi carne, así es mi mente: / un cuerpo largo, largo, de serpiente, / vibrando eterna, voluptuosamente!") (159) had to face the consequences of her boldness, according to Manino. Agustini wrote her own body, created her own body, because mind and body were together. Her culture protested, she was going too far! She was not only writing, obtaining her own voice, but she was also creating her own self. The male poet, although much inferior to Agustini, wrote: "I want to be the visionary prophet / of your ritual flesh in which throbs / the rhythm of pleasure and of life" (Quiero ser el profeta visionario / de tu carne ritual en que palpita / el ritmo del placer y de la vida") (from "To Delmira Agustini" by Manino). He wanted to regain the voice that had been man's property for so long; therefore, he had to be the "visionary prophet," the one who understood the mysteries of the woman's traditional ("ritual") body. Manino interpreted Agustini's poetry as the cry of the female in heat for the male. To the properly naive woman who returned after her divorce to her parents' house and remained "La Nena" thereafter, Manino's poem and letters should have been scandalous; they should have seemed her well-deserved punishment for her erotic frankness. But Agustini answered Manino's letters and enjoyed in his letters the presumptuous claims of the male.

Agustini's brief but complex life produced three volumes, *El libro blanco* (*The White Book*, 1907), *Cantos de la manāna* (*Morning Songs*, 1910), *Los cálices vacíos* (*The Empty Chalices*, 1913), and a series of poems collected and published posthumously under the title *El rosario de Eros* (*Eros Rosary*, 1924). In these works the writer's self-conscious process of becoming both woman and writer is evident as is Agustini's use of female masks or disguises— child, "femme fatale," and lover—to procure her poetic freedom and find her own voice. Believing that Agustini was always a passionate woman who felt a need to mask her sexual impulses owing to familial and societal pressures, Visca sees in Agustini an evolutionary process of unmasking and liberation, a process reflected in the composition of *Los cálices vacíos* and *El rosario de Eros*.

In the beginning, Agustini made the male other/lover in her poetry the source of her voice, her creator:

Hoy abriré a tu alma el gran misterio;	Today I will open to your soul the great mystery;
ella es capaz de penetrar en mí.	she will be able to penetrate me.
En el silencio hay vertigos de abismo:	In the silence there are whirling abysses:
yo vacilaba, me sostengo en ti.	I was vacillating, I'm supporting myself in you.
	(From "Intima," 78)

Clearly, Agustini was not able to start living and writing independent of what Lacan calls "the Law of the Father." Like the New England poet Emily Dickinson, who more than half a century earlier invented male preceptors for her verse, Agustini initially dubbed Rubén Darío "God of the Art," "Master," "Father" and "broke" her "pride" like "a beautiful statue, destroyed at his feet." Darío understood the tormented soul of a young woman poet and sent Agustini a "paternal word," the father poet's approval of his daring daughter (Visca 63–66). Later she discovered that she did not have to depend on the approval of the male-other, but neither did she have to deny his existence.

In "Vision," one of the most beautiful poems of *Los cálices vacíos*, the "other" appears, as it does in the majority of Agustini's poetry, as an imaginary lover. The poem is structured like a dream. The first stanza places the poetic "I" at night, in her "bedroom, enlarged by solitude and fear." This fear is not caused by her solitude, but by the mystery of the unknown of her creation. The other —"you"—emerges like a "giant mushroom" from the "dark" and watery ("humid") corners of her subconscious. This "giant mushroom" with its obvious phallic connotation is a threat rather than the "pillar," the "support," on which the poet once leaned.

The following two stanzas start with the line, "You leaned toward me . . ." ("Te inclinabas a mí . . .") and the poetic "I" becomes the woman-object with all the qualities and characteristics assigned her by phallogocentric culture. She is the giver of life and death. She is the origin of voice, although she is mute: "You leaned toward me like the big willow / of Melancholia / to the deep lagoon of silence" ("Te inclinabas a mí como el gran sauce / de la Melancolía / a las hondas lagunas del silencio"). She is the impulse of writing for the

male-other, although she cannot write: "You leaned toward me as
if my body / were the sign of your fate / on the dark page of my
bed" ("Te inclinabas a mí como si fuera / mi cuerpo la inicial de tu
destino / en la página oscura de mi lecho"). She takes the other to
the light . . . she is "an open window," that can be read as writing, as
the moment of transcendence through the union of the two lovers,
although she remains "in the dark page of her bed."

The traditional position of the "I" as a woman-object changes
in the fourth stanza, where the emphasis is on the "leaning" of the
"other." And from a passive attitude the "I" attracts, and animates
—gives life—to the other through her erotic desires: "And my wish
was a snake / sliding among the cliffs of darkness / to the lily statue
of your body" ("Y era mi deseo una culebra / glisando entre los riscos
de la sombra / a la estatua de lirios de tu cuerpo"). But this time the
"I" does not remain motionless in the darkness. Her desire for the
"male-other" does not kill her, but rather makes her grow: "and you
leaned so much, / that my erotic flowers are double, / and my star is
larger since then" ("y tanto te inclinaste, / que mis flores eróticas son
dobles, / y mi estrella es más grande desde entonces"). The "I" and
the "other" are equals. Both of them are alive with passion. Thus, the
"I" expects the birth of a "new race" from their union, "the greatest
embrace." But this embrace of equals is impossible since when the
dream ends the poet's vision vanishes, "you moved backwards and
wrapped yourself / in I don't know which deep fold of the shadow"
("te hacías atrás y te envolvías / en yo no sé que pliegue inmenso
de la sombra"). Although her arms seem to be filled with emptiness,
and her eyes seem to be blinded with shadows, in the movement
from absence-presence-absence, the poet obtains her language. Agustini succeeds in recreating ironically the passive image of woman in
order to subvert it and transform it into the woman creator of her
own muse. The male other-lover is the source of her poetry, the impulse of her writing, but he is created by her. Here, in my opinion,
lies the main difference between the "female muse" of the male poet,
let's say Darío, and Agustini's male muse. For Darío the female muse
corresponds to the primary signified, the mother, in the symbolic
order of language. She exists as the seed of language, although she
is mute and she only germinates through union with the male poet.
She germinates and language is born in him, the bearer of language.
Agustini's muse does not preexist her language. Agustini creates the

muse as "other" in the moment that she speaks/writes, liberating herself from the symbolic order that constrains the male poet.

III

By the time that Argentine Alfonsina Storni published her first book of poetry in 1916, two years after Agustini's death, other Spanish American women had followed Agustini's path and were being recognized in literary circles. Among them were the Uruguayan Juana de Ibarbourou, the Chilean Gabriela Mistral, recipient of the Nobel Prize in Literature in 1945, and the Cuban, Dulce María Loynaz. But these women were considered "islands," "exceptions" in the predominantly male world of Latin American literature. Storni's voice was the only feminist voice insisting upon an end to the sexual bias of her time. Like Delmira Agustini, Storni not only shocked her society with her profession—poetry—but also with her life. In the Buenos Aires of the first half of the century, which, in spite of being considered the Paris of South America, was as provincial as Montevideo, she dared to give birth to a child out of wedlock and, in 1938, knowing that she had a fatal illness, she took her life in the muddy waters of the River of the Plate.

The style of Storni's poetry shows her great mastery of poetic technique. Sometimes satiric and sometimes elegiac, above all, her poetry was "thorny," and, like her own attitude toward men, loaded with disdain and resentment. As was the case with any Hispanic woman who did not fit into her traditional role, Storni was branded a feminist and a Socialist; her cross/curse was to consider man her inferior but to need him. Her cry for equality in literature and in society made her contemporaries uneasy. No one denied that in her anguish at sexual injustice lay the power and tormented beauty of her poetry. But many found her claim too open and too loud. Unlike Agustini, whose poetry revealed a largely unconscious subversion of patriarchal poetics, Storni was a woman poet who wrote her mind. Until the end of her life, she pointed out the unfairness of phallic power. But her poetry—even her satiric poetry—is always transcendent with love and understanding.

Storni did not want to invert the order of power. She did not want to place men where women were and had been, in an inferior position, in order for her, and for women in general, to occupy man's superior place. But this was what male writers and critics feared. However, Storni wanted to replace the terms superiority/inferiority with the term equality. In her body of work: *La inquietud del rosal* (*The Anxiety of the Rose*, 1916); *El dulce daño* (*The Sweet Harm*, 1918); *Irremediablemente* (*Hopelessly*, 1919); *Languidez* (*Languor*, 1925); *Ocre* (*Ochre*, 1925); *Mundo de siete pozos* (*The World of Seven Holes*, 1934); *Mascarilla y trébol* (*Death Mask and Clover*, 1938), and twenty-two poems written from 1916 to 1921 and from 1934 to 1938, Storni tried to nullify men's power and freedom symbolically. In "You Want Me White" ("Tú me quieres blanca," *El dulce daño*, 1918), her anger toward sexual bias is powerfully expressed. The poem moves in crescendo from its beautiful traditional images of virginity imposed on the female speaker by the man to whom the poem is addressed to its horrifying sacramental images of death in life, the reality the woman envisions for herself if she allows the man to possess her:

Tú me quieres alba,	You want me white,
Me quieres de espumas,	Like foam,
Me quieres de nácar,	Like ivory.
Que sea azucena,	I should be a lily,
Sobre todas, casta.	Above all of them, chaste.
De perfume tenue.	Just a soft fragrance.
Corola cerrada.	Unopened corolla.
Tú que el esqueleto	You, that your skeleton
Conservas intacto	Keep untouched
No sé todavía	I don't know yet
Por cuales milagros,	By which miracles,
Me pretendes blanca	You expect me white
(Dios te lo perdone),	(God forgive you),
Me pretendes casta	You expect me chaste
(Dios te lo perdone),	(God forgive you), (120–21)

The speaker would have the traditional hierarchy Man/Woman, Superior/Inferior erased. After the poetic "I" reaches the height of her indignation, the tone of the poem changes, moving from indignation to exhortation. In spite of the use of the imperative tense in the last two stanzas, the speaker asks the man to perform a ritual voyage to the place of all origins, to the womb, to Mother Earth: "Escape to the forests / Go to the mountains / Clean your mouth; / Live in cabins; / Touch with your hands / The wet ground / . . . Renovate your skin / With salt and water" ("Huye hacia los bosques / Vete a la montaña; / Límpiate la boca; / Vive en las cabanãs; / Toca con las manos / La tierra mojada; / . . . Renueva tejidos / Con salitre y agua"). This return to the primal earth, a space untouched by civilization that has, at least in Lacanian terms,[7] made man the bearer of language, gives the male-other the possibility of a pure rebirth. Since femininity and masculinity are not innate qualities (Jones 253), a rebirth in Nature is an initiation into a space uncontaminated by "the Law of the Father," by phallogocentrism. But perhaps the speaker despairs of the man's potential for rebirth for the ending of the poem is ironical: "And when your flesh / Returns, / And when you have placed / In it your soul / Which was entangled / In so many beds, / Then, good man, / Expect me white / Expect me pure / Expect me chaste" ("Y cuando las carnes / Te sean tornadas, / Y cuando hayas puesto / En ellas el alma / Que por las alcobas / Se quedó enredada / Entonces, buen hombre, / Preténdeme blanca / Preténdeme nívea / Preténdeme casta"). In utopian Nature, the dualistic and hierarchical opposition Man/Woman is irrelevant. But Storni does not allow her readers to fantasize about Utopia; she wants to efface the double standard and to upset phallic power in her poetry and in her own day and in her own society. In "Tú me quieres blanca" the expectations of the male-other whom the speaker addresses vanish—men are left powerless. The speaker has shown the weakness of the male's phallic power. Only when true reciprocity exists and when he offers the kind of sexual purity he demands can he expect her submission and chastity.

Storni recognized that men enjoyed social power and sexual freedom denied to women and that men were also privileged to speak in ways prohibited to women. But Storni insisted on speaking herself and on speaking in a way that subjected male pretence to ridicule. In her most popular poem, ("Hombre pequeñito") ("Little Man," *Irremediablemente*, 1919), the poet appears in the figure of a canary, the singing bird, which only can live in captivity. Civilization transformed the canary, a bird that sings/cries; that sings/talks; that sings/laughs, into a symbol of captivity rather than a symbol of flight/freedom. In Storni's terms, however, men cannot hear woman's song. Like Hélène Cixous, Storni, in "Hombre pequeñito," describes man's inability to hear woman's voice. Cixous likens woman to a sphinx who "sings out because women do—they do utter a little, but they don't speak . . . they talk endlessly, chatter, overflow with sound, mouth sound: but they don't actually *speak*, they have nothing to say" ("The Laugh of the Medusa" 49). Storni likens woman to a canary who demands her freedom but cannot be heard. From the man's perspective, the canary sings to fill the silence —his silence—with music or noise he can interpret as he wishes. However, the canary does speak to the reader movingly of its plight and its desire for the freedom stolen from it.

Storni's canary speaks to its/her warden as though he is smaller than she: "Little man, little man, / Free your canary that wants to fly . . . I am the canary, little man, / Let me jump" ("Hombre pequeñito, hombre pequeñito, / Suelta a tu canario que quiere volar . . . Yo soy el canario, hombre pequeñito, / Déjame saltar"). The canary speaks as though she expects the man to understand her language though he and she are species apart. Through repetition of the word *small*, Storni emphasizes the difference that point of view makes in assigning size and status. To the man, the canary is a tiny addition to his pleasure. To the canary, the man, her jailer, is insignificant except in his role as guardian of the door of her cage, for the man can neither sing nor can he fly as she can. If we are to agree that woman, like the canary, has been domesticated in the interests of man, then man, too, at least in Storni's poem, has been reduced in human terms by the relations available to him in phallogocentric society.

Storni suggests that were the man larger he might understand woman's/the canary's desire: "I say little man because you don't understand me / Nor will you ever understand me" ("Digo pequeñito porque no me entiendes / Ni me entenderás"). "I can't understand you either" ("Tampoco te entiendo") says the canary. "Open the cage! I want to escape" ("Ábreme la jaula que quiero escapar"). With a retaliatory insistence on her incomprehension of her keeper's speech, the canary completes her process of belittling the man and by extension all men who require power to validate their masculinity. "Little man, half an hour I loved you / Don't ask me more" ("Hombre pequeñito, te amé media hora / No me pidas más"), she says. By implication the man can take the canary's liberty but he cannot constrain her to sing the song he craves.

"Tú me quieres blanca" and "Hombre pequeñito" were written at a time when Storni was seeking her position as a woman writer in the Hispanic literary world and as a woman in Hispanic society. In 1925 when *Languidez* was published, Storni had achieved enough success to foreswear what she thought was subjective poetry: "I did not have the time and calm needed, until now, to free myself from my anguish and see what surrounds me," she wrote (193). However, Storni did not succeed in abandoning the subjectivity that had been won at such cost in her earlier poetry. This subjectivity emerges in her tormented and powerful "I," though her torment now derives from her desire to be known as a woman who has achieved recognition as a poet. According to Storni, loneliness and lack of love are the price that a modern liberated woman must pay for her freedom.

Her poems present two kinds of women: the "intellectual women," the dreamers, the creators, and the "passional women" (those who play the role of the woman of man's dream). "Their heart (men's hearts) is placed not in the spiritual ones, / Who tire at the end. Like tillers / They adore what they create: they think that the best / Are those molded to their carnal ways" ("Su corazón lo ponen no en las espirituales, / Que fatigan al cabo. Como cultivadores / Adoran lo que crean: piensan que las mejores / Son aquellas plegadas a sus modos carnales") ("The Other Friend," *Ocre*, 1925).

IV

Storni recognized that women must create themselves to gain liberation. She also recognized her debt to her foremothers. Although "little men" would ignore or misinterpret women's poetry, the noise women were making was impossible to ignore. Women were reading women's works, according to Storni. They were trying to tear down the "bars of their cages." And it was inevitable that the liberation of women such as Agustini and Storni, who spoke to women through their poetry, would foster women's consciousness in general. Storni noted her debt to Agustini obliquely by suggesting the transformation of women under the spell of her writing: "The skinny doña Elvira, / The chaste doña Ines, / Today are reading Delmira (Agustini) / And Stendhal, in French" ("La flaca doña Elvira, / La casta doña Ines, / Hoy leen a Delmira, / Y a Stendhal, en francés") ("Funny Stanzas to Don Juan," *Ocre*, 1925).

Agustini's and Storni's contributions to Hispanic literary history broke ground for the next generation of Hispanic women authors. Young writers recognized in their foremothers' works a voice that enunciated their desires, their dreams, their emotions, their needs. Women writers after Agustini and Storni did not have to struggle to prove that they had a voice. They were able to write freely and unfettered.

Indeed, if we situate Agustini and Storni and their work in what Julia Kristeva has called, after Nietzsche, "monumental history" (14–15), their voices, their steps toward autonomy blaze a path for other women, not just women who would become writers, to follow. Although, but also perhaps, because they were marginalized in Hispanic culture, Delmira Agustini and Alfonsina Storni decentered the Hispanic literary discourse, providing an example for women who would turn from reading to the task of undergoing and articulating their own struggles.

NOTES

1. Virginia Woolf, "Response to 'Affable Hawk' (Desmond MacCarthy)," in *The New Statesman*, 2 October 1920; reprinted in Virginia Woolf, *Women and Writing*, ed. Michèle Barrett (New York: Harcourt, 1979), pp. 55–56.

2. For an excellent discussion of Spanish-American Modernism see Angel Rama, *Rubén Darío y el modernismo* (Caracas: Universidad Central de Venezuela, 1970).

3. Symbolism and Parnasism were the two French literary movements of the late nineteenth century adopted and adapted by Hispanic modernist poets. Symbolism was characterized by bold metaphors and images; the musicality and freedom of the verse; and especially by the power of suggestion (as Mallarmé, well-known Symbolist, said: "Do not name, but suggest"). Parnasism was characterized by plastic objectivity and perfection of form. For a detailed study of the critical history of Hispanic Modernism see Ned Davison, *The Concept of Modernism in Hispanic Criticism* (Boulder, Colorado: Pruett Press, 1966).

4. Arturo Sergio Visca, *Correspondencia Intima de Delmira Agustini y Tres Versiones "De Lo Inefable"* (Montevideo: Biblioteca Nacional, 1978), p. 41. In this letter to Enrique Reyes, her fiance, Delmira Agustini wrote: "Now they are going to take her ("La Nena") out. Today very early they took her ("La Nena") to the Recoleta which is the paseo where people take their kids."

5. See "Introduction III: Contexts of the New French Feminisms," in *New French Feminisms: An Anthology*, eds. Elaine Marks and Isabelle de

Courtivron (New York: Schocken Books, 1981): "This pleasure, when attributed to a woman, is considered to be of a different order from the pleasure that is represented within the male libidinal economy often described in terms of the capitalist gain and profit motive. . . . It is a kind of potlatch in the world of orgasms, a giving, expanding, dispensing of pleasure without concern about ends or closure" (pp. 36–37, n. 8).

6. In "A Desire of One's Own," in *Feminist Studies, Critical Studies*, ed. Teresa De Lauretis (Bloomington: Indiana University Press, 1986), pp. 78–101, Jessica Benjamin speaks of the difficulty of our accepting that a woman may want to experience herself as a subject (rather than an object) of desire.

7. For a detailed discussion of this topic see Anika Lemaire, "The Role of the Oedipus in Accession to the Symbolic," in *Jacques Lacan*, trans. David Mackey (London: Routledge and Kegan Paul, 1977).

STEPHEN H. CLARK

Testing the Razor:
T. S. Eliot's Poems 1920

The familiarity of "Tradition and the Individual Talent" breeds not so much contempt as staleness. Eliot's "Impersonal theory of poetry," in which so much was invested by the New Criticism, now seems a known quantity, thoroughly absorbed and largely superseded, and his verse, so readily assumed to vindicate and be vindicated by this aesthetic, tends to be greeted with a similar weary recognition. Anything so firmly lodged within the canon, it is supposed, can only represent an orthodoxy against which to rebel. I wish to dispel this complacency by stressing what is "perverse" in Eliot's early poetry, in particular *Poems 1920*. There's a virtual conspiracy of silence concerning the violently repudiatory sexuality prevalent in these texts. "His persistent concern with sex, the problem of our generation"[1] is granted a representative and even heroically diagnostic status; and yet explicit sexual reference is customarily recuperated as demonstrating a broader social degeneration, or simply ignored. Perhaps the decorum of such lacunae may be approved, but more is at stake than the occasional suppression of a lurid detail: I shall argue that the strength of this phase of Eliot's poetry lies in the virulence of its misogyny, and its capacity not only to shock and repel, but also to implicate.

This in turn poses with great force the issue of gender-based readings. I do not see how a feminist response to Eliot's vehement campaign of defamation can avoid a stance of counteraccusation: to read these images "as a woman" would necessarily demand a movement of resistance, anger, and repudiation. In contrast, the (male) critical consensus would seem to be, yes, he's screwed up, but aren't we all, with a corresponding reluctance to cast the first stone against him.[2] I think the importance of this protective solidarity cannot be overrated. In this essay, I wish to respond to Eliot's implicit appeal to a specifically masculine audience—"You! hypocrite lecteur!—mon semblable,—mon *frere!*"[3]—and explore the vicarious satisfactions offered by his texts. Why has it been so important to preserve the ideal of ontological autonomy in relation to this poetry? What happens if the aesthetic contract that guarantees impersonality and immunity to both poet and reader is transgressed? What does it mean to read Eliot not as an exegete but "as a man"?

> One error, in fact, of eccentricity in poetry is to seek for new human emotions to express; and in this search for novelty in the wrong place it discovers the perverse. The business of the poet is not to find new emotions, but to use the ordinary ones and, in working them up into poetry, to express feelings which are not in actual emotions at all. . . . Poetry is not a turning loose of emotion, but an escape from emotion; it is not the expression of personality, but an escape from personality. But, of course, only those who have personality and emotions know what it means to want to escape from these things.[4]

The classic status of "Tradition and the Individual Talent" has remained largely unchallenged despite the quite remarkable slippages in Eliot's terminology: even in this short extract, the relation between "emotion" and "feeling" must remain, I think, permanently insoluble. The gist, however, is reasonably clear: the "medium" of poetry is uniquely attuned to experiences screened out by the "personality." It allows one's subtlest and most elusive perceptions to be articulated; and then, just as importantly, to be disowned. Three modes of "escape" from the "eccentricity" of the merely personal are suggested. First, and most famously, through submission to the discipline of a common heritage, "the historical sense" that "compels a man to write not only with his own generation in his bones" (p. 14). It should be noted, however, that the "simultaneous order" that is here invoked is an exclusively masculine enclave. To participate in the "mind of Europe" involves the perpetuation of a patriarchal authority stemming back beyond Homer to the "Magdalenian draughtsmen" (p. 16). The second rationale is less lofty and so more disturbing: by employing commonly available, even commonplace, emotions, the poet may escape out of perversity into the "ordinary." He may enforce a complicity of recognition, not as spokesman for

an androgynous human condition, but for men, male sexual experience. And this is painfully difficult to acknowledge: that Eliot might
speak for us, for me.[5]

The third option involves the adoption of an experimental detachment toward one's own mind. "It is in this depersonalisation
that art may be said to approach the condition of science" (p. 17);
and the change of prefix is significant. The famous analogy between
the creating mind and a catalyst is elaborated in order to establish
art as a realm not of objectivity but of clinical anonymity. What
is produced, though, is "sulphurous acid," and I now wish to turn
to the passage from Tourneur that Eliot offers as exemplifying this
achieved impersonality:

> And now methinks I could e'en chide myself
> For doating on her beauty, though her death
> Shall be revenged after no common action.
> Does the silkworm expend her yellow labours
> For thee? For thee does she undo herself?
> Are lordships sold to maintain ladyships
> For the poor benefit of a bewildering minute?
> Why does yon fellow falsify highways
> And put his life between the judge's lips,
> To refine such a thing—keeps horse and men
> To beat their valours for her?
> (Tourneur, *The Revenger's Tragedy* 3:5:68–78)

In this passage (as is evident if it is taken in its context) there is a
combination of positive and negative emotions: an intensely strong
attraction toward beauty and an equally intense fascination by the
ugliness which is contrasted with it and which destroys it. This balance of contrasted emotion is in the dramatic situation to which the
speech is pertinent, but that situation alone is inadequate to it. This
is, so to speak, the structural emotion, provided by the drama. But the
whole effect, the dominant tone, is due to the fact that a number of
floating feelings, having an affinity to this emotion by no means super-
ficially evident, have combined with it to give us a new art emotion.
(Eliot p. 20)

The "attraction," "affinity," and "combination" of the "balance of
contrasted emotion" at the "positive and negative poles" of beauty
and ugliness give a precipitate of "a new art emotion": presumably
opposed to a merely human one. But even a cursory glance at the

passage cited will confirm the complete absence of any such equilib-rium.[6] To ask an obvious but neglected question, what is the "struc-tural emotion" that has been superseded by the "dominant tone"? It will be helpful to restore the passage to its context. Vindice, who has sworn to avenge his poisoned betrothed, Gloriana, has just un-covered "the masked skull of his love" and proceeds to contrast her past beauty and present mortality.[7] As an isolated verse extract, the repeated "for thee" might be understood as addressing a still sur-viving spirit of loveliness. But the presence of the skull makes any such idealization impossible. There is no attempt to evoke past hap-piness, no shared memories or lost future. Instead Vindice "chides" himself for "doating," for having allowed himself to "expend" and "undo" himself in her service: his efforts to "maintain" and "refine such a thing" are acknowledged to be as futile as the 'yellow labours' of the silk-worm.[8] There are certainly "floating feelings" drawn into the soliloquy, of pawned estates and hanging judges; they represent not the ugliness that destroys beauty, but the practical consequences of being seduced by its power. The speech marks a casting off of obligation: Vindice will henceforth participate freely and indepen-dently in the intricate choreography of the play's intrigue. And so a kind of aesthetic repletion becomes possible in contemplating the victim: she no longer has the deceiving beauty of the living, but an alternative and more potent allure in death. Here, as often in Eliot, fear of mortality can be tamed, utilized almost, through the viola-tion and sacrifice of the female body: the propitiatory offering to a new spiritual or symbolic order.

Coincidental perhaps: but let's turn to a more famous expres-sion of the same fascination with the Jacobean ethos of death-in-lust in "Whispers of Immortality" (CP pp. 56–57). The first half of the poem depicts a macabre but authentic seventeenth-century intel-ligence situated within the desires and corruptibility of the body: the second presents an opposition, banal yet apparently insuperable, between the engulfing bosom and "feline smell" of Grishkin and the modern mind's preoccupation with the "Abstract Entities." This contrast has frequently been read as an almost programmatic cele-bration of the undissociated sensibility of Metaphysical poetry: an accomplished versification of a literary manifesto. But it is not The Duchess of Malfi but John Webster who is said to be "possessed by death": we are invited to contemplate not texts but individuals, and specifically the sexual "experience" of our fellow men. "Death" has its inevitable Jacobean pun on climax, a moment of revelatory intensity in which we are most aware of ourselves as bodies and therefore mortal. Only an immersion in "sense" so total that it will exhaust the possibilities of the flesh can release us from the bondage of its desires.[9] But "to seize and clutch and penetrate" only preserves its existential glamour so long as it is done by and not to us. The combined transitive force of these verbs demands an object: Eliot's sexually charged meditation on death both presupposes and suppresses reference to a woman's body. The very absence of breasts and lips confirms the "creatures under ground" to be female: "leaned" implies both the stasis of rigor mortis and the seductive beckoning of a compliant response. Their furtive concealment accentuates rather than diminishes their erotic attraction, and hence their power. To see "the skull beneath the skin" is to see the female body as prefiguring death, enticing toward it, and therefore demanding a further violence of repudiation. The resultant "lusts and luxuries," though qualified by the supposedly neutral "its," are anything but suprapersonal. "Thought" first "clings," child-like, dependent for nurture, eager for security: then reasserts itself through "tightening," a verb evoking both male sexual arousal and the contracting grip of strangulation. The scene is left suspended in this participle of increasing menace: notice how the "creatures" through this action are reduced to inert "dead limbs."

In the second half of the poem, the female has seized control: a triple repetition of "Grishkin" suggests that this is the inevitable consequence of dignifying her with a name, an identity. "Couched" simultaneously endows Grishkin with drawing-room languor and the alertness of a predator poised for the kill. The ascendent woman is immediately translated into Swinburnian terms, with a queue of suburban Severins eager to be disciplined: both "compels" and "crawls" carry titillating intimations of the flagellating brothel. What the example of the Jacobeans shows is that desire heightened to sufficient intensity, ruthlessness, can reverse this submission. Eliot's insistent series of parallels suggests that Grishkin's covering of flesh is only camouflage. Behind the "Russian eye" lie the "sockets of the eyes"; the "friendly bust" conceals one of the "breastless creatures", and the "subtle effluence" blends into the stench of "dead limbs." Grishkin's carnal mastery must be countered through commitment to the "pneumatic bliss"; the soft inflatibility of her body demands to be punctured by the phallic response of the compressed air drill.[10] This is the modern equivalent of the knowledge of Webster and Donne, that "anguish" can be inflicted as well as undergone; that the "fever of the bone" is also a longing to reveal it; that the "skeleton" must be embraced before it may be transcended. At the moment of this stripping away, it is bluntly asserted: "No contact possible." This is the point of triumph, of proclaimed immunity. The sexual act becomes frankly solipsistic: its sensuality so completely devoid of reciprocation that the woman is refused even the status of object. Instead she is treated as mere occasion for the intensification of desire, reflected back upon a blameless and heroically questing male, who will move beyond dependence on the body, her body, into a higher and ascetic spiritual realm:[11] "As the soul leaves the body torn and bruised, / As the mind deserts the body it has used."

But is the role of "Brazilian jaguar" any more demeaning than that of the "scampering marmoset"? It might be argued that it requires a willful and humorless severity to pursue such a reading; that the lurid rhetoric of "Whispers of Immortality" is always held in check by the urbane propositional voice ("Donne, I suppose"), and the deftness of the ubiquitous Eliotic irony.[12] This would, I think, more or less hold good for *Prufrock and Other Observations*. The expansive, yet nervously taut, conversational rhythms of these poems immediately place us within a subjectivity, which, for all its idiosyncratic intensities, remains recognizably in the tradition of Jamesian personae. The sexual vacillations of this consciousness seem obscurely vindicated through the guarded, almost surreptitious, lyricism of which it is capable: because there are "mermaids singing," it's easy to forget that Prufrock wishes for a pair of "ragged claws" to deal with them (*CP* p. 17, p. 15). The reverie of "Rhapsody on a Windy Night" (*CP* pp. 26–28) pivots around the encounter with a soliciting whore: "The street-lamp said, 'Regard that woman / Who hesitates toward you in the light of the door / Which opens on her like a grin.' "

A moment of opportunity beckons and vanishes, "the passage we did not take / Towards the door we never opened,"[13] and the remainder of the poem meanders through a grotesque catalog of eroticized debris, the only sustenance of the solipsistic mind: the "twisted branch" and "broken spring"; the "old crab" gripping the end of a poking stick; and the depiction of the moon as "aged whore." The narrator totters home to a final assignation with his own solitude: so wryly impotent that the phallic menace of the curt imperative to "mount" in order to deliver the "last twist of the knife" scarcely registers. The female presents a perpetual challenge to the autonomy of Eliot's subjective idealism—"Beyond the circle of our ideas she stands"[14]—and his apprehension can be regarded as a form of indirect tribute to her power. The woman in "Conversation Galante" (*CP* p. 35) is dubbed "eternal enemy of the absolute"; she remains "indifferent and imperious" toward her companion's attempts to "body forth" his "own vacuity": "She then: 'Does this refer to me?' / 'Oh no, it is I who am inane.'" In both "Portrait of a Lady" and "La Figlia Che Piange," there are moments of reversal in which "self-possession" gutters, and the authority of the analytic voice is revealed as precarious, even completely illusory. This exacting self-scepticism develops into the purgatorial ideal of humility in the later poems; the cruelty of his treatment of women cannot match that directed toward himself.[15]

It's far more difficult to pursue such mitigating readings for *Poems 1920*, and, I think, misguided to attempt them. Such a response, I believe, diminishes the poetry by refusing to acknowledge where the "tentacular roots" of Eliot's language probe.[16] As satire, the collection shows no fellow-feeling or generosity, and little cultural insight; the famed telescoping of mythic past and sordid present only reveals a pondered cynicism and a self-regarding elitism of mode; the whimsical scholastic erudition appears incongruously disproportionate to the targets on which it is expended. I would argue for a simple reversal of priorities. Instead of treating these poems as a social critique into which a misogynistic language accidentally seeps, they should be read primarily as articulations of a psychology of sexual fear and desired retaliation. The "reconsidered passion" of "Gerontion" (*CP* pp. 39–41) should, I believe, be read in terms of the literal fact of impotence—how to "excite the membrane, when the sense has cooled." The poem's vision of the imminent demise of Western culture is symptom rather than diagnosis, an eloquent if ultimately futile compensation for an absolute severance from desire. Its declarations of theme could hardly be more explicit: "I would meet you upon this honestly . . . / I have lost my passion: why should I need to keep it / Since what is kept must be adulterated?"

The unsavoury metaphor of untreated meat in "adulterated" is characteristic of the continuous sexual dimension to Eliot's rhetoric: the desire to be at the "hot gates," wading "knee deep in the salt marsh, heaving a cutlass"; the opposition between "the tiger springs" and to "stiffen in a rented house"; the final flurry of emblems of cuckoldry, "gull," "horn," and "white feather," set against "Belle Isle" and the "Gulf." The terms of sententious repudiation themselves ooze with imagery of siring and ejaculation: "the refusal propagates a fear / Unnatural vices / Are fathered by our heroism / These tears are shaken from the wrath-bearing tree." I would insist that for all its sermonic inclusiveness, the intimacy and veracity of the poem lie in its embodiment of a language of male desire; its exclusive concern with sexual failure does not make it the less masculine.

The obvious contrast between the sprawling syntax and clammy and porous diction of "Gerontion" and the formal regularity of Eliot's quatrain poems should not blind us to their essential continuity. These supposedly provide a much-needed infusion of hard, dry Parnassianism into English verse; the rigor of a new classicism achieved through assiduous cultivation of the historical sense. But what is the nature of the history to which the famous choral finale of "Sweeney among the Nightingales" appeals?

> The host with someone indistinct
> Converses at the door apart,
> The nightingales are singing near
> The Convent of the Sacred Heart,
>
> And sang within the bloody wood
> When Agamemnon cried aloud
> And let their liquid siftings fall
> To stain the stiff dishonoured shroud. (CP p. 60)

The power of these lines derives from the endless vistas of sexual hostility opened behind the protagonists of the poem. The continuous present of "singing" suddenly focuses back into "sang" and "cried," the only past tenses of the poem. This temporal movement backward is fused with a prepositional thrust inward, from the "door" that is "apart" to the "Sacred Heart" that is "near," and then yet further "within." The lassitude of the preceding stanzas suddenly concentrates into a single climactic gasp: notice how "aloud," set against "within," seems to locate the "bloody wood" inside the body,

a woman's body. This, the "liquid siftings" and the "stain" are all
images of female sexuality as discharge, triumphing over the rigidity
of Agamemnon: "stiff" suggests that his sexual arousal continues
even in death, enveloped and overcome by this viscousness.[17] The
parallel with a mother's lullaby to her child further stresses female
power and male helplessness at the "bewildering moment." "Let . . .
fall" moves the tense forward again; the "siftings" merge into the narrative present of "singing," simultaneous aspects of the same event;
and "to stain" reaches ominously out into the future. The sexual act
will always repeat the same confrontation, always conclude in the
same betrayal and desecration of the male. Agamemnon is not "dis-
honoured" by the inglorious parallels the poem establishes between
past and present: for example, between the besmirched "shroud,"
the net in which Clytemnestra entraps, murders, and finally parades
him, and the "table-cloth" earlier in the poem on which a "coffee-
cup" has been overturned. The poem gives us no choice but to side
with Sweeney, who becomes, in terms of patriarchal politics, not
a degenerate descendant, but a final and even noble embodiment
—"Sweeney *guards* the horned gate."[18]

The critical consensus toward the figure of Sweeney has been
largely sympathetic. It tends to be assumed that there is a lost vi-
tality in his absence of inhibition that Eliot, as one of the "masters
of the subtle schools" (like his commentators), must regard with
scarcely concealed envy.[19] And this seems borne out by Eliot's own
later description: "a man who in younger days was perhaps a pugilist,
mildly successful; who then grew older and retired to keep a pub."[20]
Against this benign domestication, I would stress two things. Firstly,
the sentiment expressed in *Sweeney Agonistes*: "I knew a man once
did a girl in / Any man might do a girl in / Any man has to, needs to,
wants to / Once in a lifetime, do a girl in" (*CP* p. 134). Secondly, the
most obvious source for the name is the folk-hero of popular music
hall, Sweeney Todd, demon barber, razor murderer, and pie maker
extraordinaire. The running implication is someone's going to get
slashed, soon.

At this point, I need to give a detailed reading of the poem that
I feel most fully reveals the visceral force of Eliot's sexual rhetoric:
"Sweeney Erect" (*CP* pp. 44–45). To pause on the title: the genus
Sweeney, a zoological classification that endows the narrator with
the forensic detachment and control of a taxonomist. "Erect": erec-

tus, standing upright in contrast to the stooping of anthropoids and primates, and thus distinctively human, and tumescent (a pun so blatant that it is seldom acknowledged), a sexual and therefore animal being. A challenge is immediately thrown down to the idealizing view of man expounded in Emerson's essay "Self-Reliance," from which the seventh stanza will later be adapted.[21] "He who knows that power is inborn, that he is weak because he has looked for good out of him and elsewhere, and so perceiving, throws himself unhesitatingly on his thought, instantly rights himself, stands in the erect position, commands his limbs, works miracles" (p. 50).

Sweeney's spontaneous and unrestrained appetite fulfills Emerson's demand for complete self-trust: man "cannot be happy and strong until he too lives with nature in the present, above time" (p. 39). Thus on one level, the poem argues for original sin and the necessity of conformity and self-suppression against Emerson's doctrine of innate goodness. "On my saying, What have I to do with the sacredness of traditions, if I live wholly from within? my friend suggested—But these impulses may be from below, not from above. I replied, They do not seem to me to be such; but if I am the Devil's child, I will live then from the Devil" (p. 30). So Sweeney is an object lesson in impulse from the devil: a grim alternative version of the "aboriginal Self" (p. 37) with a salutary "insistence upon the degraded and helpless state of man."[22]

The epigraph from Francis Beaumont and John Fletcher's *The Maid's Tragedy* provides a female counterpoint to this biological categorizing of the male. "And the trees about me, / Let them be dry and leafless; let the rocks / Groan with continual surges; and behind me / Make all a desolation. Look, look, wenches!" This is part of the cry of Aspatia, deserted by her betrothed: the voice of the betrayed, the anguished, the violated. (And also, it should be noted, the anonymous: it's by no means immediately obvious that the speaker is a woman.) It's useful to restore the lines to a fuller context.

> Suppose I stand upon the sea breach now,
> Mine arms thus, and mine hair blown with the wind,
> Wild as that desert, and let all about me
> Tell that I am forsaken. Do my face
> (If thou hadst ever feeling of a sorrow)
> Thus, thus, Antiphila: strive to make me look,
> Like Sorrow's monument; and the trees about me,

> Let them be dry and leafless; let the rocks
> Groan with continual surges; and behind me
> Make all a desolation. Look, look wenches,
> A miserable life of this poor picture! (2:2:68–78)

How is the passage altered by Eliot's contraction? Most obviously, the "structural emotion" vanishes: it is no longer apparent that Aspatia is instructing her gentlewomen to use her as model for the tapestry of Ariadne that they are weaving. The self-dramatization, the stasis, the indulgence of wishing to serve as "Sorrow's monument," all go. The epigraph taken in isolation sets up an immediate sexual dichotomy between the trees and the waves. But not a balanced one: the "continual surges" increase in power at the expense of the permanent sterility of the "dry and leafless" trunks. Eliot has edited a lament down into a threat: the spell of destructive passion of the sorceress. This establishes the logic of the poem. The victim threatens "desolation" and so justifies her desertion: the reality of the woman is only fully revealed through violation and betrayal, which she is therefore seen as inviting.[23]

The disruptive voice of female grief is immediately appropriated and suppressed. "Look, look, wenches" becomes a dare, a challenge, a taunt from the narrator, to be pondered later in the poem by the "ladies of the corridor," and Aspatia's lament is both preserved within and mocked by the opening stanzas.[24] "Paint me a cavernous waste shore / Cast in the unstilled Cyclades, / Paint me the bold anfractuous rocks / Faced by the snarled and yelping seas. / Display me Aeolus above / Reviewing the insurgent gales / Which tangle Ariadne's hair / And swell with haste the perjured sails."

A backdrop of a "cavernous waste shore" is provided, as requested, but there is no audience for the female voice. It merges into the "snarled and yelping seas" as an animal cry of threat and pain, to which the "bold anfractuous rocks" remain sturdily indifferent. "Yelping" is the first of many participles in the poem that suspend action in a continuous present. These allow the authorial voice to disengage, adopt the calm and analytic perspective of "Aeolus above / Reviewing." Again, reference can be made to *The Maid's Tragedy*, where, in a masque in the first act, Aeolus receives instructions from Cynthia: "Hie thee then, / And charge the Wind go from his rocky den, / Let loose his subjects; only Boreas / Too foul for our intentions as he was, / Still keep him fast chain'd" (1:2:172–76).

But Boreas is out, and throughout the rest of the play, the sea provides images of turbulent and destructive passion. And in Eliot's poem, Aeolus, for all his apparent composure, unleashes and condones the "insurgent gales," which, as they "tangle Ariadne's hair," assist the escape of her lover, Theseus.[25] The passionate woman provokes, deserves, betrayal. There's a paradoxical arousal through the very act of abandonment; the tumescence of "swell with haste" refers to flight rather than to consummation. But to where? "Morning stirs the feet and hands / (Nausicaa and Polypheme). / Gesture of orangoutang / Rises from the sheets in steam."

Morning still has something of the "rosy-fingered dawn" about it rather than the more typically Eliotic "comes to consciousness."[26] The sexual impulse present in "insurgent" and "swells" is continued in "stirs" and "rises": the "perjured sails" become "sheets," as if the fleeing Theseus has literally been blown in. The casual mingling of Homeric reference suggests no more than an incongruous coupling, with sluggish vowels and a faint pun on nausea. More important is the reassertion of detachment through this facetious interjection, at the point when the wind and spray of the open sea thicken into a dank tropical "steam" and the poem becomes menacingly opaque.

"Gesture of orang-outang" reinforces the separation of poised narrator from what is recounted, by suggesting a language of the body, and hence of animal desire, yet also a controlled performance beckoning outward to the reader, to observe, to ponder, and to imitate. The phrase also brings in a third relevant source for the poem, The Murders in the Rue Morgue.[27] In Poe's tale, the mysterious killings, which displayed "an agility astounding, a strength superhuman, a ferocity brutal, a butchery without motive, a grotesquerie in horror absolutely alien from humanity" (p. 334), are revealed to have been performed by an orang-outang, brought back from Borneo by a visiting sailor to Paris. "Returning home from some sailor's frolic on the night, or rather in the morning, of the murder, he found the beast occupying his own bed-room, into which it had broken from a closet adjoining, where it had been, as was thought, securely confined. Razor in hand, and fully lathered, it was sitting before a looking-glass, attempting the operation of shaving, in which it had no doubt previously watched its master through the key-hole of the closet" (pp. 338–39).

The orang-outang, afraid of being punished by whipping, breaks out, and makes his way into the room of two women in the Rue

Morgue. "As the sailor looked in, the gigantic animal had seized Madame L'Espanaye by the hair (which was loose, as she had been combing it), and was flourishing the razor about her face, in imitation of the motions of a barber. The daughter lay prostrate and motionless; she had swooned. The screams and struggles of the old lady (during which the hair was torn from her head) had the effect of changing the probably pacific purposes of the Ourang-Outang into those of wrath" (p. 340). And provokes him to the slaughter so clinically described by Poe earlier in the story. There are several obvious points of reference with "Sweeney Erect": the orang-outang itself; the act of shaving; the motions subsequent to "flourishing the razor"; and the "screams and struggles" of the old lady and the swooning of her daughter. By far the most important, however, is the ape's transformation through gazing into his master's "looking-glass." Is he liberated or unleashed through seizing the mirror? Is he frustrated by his own animality, the impossibility of being other than a beast? Or, more alarmingly, must the orang-outang become human to become inhuman, act out his master's secret fantasies? Numerous textual points support the second reading. The ape is first encountered through passing "into the interior on a voyage of pleasure"; it falls into the sailor's "own exclusive possession"; despite its "intractable ferocity," he manages to keep it "carefully secluded" in his Paris residence, only concerned not to attract "unpleasant curiosity" (p. 338). The ape doesn't simply flee; it encourages pursuit by "occasionally stopping to look back and gesticulate at its pursuer" (p. 340). The sailor is initially "rejoiced and perplexed" when it breaks into the women's room; he ascends a convenient (and extremely phallic) lightning-rod that allows "a glimpse of the interior of the room" and an intimate witnessing of the subsequent events. And in Poe, it should be noted, the orang-outang gets off unpunished, or at least with nothing worse than recapture by its master and being sold to the Jardin des Plantes. The whole purpose of Dupin's, and by implication the reader's, search was to locate and define the animal, but not to reprimand or change it. "As the strong man exults in his physical ability, delighting in such exercises as call his muscles into action, so glories the analyst in that moral activity which *disentangles*. . . . He is fond of enigma, of conundrums, of hieroglyphics; exhibiting in his solutions of each a degree of *acumen* which appears to the ordinary apprehension praeternatural" (p. 315).

A similar dualism is, I think, present in "Sweeney Erect." The analytic pleasure is one of reenactment and covert approval of the "exercises" of the "strong man": for Poe, the ape, for Eliot, Sweeney. But the potency of Eliot's depiction of "physical ability" takes us far beyond even the carnage in the Rue Morgue.

> This withered root of knots of hair
>   Slitted below and gashed with eyes,
> This oval O cropped out with teeth:
>   The sickle motion from the thighs
>
> Jackknifes upward at the knees
>   Then straightens out from heel to hip
> Pushing the framework of the bed
>   And clawing at the pillow slip.

If only on grounds of syntactic peculiarity, this passage should have attracted considerable critical attention. But instead it's invariably passed over, hushed up. It fully reflects what Hugh Kenner called "Eliot's besetting vice, a never wholly penetrable ambiguity about what is supposed to be happening."[28] Who does what to whom? The customary reading, if one could be said to exist, is that this is a peculiarly tortuous description of Sweeney gazing in a mirror prior to shaving. I take the first three lines as referring to the woman, or rather the male perception of her: the next two to the masculine response; and the final three to the woman's movements, though I accept that any distinction can only be tentative. Face, hair, razor, mirror, and reflection are all elements of a language of male sexuality intense and violent and brutally explicit. The dominant trope of the passage, and indeed of the poem, is of the phallus as blade wielded on a female body both already maimed and inviting further mutilation.

Ariadne's "tangled hair" has become "knots" of pubic hair; the "withered root" a remarkably direct depiction of the clitoris as stunted penis; the "oval O" of the vagina, "slitted below," instantly develops protective "teeth."[29] These are assimilated into a single face that gazes back in a terrifying mirroring premonition. (Recalling the "snarled and yelping seas" that earlier "faced" the rocks). Freud argues no man can look at female genitals without fear of castration;[30] for Eliot, that fear is alleviated by inflicting a comparable wound. The past participles seem to displace violence into a primordial act —"slitted," "gashed," and "cropped"—but also prefigure the imminent "sickle motion." "Cropped" is an action already completed yet about to be performed. The abrupt staccato "jackknifes" continues the blade motif; almost slicing from "heel to hip," straightening out in the body. (The colon makes no syntactic sense unless the preceding three lines are taken as a collective object.) The focus then returns to the woman's body, unnamed, a mere site for the transference of "motion" into "pushing" and "clawing." There are no gender pronouns, no defined subject or predicate; whereas the past heroines are awarded resonant names, Ariadne and Nausicaa, the present of the poem defines woman solely in terms of voracious genitals and anonymous recoil. Notice the reverse sequence from completed past to present action to tableauesque participles, again used to contain and suspend while the authorial focus pans out.

> Sweeney addressed full length to shave
> 　Broadbottomed, pink from nape to base,
> Knows the female temperament
> 　And wipes the suds around his face.
>
> (The lengthened shadow of a man
> 　Is history, said Emerson
> Who had not seen the silhouette
> 　Of Sweeney straddled in the sun).

A sudden pause: the male figure is named as Sweeney, presumably erect and thus "full length." The syntax is again difficult, but I think "pink from nape to base" must refer to the woman viewed from behind prior to penetration. First, because Sweeney has already been compared to a (presumably hairy) orang-outang; second, because it is the mating position of apes; and third because Sweeney is subsequently described as "straddled," mounted, towering over. Again the female is elided even as a pronoun, merely "broadbottomed," her "temperament" humiliatingly equated with mere "suds," whether epileptic foam, shaving cream, or sexual juices. The absence of a comma after "shave" means the transitive force of the verb carries over the line ending, slicing into the adjective. What also should be stressed is the deliberation, the savouring of dominance: "addressed," poised, attentive, aimed.[31] The moment "between the desire / And the spasm"[32] is prolonged by another supercilious interpolation, this time a conflation of a sentence from Emerson's "Self-Reliance": "An institution is the lengthened shadow of one man; . . . and all history resolves itself very easily into the biography of a few stout and earnest persons" (pp. 35–36).

"Institution" is significantly absent: discipline, tradition, control. "Lengthened" continues the previous sexual pun: the shadow cast, by a man and man only, one of couplings and sirings (emphasized by the son/sun rhyme).[33] The scene suddenly opens up out of a sweaty bedroom as Sweeney expands, swells: like Antony in Cleopatra's dream, "His legs bestrid the oceans, his rear'd arm / Crested the world" (5:2:11.82–83)—a hero at his moment of triumph. For all the narrator's erudition, it is Sweeney who possesses the truly effective knowledge. "Tests the razor on his leg / Waiting until the shriek subsides. / The epileptic on the bed / Curves backward, clutching at her sides."

The deferral of "tests" and "waiting" accentuates the pleasure of mastery and enforced submission. I think we're obliged to read "the razor on his leg" as a periphrasis for erection. (Why the "shriek" if he's trying out the blade's sharpness on himself?) The woman is dubbed "epileptic," and so presumably "snarled and yelping": her spinal contortions suggest an almost literal disembowelment, a response to a slashing and a maiming. Again, the scene is suspended on a present participle of violent action—"clutching"—which permits a movement away from the body to a wider environment.

> The ladies of the corridor
>   Find themselves involved, disgraced,
> Call witness to their principles
>   And deprecate the lack of taste
>
> Observing that hysteria
>   Might easily be misunderstood;
> Mrs Turner intimates
>   It does the house no sort of good.

It seems to me comparatively unimportant whether the poem is set in a brothel, with Mrs Turner (turner over, presenter of turns, performances) as madam[34]; or in a cheap boarding house, with her as landlady. In both cases, there is an outward address to a specifically female audience.[35] "Witness," "principles," and "observing" are all authorial terms, comparable to the earlier "reviewing": the narrator seeks to abstain from involvement and also to forestall protest by displacing his moral language onto "the ladies of the corridor." It is a matter to be decided among themselves. But on their lips, these words serve as no more than a fund of euphemism to diffuse the "lack of taste" of the preceding scene. The "corridor" has an obvious sexual reference:[36] "involved" also contains a pun on vulva. The women are implicated by their very bodies: hence "disgraced" by the enforced recognition of the poem. They are presented as actively complicit with the designation of their own sexuality as hysteria and epilepsy: the "it" that can be "intimated" but never voiced, "easily misunderstood." "But Doris towelled from the bath, / Enters padding on broad feet, / Bringing sal volatile / And a glass of brandy neat."

The arrival of Doris has often been read as a positive intervention, but I feel skeptical. She is "towelled from the bath," cleansed of the blood and suds, purged by a perhaps not dissimilar "steam." As she "enters," in bovine fashion, "padding on broad feet," impassive and compliant and unsuspecting, she appears the complementary, functioning side of the convulsing "epileptic on the bed." Smelling salts versus the razor seems a mismatch: for all her good intentions and stolid pragmatic aid, there appears to be every possibility of a further violent incision.

There can be no comfortable detachment or "objective" stance toward such a poetry: it raises the question of gendered readings in a particularly acute and irrevocable fashion. I would imagine that it is impossible to read this text "as a woman" in any naive sense: to attempt an immediate identification with the "epileptic on the bed" can surely only be a traumatically masochistic exercise. But other options are available. "Sweeny Erect" could be treated as yet another of Eliot's dialogues between body and soul, a black comedy showing once again that "Flesh and blood is weak and frail, / Susceptible to nervous shock."[37] The spirit is most certainly phallic, and the weakness of the flesh correspondingly female. Yet if it is accepted that women feel a degree of hate and resentment against their own bodies,[38] then perhaps they too may participate in the spiritual pilgrimage enacted through this savage excoriation of the flesh, their flesh.[39] Alternatively, Eliot's presentation of women could be shown to rely on banal and easily dismissable stereotypes. Thus his depiction of their threatening power would be yet another appeal to automatic outrage at any inversion of gender hierarchies, and his eagerness to enlist in the "army of unalterable law" that scowls down on even the most minor liberties of Miss Nancy Ellicot[40] no more than a further confirmation of the reactionary nature of classic modernism.[41] From this perspective, it is the failure of Eliot's language that is to be celebrated; woman remains perpetually elusive, outside, subverting the structures in which he seeks to incarcerate her. And certain of the stylistic features that I've detailed—the omission of gender pronouns, the use of transitive verbs without objects, and the suspension of participles in a virtual gerundive form as if their action will never be carried through—would support such a deconstructive emphasis. This would stress the frustration and bafflement felt toward the "epileptic": the possibility that the sensual grace of "curves" and even the "shriek" might be of genuine ecstasy; that the "ladies of the corridor" know exactly what lies behind "hysteria" but they're not letting on. At the moment when female sexuality seems most rigidly confined in imagery of madness and disease, it retains an imperviousness and self-sufficiency from which the male remains permanently excluded.[42]

But to return to my opening question, what does it mean to read *Poems 1920* "as a man"? Any apotheosis of woman as unknowable, undefinable, infinitely fluid and metamorphosing, is surely eminently compatible with traditional forms of gender idealization: I can think of nothing more predictable than being perpetually enigmatic.[43] It is mistaken, I think, to read Eliot's poetry for what it tells us about women: instead we should concentrate on the more difficult kind of awareness that it promotes of masculinity. I'm inclined to respect Eliot's proclamation of impersonality; although I appreciate the urge to pull Old Possum off his institutionally sanctioned pedestal, I feel that much of the recent psycho-biographical emphasis teeters on the prurient and voyeuristic.[44] In its indefatigable search for a causal origin of the poetry, it merely duplicates Eliot's own project of disengagement toward "stuff that the writer could not drag to light, contemplate, or manipulate into art."[45] I feel it is self-righteous, self-protective, even fundamentally dishonest, to seek to confine and isolate and diagnose Eliot as an external phenomenon, an eccentricity. His poetry simply does not permit any such position of assured superiority or analytic authority to be adopted.[46]

What I feel should be challenged is not the impersonality of the author, but of the reader. B. Ruby Rich gives an acerbic aside in a recent article on pornography. If the "legions of feminist men" want "a proper subject," they can "undertake the analysis that can tell us why men like porn (not, piously, why this or that exceptional man does *not*)."[47] Insofar as I understand these "thousand sordid images,"[48] I am implicated in them, indicted by them. But I think any useful response to feminism by male critics must involve acceptance of this double bind: reading more honestly, more forthrightly, in a sense more culpably. Emerson has a fine sentence at the opening of "Self-Reliance": "in every work of genius, we recognise our own rejected thoughts: they come back to us with a certain alienated majesty" (p. 27). I still believe that there is majesty in Eliot's early writing, in the courage necessary to give expression to such "stuff." But the point is not to savor a momentary frisson of recognition and promptly consign those thoughts into oblivion again. That is to abandon any hope of change. I would justify this poetry, in all its negativity and horror, for the effort of recognition that it invites. As men, we can't glibly denounce Eliot in the name of Life or Love or Eros or any other of those pompously capitalized abstractions that tend to come into play until we have honestly acknowledged the extent to which we participate in these "feelings which are not in actual emotions at all," and "know what it means to want to escape these things."

But after such knowledge, what forgiveness?

NOTES

1. I. A. Richards, "On Mr. Eliot's Poetry," in Appendix B to *Principles of Literary Criticism*, 2d ed. (London, 1926), p. 292.
2. In *A Half-Century of Eliot Criticism* (Lewisburg, 1972), compiled, it must be said, by a woman, Mildred Martin, there are no entries under disgust, eroticism, female, femininity, impotence, misogyny, obscenity, sexuality, or woman. Compared to, for example, seven articles on the influence of Conan Doyle. And eight years later, Beatrice Ricks, in *T. S. Eliot: A Bibliography of Secondary Works* (New Jersey and London, 1980), does little better, recording one article on impotence—Reginald Fitz, "The Meaning of Impotence in Hemingway and Eliot," *Connecticut Review* 4 (1971), pp. 16–22; one on disgust—Maurice Johnson, "T. S. Eliot on Satire, Swift, and Disgust," *Papers on Literature and Language* 5 (1969), pp. 310–15; and a solitary solicitous cataloguing of instances of misogyny—Arthur M. Sampling, "The

Woman Who Wasn't There: Lacunae in T. S. Eliot," *South Atlantic Quarterly* (1968), pp. 603–10.

3. From Baudelaire's Preface to *Les Fleurs du Mal*, cited by Eliot in *The Waste Land* l. 76, *Collected Poems, 1909–1962* (London, 1963), p. 66.

4. *Selected Essays*, 3rd ed. enlarged (London, 1951), p. 21. Hereafter, *SE*.

5. Bernard Bergonzi, for example, though prepared to acknowledge Eliot's "intense sense of erotic failure and bewilderment," feels obliged to elevate this immediately into "a perennial aspect of the human condition" without seeing it as in any way gender specific. *T. S. Eliot* (London and New York, 1972), p. 22.

6. Compare Eliot's fuller account of *The Revenger's Tragedy* in his essay, "Cyril Tourneur," *SE*, pp. 182–92. "Its motive is truly the death motive, for it is the loathing and horror of life itself. To have rendered this motive so well is a triumph; for the hatred of life is an important phase—even, if you like, a mystical experience—in life itself" (p. 190).

7. Described at the opening of the play as "Thou sallow picture of my poisoned love, / My study's ornament, thou shell of death, / Once the bright face of my bethrothed lady" (1:1:14–16).

8. This is made explicit in the concluding couplet omitted by Eliot: "Surely we're all mad people, and they / Whom we think are, are not: we mistake those; / Tis we are mad in sense, they but in clothes" (3:5:79–81).

9. For a more detailed exposition of sensuality as a necessary stage toward religious comprehension, see "Baudelaire," *SE*, pp. 419–30: "Baudelaire has perceived that what distinguishes the relations of man and woman from the copulation of beasts is the knowledge of Good and Evil . . . that the sexual act as evil is more dignified, less boring, than as the natural, 'life-giving,' cheery automatism of the modern world" (pp. 427–28).

10. A fine example of the aetherealizing of Eliot's imagery comes in B. C. Southam's *A Student's Guide to the Selected Poems of T. S. Eliot* (London, 1968), p. 71: "*pneumatic:* derived from a Greek word meaning 'spiritual,' a joke which is taken up in the next word and in the last four lines of the poem."

11. "La Figlia Che Piange," *CP*, p. 36.

12. "The indecent that is funny may be the legitimate source of innocent merriment, while the absence of humor reveals it as purely disgusting." *After Strange Gods: A Primer of Modern Heresy* (New York, 1934), pp. 55–56.

13. "Burnt Norton," *CP*, p. 189.

14. "On A Portrait," *Poems Written in Early Youth* (London, 1967), p. 27.

15. Marianne Moore wrote of "Portrait of a Lady": "It may as well be

admitted that this hardened reviewer cursed the poet in his mind for this cruelty while reading the poem; and just when he was ready to find the usual extenuating circumstances—the usual excuses about realism—out came this 'drunken helot' . . . with that ending. It is hard to get over this ending with a few moments of thought: it wrenches a piece of life at the roots." "A Note on T. S. Eliot's Book," *Poetry*, xii (April 1918), pp. 36–37.

16. Eliot describes the language of the contemporaries of Jonson as possessing "a network of tentacular roots reaching down to the deepest terrors and desires": "Ben Jonson," *SE*, p. 155.

17. In "Mr. Eliot's Sunday Morning Service" (*CP* p. 57), what renders Origen "enervate" is the "mens(tr)ual turn of time": a repulsion exacerbated by the running conceit on the multiple impregnation of the ovary in such terms as *polyphiloprogenitive* and *superfetation*.

18. And certainly wiser than Agamemnon as he "declines the gambit," though this may not be enough to save him. At such points, the resonance of the King Sweeney of Irish legend also seems activated: see Herbert Knust, "Sweeney among the Birds and Beasts," *Arcadia* 2 (1967), pp. 204–17.

19. "The double feeling of repulsion from vulgarity, and yet his shy attraction to the coarse emotions of common life have found their complete symbol in Sweeney." F. O. Matthiessen, *The Achievement of T. S. Eliot: An Essay on the Nature of Poetry* (London, 1935), p. 58.

20. Reported by Neville Coghill, *T. S. Eliot: A Symposium*, edited by R. Marsh and Tambimuttu (London, 1948), p. 86.

21. *Essays: First Series*, in *The Collected Works of Ralph Waldo Emerson*, edited by Joseph Slater, Alfred R. Ferguson and Jean Fergusson Carr, 2 vols. (Cambridge, Mass. and London, 1979), 2, pp. 25–51.

22. For which Eliot praised Jansenism: "Pascal's *Pensées*," *SE*, p. 414.

23. Immediately before this passage, Aspatia has been more explicitly vengeful: "You have a full wind, and a false heart, Theseus. / Does not the story say his keel was split, / Or his masts spent, or some kind rock or other / Met with his vessel?" (2:2:45–49); "Antiphila, in this place work a quicksand, / And over it a shallow smiling water, / And his ship plowing it, and then a Fear: / Do that Fear to the life, wench" (2:2:54–56).

24. Compare the insertion of Ophelia's parting words at the close of "A Game of Chess": "Goodnight, ladies, good night, sweet ladies, good night, good night" (*CP*, p. 69). The line both juxtaposes an idealized version of female suffering with an actuality of fatigue and abortion, and transforms its plangency into a bitterly sarcastic authorial address that refuses to acknowledge any distinction between them.

25. Identifying her with the seas that threaten him through "snarled," a synonym for *tangled* in American usage, OED 2.

26. "Preludes," *CP*, p. 23.

27. *The Complete Poems and Stories of Edgar Allan Poe*, edited by Arthur Nelson Quinn and Edward O'Neill, 2 vols. (New York, 1946), 1, pp. 315–41.

28. *The Invisible Poet* (New York, 1959), p. 92.

29. Compare the vagina dentata image in "Ash Wednesday": "There were no more faces and the stair was dark, / Damp, jagged, like an old man's mouth drivelling, beyond repair, / Or the toothed gullet of an aged shark" (*CP* p. 99).

30. The classic exposition comes in the 1924 essay, "The Dissolution of the Oedipus Complex," in *The Standard Edition of the Complete Psychological Works*, XIX (London, 1961), pp. 171–79. For powerful revisionist readings of the female castration complex as a masculine projection, see Hélène Cixous, "Castration or Decapitation?" translated by Annette Kuhn, *Signs* 7:1 (1981), pp. 41–55; and Luce Irigaray, "Another 'Cause' Castration," in *Speculum of the Other Woman*, translated by Gillian C. Gill (Ithaca, 1985), pp. 46–55.

31. The erotic epiphany of "Dans le Restaurant" (*CP* p. 53) celebrates "un instant de puissance et de délire."

32. "The Hollow Men," *CP*, p. 92.

33. See also the epigraph to Emerson's essay taken from the epilogue to Beaumont and Fletcher's *Honest Man's Fortune*: "Our acts our angels are, or good or ill, / Our fatal shadows that walk by us still."

34. "Women are caught as you take tortoises, / She must be turn'd on her back": John Webster, *The White Devil* (4:2:151–52).

35. This device is apparent in the early sonnet "Nocturne," in *Poems Written in Early Youth* (p. 27). Here Romeo's serenading of Juliet is abruptly terminated by the narrator's intervention: "I have some servant wait, / Stab, and the lady sinks into a swoon." Far from protesting, "the hero smiles" at this "perfect climax," a response accompanied by a similarly provocative outward address to the "female readers" who "all in tears are drowned."

36. Compare the "cunning passages, contrived corridors / And issues" of Gerontion's extended apostrophe to the whore of History. (*CP*, p. 40)

37. "The Hippopotamus," *CP*, p. 51. One of the Latin meanings of *sal* is "wit."

38. See Dorothy Dinnerstein, *The Mermaid and the Minotaur: Sexual Arrangements and Human Malaise*. (New York, 1976), pp. 91–97.

39. Helen Gardner, for example, views Eliot's imagery of tedium and dis-

gust with a chilling equanimity: *The Art of T. S. Eliot* (Oxford, 1949), especially "The Dry Season," pp. 78–98.

40. "Cousin Nancy," *CP*, p. 32.

41. See Lyndall Gordon, *Eliot's Early Years* (Oxford, 1977), pp. 25–28, pp. 61–62; and Sandra M. Gilbert, "Costumes of the Mind," *Critical Inquiry* 7 (1980–81), pp. 391–417; reprinted in *Writing and Sexual Difference*, edited by Elizabeth Abel (Hassocks, 1982), pp. 193–220.

42. Thus the importance of the Tiresias persona for Eliot in "The Waste Land" would lie in his revelation of the greater sexual pleasure of the female. He was subsequently blinded by Juno, for giving away the most precious of her secrets, and compensated by Jupiter with the gifts of prophecy and long life. Eliot considers the story sufficiently important to quote Ovid's version in full in the notes to the poem. (*CP*, pp. 82–83)

43. A charge to which Derrida himself is far from invulnerable. "Elle engloutit—envoile par le fond, sans fin, sans fond, toute essentialité, toute identité, toute propriété" ("Out of the depths, endless and unfathomable, she engulfs and distorts all vestige of essentiality, of identity, of property"). In *Éperons: Les Styles de Nietzsche*, translated by Barbara Harlow as *Spurs: Nietzsche's Styles* (Chicago, 1979), pp. 50–51.

44. The chief cornerstone of offense in this respect is James E. Miller, Jr.'s study of the role of Jean Verdenal, *T. S. Eliot's Personal Wasteland: Exorcism of the Demons* (Pennsylvania, 1977).

45. "Hamlet," *SE*, p. 144.

46. See, for example, Tony Pinkney's employment of the work of Melanie Klein in *Women in the Poetry of T. S. Eliot: A Psychoanalytic Approach* (London, 1984).

47. "Anti-Porn: Soft Issue, Hard World," *Feminist Review*, 13 (Spring, 1983), p. 66. See also Elaine Showalter, "Critical Cross-Dressing: Male Feminists and the Woman of the Year," *Raritan* 3 (Fall, 1983), pp. 130–49.

48. "Preludes," *CP*, p. 24.

PART THREE

L'Écriture féminine:
The Language of Women

S. JARET McKINSTRY

"How Lovely Are the Wiles of Words!"—or, "Subjects Hinder Talk": The Letters of Emily Dickinson

"Biography first convinces us of the fleeing of the Biographied" writes Emily Dickinson (Letter 972).[1] Her 1,049 letters and 1,775 poems seem to illustrate her belief that language cannot capture a life, for they are full of aphorisms, witticisms, and disguises that obscure the speaker and make biography difficult to construct. Even so, readers' desire to translate her work into biography is nearly irresistible. Dickinson's writings do include enough apparent autobiography to create the "Myth of Amherst," as Mabel Loomis Todd named Dickinson in 1881,[2] complete with the famous white dress and virtual confinement to her father's house. Despite these picturesque clues, Dickinson's self-mythologizing inscription of herself as a text is not easy to decipher, for the biographied Dickinson flees even as she reveals herself, and readers seeking biographical truths or literary gems struggle to read her message. And they often misread. Charles Anderson argues that "her letters were rarely concerned with straightforward autobiography,"[3] while David Higgins complains that "the trouble with Emily Dickinson's letters is that they are so full of domestic detail. Only at rare moments are there glimpses of the poet-to-be."[4]

Undoubtedly Dickinson's letters should be read as something between autobiography and poetry, a unique genre that Dickinson creates in order to balance the poetic self-expression demanded by her art and the female self-repression demanded by her society. The letters do argue for themselves as more than daily recordings: Dickinson's habit of enclosing poems in the letters, or using lines from the letters in later poems, indicates her concept of the relationship between the literary and the epistolary genres. And readers notice this similarity—with pleasure and frustration. As Mark Van Doren notes, "It is sometimes recognized that the power of her letters is like the power of her poetry—the two are from the same source, certainly, whatever their final difference."[5] He goes on to argue that the "life of Emily Dickinson was invisible to most eyes and left little record of itself outside the poems and letters. That record is blinding in its brilliance, but it seldom goes into what we call detail."[6]

Perhaps the detail *is* there. We must learn to read it by reevaluating, in Van Doren's words, "what we *call* detail" (my emphasis), for such strict naming is precisely what blinds us to the details that the letters do provide. The details that have captured critical attention turn Dickinson into an eccentric, perhaps lovelorn maiden, and the central question seems to be how she wrote such powerful poetry from such limited experience. "To shut our eyes is Travel," she writes (Letter 354). Clearly we underestimate the power of Dickinson's imagination if we limit ourselves to the details of her existence. Her life as woman and life as poet cannot be so decisively separated, perhaps, as her letters seem to indicate. Reading Dickinson's works teaches us to break down the genre distinctions between letters and poetry, to stop dividing them by naming one text biographical fact and the other literary play. Dickinson's self-awareness as speaker in both poems and letters makes the line between fact and fiction, between biography and autobiography, extremely thin. Only the genre of the letters allows critics to expect biographical truth from them; whatever the connection between the poems and letters, the poems are exempted from recounting the factual details that the letters are mined for—and blamed for failing to provide.

What the letters *do* reveal, aside from some delightful domestic detail, is a great awareness of the power of language. The letters do not just record a woman's life in Amherst in the nineteenth century, although some of those sociological aspects are evident; they do not simply trace the development of the woman's, or poet's, mind, even though they provide tantalizing personal details. Mainly, they show a poet concerned with sharpening her linguistic tools in every way possible. The letters fall into three basic categories: the general letters written throughout her life to family and friends; the numerous letters written to her literary "Preceptor," Thomas Higginson (written between April 1862 and 1885, shortly before Dickinson's death); and the three so-called Master letters, which Dickinson did not address to any known person (written presumably between 1858 and 1862; the letters are undated). All of the letters, to varying degrees, reveal Dickinson's ability to speak in the contrasting voices of ingenuous child and ingenious autobiographer.

Genevieve Taggard writes, "When Emily Dickinson's letters are carefully assembled and studied, and three or four downright and candid sentences of her own about herself taken seriously, we have a story which tells itself, and a life the poems verify."[7] Yet the verification comes only in terms of our ability to read Dickinson's clues (notice Taggard's own judgments: "downright," "candid," "taken seriously"). The story does not "tell itself," but rather entices readers into constructing (auto)biography out of the literary through Dickinson's interweaving of the genres of letters and poetry. By reinterpreting these genres, by translating domestic detail into poetic moment, Dickinson can circumvent her society's expectations for female silence and enable herself to speak. Mastery over the "wiles of words" (Letter 462) provides the means for her linguistic rebellion. Haunted by a paradoxical desire for silence and revelation, referentiality and circumference, isolation and communication, Dickinson uses her letters to create the myth that both reveals and veils her, as her preceptor Thomas Higginson complains: "You only enshroud yourself in this fiery mist and I cannot reach you, but only rejoice in the rare sparkles of light" (Letter 330a). The purpose of Dickinson's words is not to reveal her biography, but to celebrate her linguistic costuming, pose, and self-creation.

This language turns autobiography into biography, for Dickinson interprets herself. "As she recites her story, we see her engaged in artifice, formulating a legend or mythology about her life," writes Barbara Mossberg.[8] The well-known aspects of the "Myth of Amherst," such as the white dress and functional agoraphobia, are translated into the language of the letters: just as she presented herself as a unique eccentric in Amherst, she writes eccentric letters that are epigrammatic, often poetic, and certainly hard to read as merely domestic statements. " 'House' is being 'cleaned,' " she writes in Letter 318 (her emphasis). "I prefer pestilence. That is more classic and less fell." She manipulates language's ability to surprise us by renaming objects and thus heightening the power of the speaking subject.

Writing about her young nephew, for example, she says that "Ned tells that the Clock purrs and the Kitten ticks. He inherits his Uncle Emily's ardor for the lie" (Letter 315). Ned's childish linguistic reversal becomes Dickinson's conscious gender reversal, transforming the anecdote from mere humor to a comment on the constructedness of language itself. Everyday details—including Dickinson's famous bread recipe—are interrupted by snatches of poetry, apparent *non sequiturs* that have little relation to the rest of the letter aside from their inherent linguistic beauty. "The Papers thought the Doctor was mostly in New York," she writes in Letter 354, and then continues: "Life is the finest secret. / So long as that remains, we must all whisper. / With that sublime exception I had no clandestineness. / It was lovely to see you and I hope it may happen / again." Careening between event and fancy, the letters indicate Dickinson's construction of her life as poetic biography.

Indeed, the letters reveal a great deal about Dickinson's interpretive language, which often cloaks meaning by using words to disguise rather than invite referentiality, to obfuscate any relationship to the world. The letters become Dickinson's means of self-concealing and self-revealing, allowing her to balance the conflicting desires for silence and speech. It is not an easy balance. Sharon Cameron claims that "the more vested the relationship with the letter recipient, the more aphoristic, epigrammatic, and explicitly literary the letters become . . . the letters may, in fact, tell us more about the postures that replace relationship than about the relationships themselves."[9] And the most interesting of the letters are the Higginson letters and the Master letters, for Dickinson's posture— or imposture—is most evident in these letters as she struggles between the desire to reveal and conceal herself, or rather her selves— woman and poet.

Clearly part of Dickinson's pose is to represent herself as a naive little girl, a reliable self-narrator who is anxious for guidance and approval. This disguise is produced by a consummate user of language who, Richard Sewall complains, "surely with willful cunning and surely with an artist's skill, . . . avoided direct answers to the major questions that anyone interested in her as poet or person might have been moved to ask."[10] Thomas Higginson, whose long correspondence with Dickinson yields some of her most complex phrases of self-exposure and self-effacement, wrote that he asked questions "which she evaded . . . with a naive skill such as the most *experienced and worldly coquette* might envy"[11] (my emphasis)—a fascinating analogy, since Dickinson's pose relies on presenting herself as a little girl, thus female—submissive, dependent—but still unsexual (or at least sexually unformed). Yet this poet-as-little girl is not naive, as Higginson notes, but skillfully manipulates her sexuality through her use of language.

Higginson unwittingly recognizes the crux of Dickinson's artifice. Understanding, as Sandra Gilbert and Susan Gubar note, "the social laws, masquerading as cosmic laws, which obliged every woman in some sense to enact the role of nobody,"[12] Dickinson exploits her femaleness to gain a Preceptor-Master-Tutor and still retain the pose of an ungendered—childlike and sometimes, in fact, male—artistic voice. By attracting Higginson with her pose of helpless girl, and with her words, she can become the speaker-poet who puzzles Higginson, who teaches her tutor. In a letter, he recalls that "It would seem that at first I tried a little—a very little—to lead her in the direction of rules and traditions; but I fear it was only perfunctory, & that she interested me more in her—so to speak—unregenerate condition" (Letter 342b). He writes to her that he feels "timid lest what I *write* should be badly aimed & miss that fine edge of thought which you bear. . . . I think if I could once see you & know that you are real, I might fare better" (Letter 330a).

After meeting her, Higginson comments on her combination of power and pose: after handing him lilies "in a sort of childlike way" and claiming "in a soft frightened breathless childlike voice" that "I never see strangers & hardly know what I say," he writes that Dickinson "talked soon & thenceforth continuously—& deferentially—sometimes stopping to ask me to talk instead of her—but readily recommencing" (Letter 342a). Thus the self that Dickinson reveals in her many texts (letters, poems, and physical body) balances the reticence of the female voice with the speaking (male) poet's voice in order to escape from the restrictions of gender and genre. The result is precisely that constructed self who flees from biographers. Robert Weisbuch claims that the "hectic rhetoric"[13] of the Master letters, like much of her poetry, "contrasts and sometimes, remarkably, combines a self which is powerful, autonomous, godlike with a self which is all-vulnerable, limited, and victimized,"[14] resulting in a "sumptuous destitution" that reflects both powerless child-woman and powerful poet.

Yet that destitution is precisely Dickinson's wealth. "My Busi-

ness is—Circumference" (Letter 268), she writes to Higginson; this
sets Dickinson on a marginal edge and encloses the rest of the world
within a circle *she* inscribes. Such marginality can be more empowering than inclusion in and obeisance to the restrictions of the
circle, as many feminist theorists have noted, and Dickinson plays
with language as a means of marking out her periphery. Speech becomes her escape, not her prison. "You see my posture is benighted,"
she writes to Higginson (Letter 268), seeking light from him but
also giving herself power through punning to be rescued by a knight
or honored as a knight, to be victim or rescuer. Hers is no passive
role. Dickinson's indirection becomes a control over creation and
interpretation, as she names herself and the world she encircles.

Marginality can be misunderstood, however, and part of Dickinson's goal is to be understood by Higginson and, indeed, formed
by him: "Your opinion gives me a serious feeling. I would like to be
what you deem me," she writes (Letter 319). And she recognizes the
problems her unconventional linguistic style can create: "I think you
called me 'Wayward.' Will you help me improve?" she asks Higginson (Letter 271). Louis Untermeyer complains that she writes "tele-
grams" that "seem not only self-addressed but written in code,"[15] and
Adrienne Rich writes that "Wherever you take hold of her, she pro-
liferates."[16] The difficulty readers discover when they "take hold of
her" arises because she is not restricted to conventional roles or conventional language. For example, Dickinson defines herself as both
subject and object of her letters, talking about herself in both first
and third person: "I got a bad whim. Please don't leave Emily again,
it gnarls her character!" (Letter 317). She refers to herself as "Daisy,"
"she" and "it" in the Master letters, "your obedient child" in the
Higginson letters, mixing poems and aphorisms with her pleas for
help with writing. Through these poses, Dickinson can become as
many selves as she pleases, as the Higginson letters illustrate: sign-
ing herself "Your Scholar" (Letter 271), she uses that dichotomous
term to define herself as both student *and* teacher, clearly training
her "Preceptor" to read and value her words. (And his responses indicate that the lesson was well taken indeed—"She was much too
enigmatical a being for me to solve in an hour's interview," he wrote
in October 1891 [Letter 342a]). Her use of letters to convey herself
appropriately empowers her as both sender *and* message: although
the epistolary form generally demands specific roles (reader/writer,

receiver/sender, recipient/creator), her letters to Higginson conflate these roles, and Dickinson's Master letters do not indicate an addressee, and were perhaps never sent. Thus the reader enclosed in the Master letters is Nobodaddy,[17] or somebody (male? a lover? an ideal, later replaced by Higginson?—the critics' enigma), or even Dickinson herself as her own sender and interpreter, taking both roles.

The Higginson letters illustrate Dickinson's linguistic ability to manipulate the roles conventionally assigned to woman, letter writer, or poet(ess). The letters reinforce Dickinson's child role, emphasizing her female dependence, and cast Higginson as an earthly, literary father or Master to whom she gives herself in language: "The Mind is so near itself—it cannot see, distinctly—and I have none to ask—" she tells Higginson, and she flatters him by asking, "if you please—Sir—to tell me what is true?" (Letter 260). Although she claims that "I could not weigh myself—Myself" (Letter 261), she weighs her words carefully, often, as I pointed out earlier, using puns and double entendres to distinguish between the girl student and the poet scholar. She responds to Higginson's advice in "Letter to a Young Contributor" in the *Atlantic Monthly* of April 1862 "to cut and contrive a decent clothing of words" by clothing herself in language that reveals and conceals, creating a literary striptease of sorts. Requesting help with her poems, she tells him that "While my thought is undressed—I can make the distinction, but when I put them in the Gown—they look alike, and numb" (Letter 261). She seemingly empowers him to "clothe" her: "And if at any time— you regret you received me, or I prove a different fabric to that you supposed—you must banish me" (Letter 268). Yet she has shifted his analogy to give herself all the power; she is both the "undressed" thinker and the "fabric" that can decently clothe those thoughts, thus leaving little for Higginson to do but admire her talent.

And her talent—"Melody, or Witchcraft" (Letter 261)—rests precisely on this power to transform herself into a text. "I enclose my name," she writes (Letter 260); in response to Higginson's request for a picture of her, she gives a self-portrait in words: "Could you believe me—without?" (Letter 268). The self-as-text is not the unadorned self that biographers seek: "When I state myself, as the Representative of the Verse—it does not mean—me—but a supposed person," she warns Higginson (Letter 268). Yet this "supposed person" has incredible powers of self-creation and disguise. Dickinson translates herself into powerless natural images—a wren, a "Kangaroo among the Beauty"—that seem to conform to a social view of her as a (plain) woman. At the same time, she makes herself unique—"a Kangaroo" —and celebrates her isolation by claiming that, like her, "Nature, it seems to myself, plays without a friend" (Letter 319). She thus becomes, in her letters, both natural object and Nature itself, both created and creator, both word and speaker.

And both powerless and powerful. Dickinson retains the pose of the needy child who is alone and frightened, and thus empowers Higginson, her "Preceptor," as the one whose teaching—presence through epistolary advice—can replace her autobiography of absence (she writes in the letters that she loses three teachers, her father, her mother, her dog Carlo, and God—"an Eclipse," making herself the perfect nineteenth-century heroine). Thus loss becomes, for Dickinson, the right to learn from her "Tutor," as the complete text of Letter 314 indicates. "Carlo died— / E. Dickinson / Would you instruct me now?" (Letter 314). Death is paralleled with instruction in this seeming *non sequitur*. In an earlier letter, Dickinson writes that "My dying Tutor told me that he would like to live till I had been a poet, but Death was much of Mob as I could master—then" (Letter 265). These letters, for Dickinson, allow a mastery of balancing powerlessness and power by replacing loss with language, translating personal contact into textual contact, and speaking in poetry rather than autobiography.

Textuality has its dangers, however. Like her father, who "buys me many Books—but begs me not to read them" (Letter 261), Dickinson fears the literary attention and the linguistic power she desires. She claims that publication is as "foreign to my thought, as Firmament to Fin," and that "My Barefoot-Rank is better." Even so, she writes frequently to Higginson and seeks his recognition, for "if I told it clear—'twould be control, to me" (Letter 265). Self-control and textual control are paralleled. Person and poet cannot be completely separated. Higginson's critical advice about her writing becomes "surgery," and although "it was not so painful as I supposed" (Letter 261), and "perhaps the Balm, seemed better, because you bled me, first" (Letter 265), the image reflects a painful operation on the physical rather than the textual body. She sees this pain as necessary, however: "I had rather wince, than die," she argues. "Men do not call the surgeon, to commend—the Bone, but to set it, Sir, and fracture within, is more critical. And for this, Preceptor, I shall bring you—Obedience—" (Letter 268).

Increasingly, Dickinson uses the image of Higginson as a language doctor to empower him as critic and to reinforce her need, as patient-child, of his literary medicine: "I will be patient—constant, never reject your knife and should my my [sic] slowness goad you, you knew before myself that Except the smaller size / No lives are round— / These hurry to a sphere / And show and end— / The larger —slower grow . . ." (Letter 316). Even as she invites his cutting, she continues to write poetry in her own way. She is both a constant patient and constantly patient, both "smaller size" and "the larger" that "slower grow." Higginson's advice functions as a sort of worldly second opinion, a measure of the ways readers might view her, and is therefore invaluable to her not because he is superior to Dickinson but because he is *not* Dickinson. Dickinson's letters cast Higginson and herself in the roles of doctor-patient, reader-writer, preceptor-scholar, yet the relationships are not as precisely powerful-powerless as they initially seem. "The Vein cannot thank the Artery—" (Letter 352), she tells him: as vein, she is dependent on his prior efficacy as artery, but they are both necessary parts of the (same) body. Without both, the body dies. He is, finally, not all-powerful doctor but embodied reader, empowered by the language of the writer, and she uses him to diagnose her poetic powers.

Her insistence on addressing him as doctor, reader, and teacher reflects a refusal to lose the apparent childlike dependence that justifies her ingenuous pose. "I ask you to forgive me for all the ignorance I had. I find no nomination sweet as your low opinion. Speak, if but to blame your obedient child," she begs Higginson (Letter 352). Despite the obvious impact of her language—on Higginson as well as others—she pretends to be incapable of judging herself (as person and poet) for herself. Asked "for my Mind" to "use it for the World," she claims that "I could not weigh myself—Myself—My size felt small—to me" (Letter 261). Sending Higginson two poems, she asks, "Are these more orderly?—I thank you for the Truth—I had no Monarch in my life, and cannot rule myself, and when I try to organize —my little Force explodes—and leaves me bare and charred—" (Letter 271). Gilbert and Gubar argue that Dickinson's dependent pose overcame her, that "what was habit in the sense of costume became habit in the more pernicious sense of addiction, and finally the two habits led to both an inner and outer in*habit*ation—a haunting interior other *and* an inescapable prison."[18]

But that "little Force" clearly has linguistic power—destructive and creative. Her submissive language masks a recognition of the strength of her voice. "You ask great questions accidentally," she tells Higginson. "To answer them would be events. I trust that you are safe" (Letter 352). The *non sequitur* becomes a warning about the dangerousness of her possible answers to the questioner: that "little Force" can indeed explode. Her poses restrain her own speech. Her letters then control Higginson by assigning his roles and ironically refining his comments. For example, she writes a metered poem in response to his complaint that her "gait" is " 'spasmodic' " even as she pleads for his assistance: "You think my gait 'spasmodic'—I am in danger—Sir— / You think me 'uncontrolled'—I have no Tribunal" (Letter 265).

Her irony does not veil her sincere desire to gain more linguistic ability through her correspondence with Higginson, for Dickinson knows that language is hard to control; the child-Dickinson can "never try to lift the words which I cannot hold" (Letter 330). However, the artist-Dickinson claims that "the broadest words are so narrow we can easily cross them—but there is water deeper than those which has no Bridge" (Letter 413). Dickinson's struggle to use language to span her thought indicates both her depth of thought and her understanding of the limits of language. The narrow text does not bridge the speaker's meaning. Even so, Dickinson's voice does give her power over speech and speaker. Although Terence Diggory claims that she casts Higginson as a "god of scalping ecstasy and searing judgment,"[19] Dickinson's use of him as the object of her prose makes him part of the "Supernatural" that is "only the Natural, disclosed" (Letter 280) through her ability to name it. She is not victim of her dependence, but victor through the roles she imposes on him and herself in the language of the letters. "I have no Saxon, now —" (Letter 265) she tells him; but clearly she has used language— her own language, indeed—to create herself as child-poet, Higginson as Preceptor-admirer. "I would like to be what you deem me" (Letter 319), she claims, even as she becomes what she deems herself.

The Master letters reveal a different pose. Although they were, apparently, written before the letters to Higginson, and it seems likely that the correspondence with Higginson in some sense re-

placed the one-sided correspondence with the Master (she does address Higginson as "Master" in several of the letters she wrote to
him), the Master letters reveal Dickinson's initial struggles with
language and self—with, finally, the disguise that language allows,
or demands, for a woman poet. Unlike Higginson, the Master is an
unknown other—to critics and, possibly, to Dickinson herself—who
cannot be so easily controlled by language. Unlike the later Higginson letters, which illustrate Dickinson's control over her language,
her pose, and her reader, the Master letters point out a continual
failure of expression and communication, and Dickinson's prose de-
teriorates due to her inability to balance the roles of child-woman
and poet, as she does in the Higginson letters. The Master letters,
therefore, are evidence of the painful process of self-disguise and self-
creation that is completed and celebrated in the Higginson letters.

   In all three Master letters, Dickinson presents herself in only
one guise. Instead of the child-scholar of the Higginson letters, balancing repression and expression, Dickinson here becomes "Daisy,"
a conventional female image linking woman and natural object, and
she does not transcend that role. Her self-identification with nature
limits her, for she is unable to express herself linguistically; her
dialectical ability to use—and be—Nature, evidenced in the later
Higginson letters, falters. She writes in despair that "even the wren
upon her nest learns (knows) more than Daisy dares" (Letter 248).
In Letter 187, Dickinson is translator between nature ("my flowers")
and the uncomprehending Master who cannot read their (her) "messages," but she has no power to make nature speak to him: "You
ask me what my flowers said—then they were disobedient—I gave
them messages." And she is incapable of communicating with the
Master, for she is caught in language that he cannot understand: "If
you saw a bullet hit a Bird—and he told you he was'nt shot—you
might weep at his courtesy, but you would certainly doubt his word,"
she writes. "One drop more from the gash that stains your Daisy's
bosom—then would you *believe*?" (Letter 233). Part of the problem,
of course, is that she is speaking a female language of the body in
conflict with the cultural language of the intellect. The contrast between the physical body and language, between pain and courtesy,
parallels Dickinson's irreconcilable link with and limit in nature:
she is the wounded bird *and* the stained interpreter, trying to use
words when only blood serves as proof.

Her focus on natural images reflects her imprisonment in the physical body: "Thomas' faith in Anatomy, was stronger than his faith in faith," she claims after the wounded bird story above (Letter 233). Anatomy, Simone de Beauvoir said, is destiny; for Dickinson, sexual difference becomes undesired division from the Master. "God made me—[Sir] Master—I did'nt be—myself," she argues (Letter 233). Suffering from a heart that "outgrew me—and like the little mother—with the big child—I got tired holding him," she uses the image of pregnancy as physical proof of emotional love, and therefore loss of control over her own body (sexuality). She asks the Master, "Have you the Heart in your Breast—Sir—is it set like mine. . . ?" (Letter 233). Thus embodied, he might feel as she does, and anatomy could be power.

Gender confronts genre as she translates sexual difference into the language of disguise that we see later in the Higginson letters. Words do begin to bridge the gap between male Master and female speaker. Dickinson imaginatively transcends difference as she wonders, "if I had the Beard on my cheek—like you—and you—had Daisy's petals—and you cared so for me—what would become of you? Could you forget me in fight, or flight—or the foreign land?" (Letter 233).[20] However, her question is unanswered. Unable to use the genres of poetry and letters to linguistically confirm physical (and therefore emotional) sameness between male and female, and unable to gain power in female poses, as she does with Higginson, her translation of feeling into words fails. Even so, nature and language are inextricably linked in her perception of gender and genre, her conception of her poetic voice. She recognizes the fearful power of words: "Vesuvius dont talk—Etna—dont—[Thy] one of them—said a syllable—a thousand years ago, and Pompeii heard it, and hid forever—She could'nt look the world in the face, afterward" (Letter 233). The danger of a natural explosion so terrifies Dickinson—she equates herself with these catastrophic, uncontrollable forces—that she desires the submission and silence of female love. "Have you a little chest to put the Alive in?" (Letter 233) she asks the Master, referring to both a box for her living poems and a physical place for her emotions (for safekeeping or burial?); in Letter 460 she reopens that container and tells Higginson "to say if my Verse is alive?" In the Master letters, she desires silence and death rather than the dangers of self-expression: "I died as fast as I could" (Letter 233).

The incoherence of the last Master letter illustrates the danger of losing the female self ("Daisy," "she," "it") to another ("Master," "he," "it," "you"). She is afraid that "Daisy—offend it—who bends her smaller life to his (it's) meeker (lower) every day" (Letter 248). The multiple pronouns indicate Dickinson's confusion of roles and loss of identity as she is taken over by "a love so big it scares her, rushing among her small heart—and pushing aside the blood and leaving her faint." Her desire to please the Master becomes terror of punishment as the pain of love changes from a "wound" and "cough as big as a thimble" to "a Tomahawk," yet "(you) Her Master stabs her more—." She even silences herself for him: "I will never be noisy when you want to be still. I will be . . . your best little girl—nobody else will see me, but you" (Letter 248). The Lacanian incoherence— repeated pronouns, chains of signifiers without any precise reference —shows Dickinson's understanding of the inability of language to contain her desire for—and fear of—the Master. Seemingly language fails to transcend the difference she perceives, fears, and desires, and she is trapped in the role of Daisy—a fragile, short-lived girlflower.

"Language is an inherited system, an imposed Master, but Dickinson can jostle it to master the Master," claims Weisbuch.[21] The Master is, in these letters, only a self-imposed verbal construct. And Dickinson, despite the incoherent pleading of the final Master letter, is still the writer, even if she cannot get the response from the Master that she desires. The poet's voice does not die. Indeed, the Master letters seem to be rehearsals for the Higginson letters, in which Dickinson's role as "best little girl" empowers her speaking voice as masterful poet. Cameron writes that "language does not fulfill the desire it can learn how to express" because it must always mediate between the object and its naming; "presence must suffer a translation into language."[22] The Master letters indicate Dickinson's discovery of, and finally mastery of, that translation. The pain of these letters is resolved in the Higginson letters, which show a speaker in control of her voice and her audience, her gender and her genre. The Master, like Higginson, is contained in Dickinson's "Circumference" and becomes what she deems him to be: a linguistic object of desire.

Dickinson writes a new language, perhaps; her epigrammatic style, veering between inhibition and exhibition, empowers her to speak herself through her linguistic mask as both "Representative of the Verse" and "a supposed person" (Letter 268). Perhaps Cixous would applaud; Dickinson effectively inverts female humility so that it conceals irony and reveals power in female disguises—child, flower, nature, lover. Like "a treason of Progress—that dissolves as it goes" (Letter 280), Dickinson's message is self-effacing—or self-multiplying, as Rich believes. Her letters, like her poems, move from present(ce) to absence to poetry, and somewhere in that circle's circumference we can read—reach—Dickinson.

NOTES

1. *The Letters of Emily Dickinson* in three volumes, edited by Thomas Johnson and Theodora Ward (Cambridge: Belknap Press, 1958). All further letters will be cited by number.
2. Mabel Loomis Todd, quoted in Millicent Todd Bingham's *Emily Dickinson: A Revelation* (New York: Harper and Row, 1954).
3. Charles Anderson, *Emily Dickinson's Poetry: Stairway of Surprise* (New York: Doubleday Press, 1966), p. 327.
4. David Higgins, *Portrait of Emily Dickinson* (New Brunswick: Rutgers University Press, 1967), p. 27.
5. Mark Van Doren, "Introduction" in Mabel Loomis Todd, ed., *The Letters of Emily Dickinson* (New York: World Publishing Company, 1951), p. v.
6. Ibid., p. vii.
7. Genevieve Taggard, quoted in Barbara Antonia Clarke Mossberg, *Emily Dickinson: When a Writer Is a Daughter* (Bloomington: Indiana University Press, 1982), p. 5. For further discussion of the conflict for female writers and narrators, see Joanne Frye's *Living Stories, Telling Lives* (Ann Arbor: University of Michigan Press, 1986) and Nancy K. Miller's "Emphasis Added: Plots and Plausibilities in Women's Fiction," *PMLA* 96 (January 1981).
8. Mossberg, *Emily Dickinson*, p. 87.
9. Sharon Cameron, *Lyric Time: Dickinson and the Limits of Genre* (Baltimore: Johns Hopkins University Press, 1979), p. 12.
10. Richard B. Sewall, *The Life of Emily Dickinson* (New York: Farrar, Straus and Giroux, 1974), p. 3.
11. Higginson, *Atlantic Monthly*, October 1891, quoted in Sewall, p. 542.
12. Sandra M. Gilbert and Susan Gubar, *Madwoman in the Attic: The Woman Writer and the Nineteenth-Century Literary Imagination* (New Haven: Yale University Press, 1979), p. 588.
13. Gilbert and Gubar, *Madwoman*, p. 602.

14. Robert Weisbuch, *Emily Dickinson's Poetry* (Chicago: University of Chicago Press, 1975), pp. xi–xii.

15. Louis Untermeyer, quoted in Cameron, *Lyric Time*, p. 33.

16. Adrienne Rich, "Vesuvius at Home: The Power of Emily Dickinson" in *Shakespeare's Sisters: Feminist Essays on Women Poets* (Bloomington: Indiana University Press, 1979), p. 121.

17. *Nobodaddy*, a term used by William Blake to denote the awful Father-God-Master, is applied to Dickinson's Master-Lover-God by Gilbert and Gubar in *Madwoman* and by Weisbuch. Thomas Johnson notes in the *Letters* that one of the candidates for the Master is the Reverend Charles Wadsworth, but that is only conjecture (Letter 248a).

18. Gilbert and Gubar, *Madwoman*, p. 591.

19. Terence Diggory, "Armored Women, Naked Men: Dickinson, Whitman, and Their Successors" in *Shakespeare's Sisters*, p. 137.

20. This claim evokes the conventional arguments about male and female feelings, epitomized by the debate between Anne Elliot and Captain Harville in Jane Austen's *Persuasion* (Volume II, Chapter XI). Anne claims that it is women's "fate rather than our merit" to love longer, for "we live at home, quiet, confined, and our feelings prey upon us. . . . You have always a profession, pursuits, business of some sort or other, to take you back into the world immediately, and continual occupation and change soon weaken impressions."

21. Weisbuch, *Emily Dickinson's Poetry*, p. 63.

22. Cameron, *Lyric Time*, pp. 190–191.

ANNA SHANNON ELFENBEIN

Unsexing Language: Pronominal Protest in Emily Dickinson's "Lay this Laurel"

(J. 1393)
Lay this Laurel on the One
Too intrinsic for Renown—
Laurel—vail your deathless tree—
Him you chasten, that is He!

Decipherers of Emily Dickinson's poetic cryptograms have always employed biographical evidence where possible to crack the poet's coded messages. But the decoding language, standard English, has been an obstacle to deeper understanding of Dickinson's licensed poetic language, a language in whose infractive power we are only now beginning to recognize a protest against the grammar of gender. "Lay this Laurel," like many of Dickinson's poems, has been interpreted biographically, since some facts concerning its composition are accessible while its meaning remains elusive. We know that it was one of a series of brief poems Dickinson wrote commemorating the death in 1874 of her father Edward Dickinson. In June 1877, following the third anniversary of his death, she sent the four-line version of the poem reproduced above to Thomas Wentworth Higginson as a redaction of "Decoration" (*Scribner's Monthly*, June 1874), an elegy that moved her intensely appearing as it did in the very month her father died. Thomas H. Johnson reproduces "Decoration" in *The Poems of Emily Dickinson* in a note following "Lay this Laurel." Since it served as a reference point for Dickinson and continues to serve as a gloss for interpreters of "Lay this Laurel," I quote it in full.

DECORATION.

"Manibus date lilia plenis."

Mid the flower-wreath'd tombs I stand

Bearing lilies in my hand.
Comrades! in what soldier-grave
Sleeps the bravest of the brave?

Is it he who sank to rest
With his colors round his breast?
Friendship makes his tomb a shrine;
Garlands veil it; ask not mine.

One low grave, yon tree beneath,
Bears no roses, wears no wreath;
Yet no heart more high and warm
Ever dared the battle-storm,

Never gleamed a prouder eye
In the front of victory,
Never foot had firmer tread
On the field where hope lay dead,

Than are hid within this tomb,
Where the untended grasses bloom;
And no stone, with feign'd distress,
Mocks the sacred loneliness.

Youth and beauty, dauntless will,
Dreams that life could ne'er fulfill,
Here lie buried; here in peace
Wrongs and woes have found release.

Turning from my comrades' eyes,
Kneeling where a woman lies,
I strew lilies on the grave
Of the bravest of the brave.

(Poems, 961)

Richard B. Sewall suggests that there was much in "Decoration" to "suggest Dickinson's father to her: his lonely death, especially; the world's failure to recognize his true virtues and to understand him; the peace after a life of dedication and self-sacrifice" (1974, 72). There is also much in "Decoration" and in Dickinson's answer to it to suggest social criticism of those public celebrations of male valor such as Decoration Day (now generally known as Memorial Day) that honor male heroism and achievement. Edward Dickinson had had his share of such public honor. He had been a prominent public figure in Amherst and in Massachusetts throughout most of his life as a representative to the General Court of Massachusetts twice (1838 and 1873), a state senator twice (1842 and 1843), a member of the governor's executive council, a major in the militia, a delegate to the National Whig Convention in Baltimore (1852), a representative to the U. S. Congress for the Tenth Massachusetts District (1852), an attorney admitted to practice before the Supreme Court (1854), a possible candidate for governor of Massachusetts (1859), and a possible candidate for lieutenant governor two years later (he refused the offer to run). When he died in his hotel after giving a speech before the General Court in Boston on June 16, 1874, the House adjourned and the news appeared in papers across the state. To Amherst he embodied public virtue. In addition to many civic benefactions, too numerous to relate, he was instrumental in bringing the telegraph and had brought the railroad to Amherst, served as president of the company, and had a locomotive named after him. During his funeral, the shops in Amherst were closed and all business was suspended in his honor (Sewall 1974, 52, 67, and 54).

   Also a public man, Thomas Wentworth Higginson, abolitionist, reformer, preacher, Civil War colonel, long-standing supporter of feminist causes, well-known arbiter of literary taste, and "Preceptor" of Dickinson's verse, wrote "Decoration" to pay tribute to "the bravest of the brave," an unknown woman lying in an untended, unmarked, "low" grave alongside the graves of the military dead. But before kneeling and strewing his lilies on the grave of this woman, Higginson evokes the epic tradition that excludes such women with a Virgilian epigraph, "Manibus date lilia plenis" (Give me handfuls of lilies to scatter).[1] The poem that follows moves beyond this tradition unexpectedly by commemorating female heroism. The anonymous woman's sacrifice and "dauntless will" are measured against and found equal to those of the most valiant of the soldiers whose tombs are flower-wreath'd and garlanded. In turning aside from the patriarchal pattern, which, as Simone de Beauvoir trenchantly noted, follows primitive practice in its valorization of violence, cursing woman by excluding her from war and according superiority "not to the sex that brings forth but to that which kills," Higginson indicts society for glorifying war and warriors and for failing to reward or to remember its courageous women (The Second Sex, 72). The grievances of these women may be inferred in "Decoration" from the lines that note the unsung woman's "dreams that life could ne'er fulfill" and the "wrongs and woes" that define her earthly existence.

The letter to Higginson in which Dickinson enclosed "Lay this Laurel" does not respond to the feminist sentiments expressed in "Decoration." Rather it connects Dickinson's rereading of the poem to reflections on her father's death and to restless contemplation of the question of immortality, her "flood subject." She writes that she recalls being troubled by the question when as a very small child she heard the minister at a funeral ask "Is the Arm of the Lord shortened that it cannot save?" (*Letters*, 583). Submitting herself to Higginson's tutelage on this spiritual point, as she had fifteen years earlier when she opened their correspondence by asking whether he was "too deeply occupied to say if my Verse is alive," she offers obliquely to share her experience of loss with him to prepare him for a loss that she seems to anticipate for him (*Letters*, 403). (Higginson's wife Mary died after a long illness on September 2, 1877, three months after Dickinson's letter.)

Both Dickinson's letter and her poem seem to repay an emotional debt she felt she owed. After her father's death she wrote Higginson that his "beautiful Hymn" had seemed "prophetic" and that it had "assisted that Pause of Space which I call 'Father'—" (*Letters*, 528). Three years later in the letter enclosing "Lay this Laurel," she extended her hopes that "the health of [his female] friend [be] bolder," adding a four-line floral tribute to her. She prefaced "Lay this Laurel" by noting her awareness that grief and tribulation can be mitigated through sharing: "It comforts an instinct if another have felt it too" (*Letters*, 583). However, if she shared "Lay this Laurel" with Higginson to steady and solace him, as seems likely, the poem nevertheless transcends its consolatory function, for it also distills the essence of Higginson's critique of sexist social custom, dramatizing Dickinson's poetic virtuosity and deconstructing the "logic" of patriarchal language.[2]

Although Higginson may have been baffled by the delicacy with which Dickinson proffered her sympathy, he must have been flattered by her response to his own work. During the period in which he and Mabel Loomis Todd consulted on the posthumous second series of Dickinson's poems, it was probably he who decided that the quatrain Dickinson had sent him should be published rather than an eight-line version of the poem written in pencil on scraps of paper. This eight-line version exists in two trial drafts. The first, showing evidence of revision, reads:

> Lay this Laurel on the one
> Lay—Triumphed—and remained unknown—
> Laurel—fell thy futile Tree
>   your
> Such a Victor cannot be—
>   could not
>
> Lay this Laurel on the one
> Too intrinsic for Renown—
> Laurel—vail thy deathless Tree
>   your
> Him thou chastenest—
> That is he—
>   was
> Him you chastened
> That was he
>
>   (*Poems*, 962)

The second draft, on a larger stationery scrap, may be a fair copy of the first with the verbs *chastened* of line seven and *was* of line eight rendered in the present tense. A parallel examination of the first four lines of this draft and "Lay this Laurel," which closely resembles its last four lines, seems to confirm Higginson's decision to publish the quatrain he had been sent in 1877. A parallel examination of the first four lines of this second draft and its last four lines seems to demonstrate a process of composition characteristic of Dickinson as she moved to ever higher levels of abstraction in revision.

> Lay this Laurel on the one   Lay this Laurel on the one
> Triumphed and remained unknown—   Too intrinsic for Renown—
> Laurel—fell your futile Tree—   Laurel—vail your deathless
> Such a Victor could not be—   Tree—
>   Him you chasten—that is he—
>   (*Poems*, 962)

Replacing the lily, a fragile and ephemeral bloom symbolic of Christian purity, with the laurel, an enduring evergreen symbolic of poetic immortality, discarding words such as *triumphed* and *Victor*, and describing the "one" at a greater psychological and emotional distance as "too intrinsic for Renown," Dickinson moved beyond language that echoed the martial diction of Higginson's poem to language that embodied her own thought. Although the first working draft recalls something of "Decoration," as Dickinson refined her language she moved further from the sentiment expressed by Higginson, evoking at last, in the memorable four lines of "Lay this Laurel," the mystery of unique human personality effaced by the mystery of human mortality. In the face of these great mysteries, Dickinson seems to say, we must confront the ineffable and the unutterable. Unable to consecrate or to hallow the departed One, the commemorative gesture must always fall short. In its recognition of this fact, "Lay this Laurel" diverges radically from "Decoration."

However, having authorized the quatrain, Higginson was the first to praise it. In May 1891, he wrote to Mabel Loomis Todd: "['Lay this Laurel'] is the condensed essence of ['Decoration'] & so far finer" (*Poems*, 961). Later, other critics championed "Lay this Laurel," but confessed or betrayed their lack of understanding of it, brandishing encomiastic phrases, subjecting individual words to scrutiny, and leaning on the poet's biography to explain their response and its meaning. Conrad Aiken observed that, evading interpretation, it "verges perilously on the riddle" and that its thought entices while "the meaning escapes" (Sewall 1963, 14). George Frisbie Whicher agrees with Higginson that Dickinson's redaction is superior to "Decoration" and notes that she had managed to say "in four lines what he had taken twenty-eight to say, leaving out the feminist sentiment in which his thought was entangled" (222). Richard Chase asserted that it "would be recognized as expressing the accent of a major poet even if she had written nothing else" (252). Thomas H. Johnson claimed that few "poets in the language have achieved fulfillment by way of the single quatrain with greater sureness than Emily Dickinson" does in "Lay this Laurel" (*Emily Dickinson*, 228). Archibald MacLeish praised it as "one of her greatest poems and perhaps the only poem she ever wrote which carries the curious and solemn weight of perfection" (Blake and Wells, 313–14). Ronald A. Sudol discovered the "best clues" to its meaning in "Decoration" and in lines from Milton's "Lycidas" and from Shakespeare's *King Lear*.[3] Interested primarily in its genesis and its place in Dickinson's opus, Sudol located it at the threshold of Dickinson's later poetry, particularly those elegies in which she implicitly rejects "the consolation of immortality" finding "comfort in the intrinsic value of the life being commemorated" (10). David Porter sums up the response of his colleagues when he observes that "[Dickinson's] minute elegy for her father, 'Lay this Laurel on the one,' continues to baffle even her ardent readers" (45).

Although these critics agree almost unanimously that "Lay this Laurel" is an important poem, they all fail to note the protest instantiated in its slight but subversive structure. At the very heart of other Dickinson poems and hidden in plain view in "Lay this Laurel," which exploits the mythological resonance of the laurel's tragic story, this protest emerges in the poem's use of language, language that Dickinson's earliest readers saw as insanely idiosyncratic and unconventional and that we are only now beginning to see as political and even radical. Making singular pronouns plural, mismatching nominatives, possessives, and reflexives, inventing oxymoronic forms such as "themself," suspending and attentuating pronoun reference, and violating conventional expectations of gender in poetic personification, Dickinson played the language against itself with fierce intensity. In this elegy and in Dickinson's letters and other poems, "ungrammatical" pronouns infract the oppressive grammar of gender.

In American Victorian society, which maintained social distinctions of gender at great psychic cost to individuals and which created an "abyss of inequality" between the sexes, enshrining white women but undermining them by exalting their silent influence, even to trifle with the rules governing pronoun use, as Dickinson did, was to refuse to be silenced.[4] This, of course, did not prevent those whom she supplicated to print her poems from refusing or from missing her point. Her charge, "All men say 'What' to me, but I thought it a fashion," aptly summarizes the response to her dissent from the rules of a language that corseted expression—women's expression most of all (Letters, 415). Ironically, it was perhaps the inability of those she addressed to comprehend her "slanting" mode of expression that made it possible for her to trifle with the language and get away with it. Her estrangement from the "sound common sense" spoken by those such as her own sister Lavinia who espoused "Plain english . . . such as Father likes" emerges in her poetic refashioning of pronominal reference (Sewall 1974, 247).

Dickinson did not merely trifle covertly with the linguistic "fashions" governing pronominal gender. Examples of infractive pronoun use abound in her work. In a letter to Higginson dated January 1884, for example, she wrote: "I always ran Home to Awe when a child, if anything befell me. He was an awful Mother, but I liked him better than none" (*Letters*, 517–18). The orphan pose and the pun on "awful" make the sex change and suggestion of child abuse acerbically witty. In "Going to Him(Her)! Happy letter!" (J. 494), which appears in two versions nearly identical except for the sexual identity of the addressee, she problematizes ascribed gender *and* number. "Going to Him(Her)! Happy letter!" calls attention to its neutering and multiplying of the poetic voice(s), first as "I," then as "it," and finally as "we," by declaiming "I only said the Syntax— / And left the Verb and the pronoun out."

Like Walt Whitman, Emily Dickinson crossed the gender barrier in some remarkable poems, figuring the "supposed person" she presented or one aspect of that person as male in such poems as "We learned to like the Fire / By playing Glaciers—when a Boy—" (J. 689), in "Her sweet weight on my Heart a Night" (J. 518), where she speaks about a lost "Bride," in "My Life had stood—a Loaded Gun—" (J. 754), in "Conscious am I in my Chamber" (J. 679), and in "I have a King, who does not speak—" (J. 103), where she explores the source of her creative/destructive impulses, bifurcating her consciousness and assigning her creative drive to a fantasmagoric voiceless "Master."

In other poems she glides from one identity to another through pronoun shifts, revealing the multiple guises of the person she designated as "Ourself behind ourself, concealed" ["One need not be a Chamber-to be Haunted—" (J. 670)]. Two such poems are "This Chasm, Sweet, upon my life" (J. 858) and " 'I want'—it pleaded—All its life—" (J. 731). In such poems we see the familiarly fragmentary and dissociated consciousness of the speaker breathlessly daring transcendence or oblivion while keeping a precarious toehold in the here and now. In " 'I want'—it pleaded—all its life—" the speaker's yearning for experience unavailable to the engendered corporeal self locates itself in the neuter pronoun *it*, the pronoun through which Dickinson also enacted her deprivation in "What shall I do—it whimpers so—/ This little Hound within the Heart" (J. 186) and "Why make it doubt—it hurts it so—" (J. 462): " 'I want' —it pleaded—All its life— / I want—was chief it said / When Skill entreated it—the last— / And when so newly dead— / I could not deem it late—to hear / That single-steadfast sigh— / The lips had placed as with a 'Please' / Toward Eternity—."

Elegiac in its lament for the loss of that aspect of the self forbidden expression except as a "single-steadfast sigh," the poem yields and then withholds subject status to *it*, the pronominal signal of a lack about which Dickinson wrote so poignantly in poems such as "A Loss of Something Ever Felt I" (J. 959) and "The nearest Dream recedes—unrealized—" (J. 319).

Still other poems stress indeterminacy of gender and number through absent, suspended, or ambiguous pronominal reference. Some of these poems subvert conventional expectations by forcing the reader to match nouns with uncertain referent pronouns and thus to confront inherently unstable assumptions about gender embedded in our language. Through her characteristic exploitation of Latin figures such as *ellipsis* and *parenthesis*, Dickinson ramified ambiguities of meaning in such poems, "moving into an apparently unrestrained realm of creative freedom," a realm in which many of the received truths embodied in language and custom could be safely scrutinized through infracted grammar and syntax (Cuddy 1978, 83–84).[5]

As Sandra M. Gilbert notes: "The fluidity of ego which gives Dickinson's rejection of genre its special fluency can be witnessed in countless poems—verses whose daring experiments with oblivion or assertions of alternative identity signal a rejection of tradition as surely as do their proliferating pronoun shifts" ("American Sexual Politics," 149). In its departure from the generic expectations governing the elegy as this form has evolved in the male tradition and in its transgression of conventional expectations concerning pronoun reference, "Lay this Laurel" is a noteworthy example of Dickinson's rejection of literary tradition and of the genres and genderized language through which that tradition has achieved expression. The poem's treatment of fame and poetic immortality lends resonance to its violation of patriarchal linguistic forms and literary formulas.

The strategy Dickinson deploys in "Lay this Laurel" reveals the way in which she frequently inscribed her subversive message at the level of grammar and syntax. Through its suspension and attenuation of pronoun reference and through its allusion to one of the most familiar of classical myths, the poem makes its subversive point. The story of the metamorphosis of Daphne, a mortal maid pursued by the god Apollo and transformed into a laurel tree by her father to save her from the god, would have been familiar to Dickinson, who loved classical literature. It is retold by Amherst professor N. W. Fiske in his translation from the German of J. J. Eschenburg's *Manual of Classical Literature* (1846 ed.), a book listed among the required texts for the classical course at Amherst Academy during Emily Dickinson's years at the school (Cleary, 122). Considering her own confined existence in her father's house, Dickinson may have identified with Daphne who frustrated the god only to be transformed into the laurel tree, whose boughs wreath the victor, glorifying both male prowess and patriarchal poetry. An emblem of female immanence and male transcendence, Daphne/the laurel of classical myth thus plays the role allotted women in the poetic process and the poetic tradition. Poet and novelist Robert Graves described this role succinctly and perhaps approvingly when he asserted: "Woman must be Muse or she is nothing" (446).

Daring to assert that she was a woman poet rather than "nothing" or "Nobody," Dickinson foregrounds the laurel's story in "Lay this Laurel" through unstable and ambiguous pronoun reference that forces the reader to cast about for the poem's hidden source in order to resolve the question of the sexual identity of the departed "One." However, the hidden source in this poem, as in other Dickinson poems, is in plain sight. It resides in the poem's ambiguity, ambiguity that is the essence of the experience depicted. Because it is mentioned twice by its feminine name, Laurel, a name perhaps less common than Lily or Daisy but nevertheless always feminine in connotation, and its story compete with the One for status as subject of the elegy. At the misty vanishing point of death depicted by "Lay this Laurel," the laurel/tree is the only identifiable and concrete noun, since the speaker, subject, and audience of the poem are shrouded by poetic apostrophe. The laurel can be known while the speaker, subject, and audience of the poem remain forever unknown and unknowable.

Much depends upon the reader's awareness of the traditionally designated gender of the laurel, for it is paradoxically connected by proximity and by exact rhyme with the closural *He*, and its gender must be decided before the male pronominal referents of the last line can be linked tentatively with the antecedent *One* of the first. A lingering ambiguity concerning this linkage frustrates final determination concerning the gender of the One, though capitalization of this indefinite pronoun and of the closural pronouns might encourage the reader to assume coreference. If indeed these pronouns are coreferential, then the fact that both Daphne (the mortal maiden who fled attempted rape by Apollo) and the deceased (ostensibly Edward Dickinson) have been unsexed by metamorphosis/Death, which finally confers equal rites on female and male, makes frustration with the ambiguity concerning sexual identity futile. Finally, neither Daphne, having become the laurel, nor *He*, having become the *One*, remains functionally gendered.

If, however, the closural *He* and the *One* of the first line are not coreferential, then the capitalized masculine pronouns of the last line direct attention to some(One) outside the text but implicated in its action. *This* One, who is close at hand in the first line, thus contrasts with *that* He, the final word of the last line, who is distant. Perhaps possessing the immortality of Apollo or of the Christian God, *He* would, if the poet had her way, be chastened by the laurel's "vailing" and by the death of the One too noble to be judged according to the world's standards.

Through the indeterminacy of such reference, the poem extends its meaning beyond the parameters of the sexual or the personal. Direct address of the presumed reader(s), who is(are) told to "Lay this Laurel," voids gender difference. Dickinson's unidentified lyrical "I" also lacks gender, as does the laurel, which is charged with covering the departed One. Once a desirable mortal woman, the laurel perhaps covers both its sexual lack and that of the One "too intrinsic for Renown" (renown means "renaming" in Latin). Through the word *intrinsic*—a word employed in the funeral sermon for Edward Dickinson to rationalize his withdrawal from the town of Amherst—the poet implicitly derides the connection of gender and fame/success/social esteem established through language and social custom. For the intrinsic (inherent, imperceptible, interior; hence, conventionally feminine) qualities of an individual have little to do with renown as tradition decides it. It is rather the extrinsic sexuality and achievement of the male that tradition recognizes by crowning him with laurel.

The poet defies this tradition. Outside the uses of tradition and beyond the claims of socially defined sexuality, but within the charmed circle of the poem, the speaker, the person(s) addressed,

the One, and the laurel resist renaming and engendering. In this resistance, the speaker identifies with audience, subject, and vehicle.
Unlike William Blake's eroticized "emanation" or Wallace Stevens's
"interior paramour," the speaker and the speaker's ungendered audience, subject, and mythological vehicle are in fact characterized by
their shared distance from the claims of gender. But such distance
cannot be absolute, since the ambiguities created by unstable reference so multiply the interpretive possibilities that all are tainted
or chastened by these claims. The laurel is also tainted by its traditional function. The word *chasten* (purified, shrunken, punished)
reminds the reader of the "chaste/chased" laurel's plight in being
robbed of its own creative potentiality and forced to confer glory on
its would-be rapist and his mortal worshippers beginning with those
who triumph in the games held in his honor.

However, if the absent but deified He had the capacity for guilt,
He too might be chastened, by the death of One so intrinsically noble
or by the abject and inanimate laurel, once a victim of his lust. The
One might also be chastened, though to be chastened by those who,
like the laurel, serve or follow an amoral deity might add posthumous insult to the injury death represents. The adverb *too* suggests
the complicity of the living One in the system of social definition
that requires both distinctions of gender and adverbial intensifiers to
enable them. When the mortal frontier is traversed, such complicity
can cease, and the One can then become One relative to none, having
transcended or transvalued gender.

It seems appropriate, considering the ambivalence with which
Dickinson seems to have regarded both her earthly and her heavenly
f(F)ather, that the word *chasten* should have paradoxical meanings
and that such a word could be applied with equal force to the One
and the He of the poem whether they are coreferential or not. The
ambiguous (perhaps defensive) doubling of male pronouns at the end
of "Lay this Laurel" is equally paradoxical, for these pronouns insist
on the masculinity of the mortal One or of the immortal He but
deny it with a neutering emphatic (but grammatically ambiguous)
that, which might be either a relative or a demonstrative pronoun.
(The ambiguity is deepened by the fact that the word bears a secondary stress.) As legatee of Edward Dickinson's memory, the poet
identified herself increasingly with him, arrogating to herself the
function of the laurel that decked the church during the funeral ser-

vice she had not attended (Sewall 1974, 69). John Evangelist Walsh tells us: "The only mark of her connection with the ceremonies was a small wreath of white daisies that lay in solitary simplicity on the otherwise unadorned coffin" (221).

The belated gesture with which Dickinson commands "this" laurel to commemorate her father suggests that earlier tributes to him were insufficient, perhaps especially those tributes paid to him by Austin and Susan Gilbert Dickinson of the Evergreens, the house next to the Homestead, where Edward Dickinson, his wife, Emily Norcross Dickinson, and his daughters, Emily and Lavinia, lived. During her father's lifetime, Emily confessed "I am not very well acquainted with father," noting elsewhere "My father seems to me often the oldest and the oddest sort of a foreigner" (Sewall 1974, 55 and 66) and observing, as she recalled her last afternoon with him: "His Heart was pure and terrible and I think no other like it exists" (*Letters*, 528). Perhaps no one would fit this description except the remote God of the Old Testament whose image Dickinson's words here and elsewhere recall in a manner perhaps typical of nineteenth-century daughters.

The poem (dis)covers the poet's ambivalence toward this man, who was and to whom she was, a beloved mystery. Less obvious than its ambivalence toward secular and spiritual (f)Fathers is the ambivalence of the poem's implied stance toward the poetic tradition. For just as Higginson's "Decoration" prompted Dickinson's poem, Horace's famous *"Exegi monumentum aere perennis"* (or perhaps Virgil's *Aeneid* from which Higginson borrowed the Latin epigraph for "Decoration") provides the sort of patriarchal Ur text Dickinson's poem subverts. A progenitor of the tradition of poetic boasting, Horace's ode concludes by asking the Muse to "willingly encircle my forehead with Apollo's laurel" (Cleary, 127).[6] The leaves that contain a poem, like the leaves that crown the laureate, would be conventionally supposed to immortalize both the poet and the poet's subject. In "Lay this Laurel," however, Dickinson analogizes the laurel and her poem, bestowing laurel instead of claiming it. Rather than conferring honor, the laurel chastens both the One it covers and the g(G)od responsible for its metamorphic existence. The poem thus takes its stand outside the patriarchal tradition, a tradition Harold Bloom has found fraught with terrors for the male ephebe whose longing for the laurel motivates poetic misprision/misreading of patriarchal progenitors.

Although it rejects this tradition rather than rereading or rewriting it in the way a male poet might, "Lay this Laurel" evinces mixed emotions about this rejection. Just as the laurel is implicated in its own tragedy, so too is the poet in the tradition that "Lay this Laurel" rejects. The playful redaction of "Decoration" and the submission of the quatrain to Higginson—the very existence of the poem—attest to Dickinson's engagement in the process of creation and her desire for recognition as a poet. Further, the deep structure of the poem places it among those Dickinson works that treat the poetic or intellectual tradition and the creative woman's vocation— poems, such as "I have a King, who does not speak" (J. 103), "Myself was formed—a Carpenter" (J. 488), "They shut me up in Prose" (J. 613), "Publication—is the Auction" (J. 709), "Fame of Myself, to justify" (J. 713), "She rose to his Requirement—dropt" (J. 732), and "My life had stood—a Loaded Gun" (J. 754), to name but a few. In these poems, as in "Lay this Laurel," Dickinson's licensed infractions of linguistic convention force readers to confront the inherent sexual biases of our language and our literature and invite them to enter Dickinson's realm of imaginative freedom beyond the engendering conventions that constrain—that constitute—human thought and emotion.

NOTES

1. This famous line #883 from the sixth book of Virgil's *Aeneid* may have suggested to Dickinson the apostrophic opening of "Lay this Laurel."

2. Ruth Miller describes Dickinson's redactive practice, that is, her repeated "distil[ling of] amazing sense" (J. 448) from the works of canonical poets and from the works of contemporary versifiers. Miller writes: "[Dickinson] does not borrow, she improves. When she reads something that is printed, she pits her skill against that which has won the public stamp of approval, she does it over, leaving it, as she thinks, with a finer finish, a greater relevance" (223).

3. Sudol hears echoes of "Lycidas" and *King Lear* in "Lay this Laurel." According to Sudol, the use of laurel as an emblem of immortality and the implied connection between the departed one and the poet, who are both denied earthly acclaim, Dickinson owes to Milton. To

Shakespeare, he asserts, Dickinson owes the description of one who is "too intrinsic." Shakespeare's lines read: "That such a slave as this should wear a sword, / Who wears no honesty. Such smiling rogues as these, / Like rats, oft bite the holy cords a-twain / Which are too intrinsic t'unloose; smooth every passion / That in the natures of their lords rebel" (II.ii.66–70). Sudol notes that Dickinson uses similar language to different effect: "man's symbols of triumph over death cannot bestow more honor than the elegist recognizes as an intrinsic value that supersedes both the immortality achieved by all and the social recognition reserved for some" (13–14).

4. The rigid socialization of males and females to assume separate spheres in Victorian America has been the subject of much recent scholarly comment. By the 1880s American society had plumbed what Henry James called an "abyss of inequality, the like of which has never before been seen under the sun" (Ziff, 275). Separated by antithetical training and values, men and women knew little of each other's interests. Men's interests were commercial, professional, or political, while women's were cultural, familial, or moral. Women's sentiments were to be felt but not heard. A moral pundit of Dickinson's day, Mrs. Lydia Sigourney, urged her women readers to practice self-control, curbing their tongues and smiling "upon every member of [their] household[s] like the dew upon the tender herb, or the sunbeam silently educating the young flower" (11).

   In such a society, violating the grammatical rules governing pronoun use constituted a defiant speech act. One need only reflect on the militant resistance to the abolition of the generic *he* in our own day to recognize the implications of Dickinson's pronominal play. In "How 'Low Feet' Stagger: Disruptions of Language in Dickinson's Poetry," Cristanne Miller observes that such play often corresponds directly to explicit thematic concerns of a given poem and notes that Dickinson "restructures [sexual] role associations perhaps most clearly through an unconventional use of pronouns" (135).

5. Three articles suggest Dickinson's debt to Latin poets: Lois A. Cuddy's "The Influence of Latin Poetics on Emily Dickinson's Style" and "The Latin Imprint on Emily Dickinson's Poetry: Theory and Practice" explore Dickinson's adaptation of the quantitative metrics and "ungrammatical" figures of Latin poetry. Vincent J. Cleary's "Emily Dickinson's Classical Education" examines Dickinson's use of classical allusion.

6. Horace's Ode 3.30 is translated by Vincent Cleary, who notes that the English translation contains almost twice as many words as the

original. This demonstrates the kind of compression possible in Latin prosody. Horace vaunts that he has "built a monument more lasting than bronze / Taller than the site of the Pyramids, / Which neither greedy rain, nor the powerful North wind / Nor the innumerable series of years, nor the flight of time, can destroy" (127). This boast reverberates throughout the patriarchal tradition. Shakespeare's boast, "Not marble, nor the gilded monuments / Of princes, shall outlive this powerful rhyme," sonnetizes the same idea.

CAROLYN A. DURHAM

Linguistic and Sexual Engendering in Marianne Moore's Poetry

Marianne Moore's poetry raises many of the same questions that currently trouble feminist readers of Marguerite Yourcenar: Who is speaking? Where is the author? Where is the woman? The selection of Yourcenar, a woman who consistently speaks in a first-person masculine voice, to break open the fraternal ranks of the Académie Française echoes the privileged status granted in anthologies and literary histories to Moore, a woman whose poetry is apparently devoid of any reference to female experience. The Yourcenar parallel in some sense questions those interpretations of literary history that place Moore confidently at a transitional stage of necessary (though for some regrettable) absorption into male culture, and begins to validate the position I propose to grant her within the mainstream of a still-developing female tradition. Assuming then that Moore may be less idiosyncratic than conventionally supposed (curiously, Moore turns out to cite Yourcenar as example in an essay on "Idiosyncracy and Technique" [*Reader* 181]), how does this self-acknowledged lover of hybrid forms manage that most difficult of all: the woman-poet?

The dictum "cherchez la femme," which has informed recent feminist criticism of Moore's poetry, has led to results as surprisingly conventional as the plot structures from which the cliché derives. On the one hand, critics such as Suzanne Juhasz, Barbara Gelpi, and even Adrienne Rich (for whom Marianne Moore "fled into a universe of forms" [qtd. in Gelpi and Gelpi xiii]) conclude that the woman is indeed absent from Moore's poetry, deliberately sacrificed to and by the poet in what Juhasz calls an effort to become "one of the boys" (35). Such a reading adds nothing feminist but disapproval to the dominant critical interpretation of Moore as a "poet's poet" whose primary interest lies in her mastery of form and technique. Yet, ironically, those critics who make the opposite assumption, often in direct reaction to the traditional position, repeat the error; thus, the attention that Bonnie Costello, Terence Diggory, and Jeanne Kammer pay to various aspects of Moore's femininity adds nothing feminist but approval to the male critical intuition that Moore's decorous plants and animals embody traditional female virtues. Moreover, in her book-length study of Moore, Costello comes full circle to rejoin Juhasz and in the process does a real disservice to feminist criticism; for Costello now denies gender any relevance, marginalizing and so dismissing it with the aside, "I have dealt with Moore's 'feminine' qualities elsewhere" (13).

Oddly enough, feminist analyses of the sociohistorical conditions that in the nineteenth century made "the very nature of lyric poetry . . . inherently incompatible with the nature or essence of femaleness" (Gilbert and Gubar, *Madwoman* 541) may, in Moore's case, provide a more productive link to the situation of the twentieth-century woman poet. Two central concerns have traditionally made poetry the most problematic of literary genres for women writers. As Sandra Gilbert and Susan Gubar argue, the writing of lyric poetry at the time of Emily Dickinson required both a self-assertion in conflict with the self-effacement expected of women and an education in the linguistic and formal tradition of the genre unavailable to most women (*Madwoman* 541–49). These two issues of self and language can be linked directly to the contemporary feminist imperative to "write the body," to claim female sexuality as the clearest sign of the female self and the most effective access to a female language. Although Gilbert and Gubar's current work on the modernist period supposes a break with the nineteenth-century female tradition, they too note that "connections between female pleasure and female power, between assertive female sexuality and assertive female speech, have been traditional ones" (*Madwoman* 568). In a characteristically hybrid gesture, Marianne Moore's poetry uses a nineteenth-century strategy of the double text to announce the themes and techniques that become overt in modernist and postmodernist women's poetry: an apparent renunciation of self overlays the subversive encoding of female sexuality; an apparently gender-free concern with linguistic and formal experimentation conceals the subversive rejection of male language. My own argument also has a twofold purpose; I seek both to uncover Moore's concealed sexual narrative and to explore the three distinct forms it takes in the course of her poetic career.

Let me acknowledge at once that it is not without some trepidation that I propose this reading of a consecrated "ladylike" poet. R. P. Blackmur assures us that "there is no sex anywhere in her poetry" (Tomlinson 85); Randall Jarrell situates Moore in a world "entirely divorced from sexuality" (Tomlinson 122); and Juhasz confirms that Moore "opt[ed] for nonsexuality" (39). Still, Moore's own reading of Ezra Pound might suggest otherwise: "I have taken great pleasure in both your prose and your verse, but it is what my mother terms the saucy parts, which have most fixed my attention" (Tomlinson 17). In "Poetry," Moore deliberately abandons the stance of the writer for that of the reader to encourage women to seek the "place for the genuine" that lies behind the male mask of a hostile genre. In her single most self-assertive poem, "O To Be a Dragon," Moore's wish surely points beyond the monster to the "fiercely vigilant and intractable woman" that is simultaneously designated by the word. Similarly, embedded in the very center of "The Paper Nautilus," a poem that turns the specifically female experience of maternity into a metaphor for poetic creation, the line break suddenly forces us to acknowledge that "she is in / a sense a devil—"; doubly concealed behind the suspended image (of the "devil-fish") and the apparent denotation of evil, Moore announces that the female poet is daring, clever, and mischievous.

Moore's early poems emphasize the more subversive aspects of her covert play. *The Selected Poems* of 1935 include her most explicit and most pessimistic rejection of maleness as encoded in both sexuality and language; Moore first defines the female self negatively, in opposition to what it is not. In "The Fish," for example, Moore exposes the destructiveness of male sexuality as experienced by the female. The poem begins with images of darkness and death that describe the wounded vagina: the mussel-shell "opening and shutting itself like / an / injured fan." The secret and hidden nature of female sexuality, next encoded in an image of submerged barnacles, provides no protection as the "shafts of the / sun, / . . . move themselves with spotlight swiftness / into the crevices— / in and out." Moore's third enactment of this sexual conflict reverses traditional gender associations of the natural world as the male sea accosts the female cliff: "The water / drives a wedge / of iron through the iron edge / of the cliff." Although Moore portrays the vagina as a "defiant edifice," its very form is determined by the injury of male sexual aggression: "All / external / marks of abuse are present" and, more explicitly, "dynamite grooves, / burns, and / hatchet strokes, these things stand / out on it." Indeed, although Moore asserts that female endurance will outlast male aggression, this passive victory comes at the price of the total destruction of female sexuality: "the chasm-side is / dead." The insistent reduction of the female principle to an unnamed, objectified "it," which results from the loss of female sexual power ("Repeated / evidence has proved that it can live / on what can not revive / its youth. The sea grows old in it"), stresses by contrast Moore's equation of the female self with female sexuality.

The final sequence of poems in this early collection encloses the specifically feminist message of "Sojourn in the Whale," to which I will return below, within parallel poems about the maleness of language. In "He Wrote the History Book," the title quotation marks the sureness with which even a five-year old boy can simultaneously name himself and the world; the child identifies with the father who, as primary signifier, author of "*The* book," is equated in turn with language itself. Moreover, Moore's play on the son's contribution to his father's "legibility" connects linguistic authority to the power of the law. The father's writing of his-story inscribes the general association of culture and maleness just as the final line of the poem —"Thank you for showing me / your father's autograph"—encodes a parallel identity between language and the individual male self. Although the female poet recognizes the child's assertion to be "sufficiently synthetic," that is, manmade, such an ideology of language functions to silence her: "I have been dumbfounded by / it oftener than I care to say." It is not surprising then that Moore ends her first volume of verse with "Silence," a poem in which every line but the last belongs to a quotation now attributed to the poet's own father. Even though the poem ends with the daughter's clear assertion that she does not dwell in the father's world ("Nor was he insincere in saying, 'Make my house your inn.' / Inns are not residences"), his words effectively dominate to drown out hers.

The intervening poem ("Sojourn in the Whale"), Moore's one example of the feminist manifesto, helps us understand how the woman poet nevertheless manages to speak in the narrow space left open between the equating of language with maleness and the inevitable call for female silence that must follow. Confronted by the male belief in dichotomous oppositions, grounded in sexual difference—"There is a feminine temperament in direct contrast to ours" —Moore "smile[s]" (the poet names her own anger only in the female metaphor of Ire-land) as she asserts the transformative power of the female who can "spin gold thread from straw" and who, like "water in motion," rises automatically to overcome obstacles. As we will see, this belief in fluidity functions centrally throughout Moore's poetry to surmount the fundamental dualism of sexuality itself. Already the opening lines of "Sojourn" not only associate clearly phallic metaphors—the sword, the needle, and the tree—with the female Ireland but ironically invert them ("Trying to open locked doors with a sword, threading / the points of needles, planting shade trees / upside down") so that each in turn is rendered impotent.

Moore's early concern with the power of the male poetic tradition to destroy the hybrid self of the woman-poet by a double-edged attack on her sexuality and her authority to speak may well explain Moore's often repeated insistence that she "never intended to write poetry" and that what she did write "could only be called poetry because there is no other category in which to put it" (Reader 256–58). Her expectation that each of her poems might be her last and her increasing disinterest in being published (Tomlinson 17) could be linked as well to frustration in face of the clearly incomplete readings her highly praised poetry was receiving. Moore's apparent change in attitude toward the term poetry—"I do not now feel quite my original hostility to the word" (Reader 238)—may then correspond to an alternative strategy that in other poems replaces negative opposition to the male with a positive inscription of the female. In an interesting parallel between feminist literature and feminist criticism, Moore's poetry reflects the distinction that Elaine Showalter has recently made between "feminist critique," the reading of literary images of women, and "gynocritics," the process of defining women's writing.[1]

Although Moore has long been read as the quintessential modernist, her reputation has been narrowly grounded in what Hugh Kenner calls "the tradition of describing accurately the thing seen"; such critical marginality leads to the equally common designation of Moore as an "inaccessible" poet as "baffling" as her poetry is reputed to be (Abbott). In fact, modernism's more central commitment to linguistic innovation better illuminates the radical self-reflection and self-generation that characterize many of her poems. In a paradox illustrative of the feminist act of re-vision, redefining Moore as a *female* modernist thus results in her simultaneous redefinition as a female *modernist;* her work underscores the crucial role that language plays not only in the definition of modernism but in an understanding of the potential difference(s) of women modernists as well. This reconceptualization of Moore's primary focus finds support in her own descriptions of a poetic process based on "spontaneous initial originality" in which she is "governed by the pull of the sentence" as "words cluster like chromosomes, determining the procedure" (*Reader* 263); and her delightful correspondence with Henry Ford over the naming of the Edsel affirms her clear commitment to self-generative language in the most unpropitious of circumstances.[2] "A Carriage from Sweden," included in Moore's 1944 collection *Nevertheless,* offers an example of her autogenerative techniques that allows us to consider the difference gender may make within what has been a predominantly male tradition of experimental writing. Hélène Cixous's theory of female language as "vol"—the theft / flight of male language—is meant to address precisely this issue.[3]

"A Carriage from Sweden" suggests that Moore's work, often praised for its attention to realistic detail, is in fact essentially antivisual and antidescriptive; the occasion for her disproportionate and detailed description is a "put-away" cart, which "no one may see." Both the linguistic and thematic development of "A Carriage from Sweden" insistently highlights the process of the poem's own composition, as does the inclusion of such generative imagery as a spruce seedling, which fans out "by itself," and a "self-lit" lighthouse. Structurally, the description of the cart engenders the woman "for whom it should come to the door— / of whom it reminds me"; the woman's "pineneedled-path deer-swift step" produces in turn the pine tree and the "runner called the Deer." The final sentence of the poem both reaffirms the generative sequence we have been reading and makes explicit the larger process that informs the entire poem:

> I understand;
> it's not pine-needled-paths that give spring
> when they're run on, it's a Sweden
> of moated white castles—the bed

> of white flowers densely grown in an S
> meaning Sweden and stalwartness,
> skill, and a surface that says
> Made in Sweden: carts are my trade.

The textual "surface" of Moore's poem, determined by the fifty words of the two-page work that begin with *s*, announces a poem "made," like Sweden, out of the letter *S*.

But is this generative poem also en-gendered, that is, encoded as a female text? In a usurpation of God's powers, the female figure in Moore's poem not only creates the natural world but both generates and names the male, thus claiming linguistic authority. The curved line of the *s* suggests a traditional association with the female, and the foregrounding of the mechanical letter generation ironically overshadows the thematic insistence on the straight lines of male stalwartness ("a vein / of resined straightness from north-wind / hardened Sweden's once-opposed-to- / compromise archipelago").[4] Moore's poetic assertion that "carts are my trade" subtly reinforces this connection between gender and language, for cart derives from the Indo-European *ger-*, base for a variety of words meaning to "curve, bend, curl." The final revelation of the cart as the structural foundation of the elegant carriage of the poem's title supports an attack on poetry as romance, which may be aimed in particular at the image of women that informs it; Moore's one overt expression of disdain —the ironic exclamation "What / a fine thing! What unannoying / romance!"—accompanies the appearance of the woman who will inspire the rest of the poem.

Moore's single most openly self-generative poem, "Saint Valentine" (published in the 1966 collection *Tell Me, Tell Me*) helps to support the dual hypotheses that she attaches meaning to the shape of letters and that her simultaneous mirroring of the generative and the gender potential of poetry often involves a reflection on and of the origins of language itself. Moore uses the *V*, a letter whose form conventionally links it to female sexuality, to create successively language ("a name beginning with 'V'"), the forgotten female poet ["Vera, El Greco's only / daughter (though it has never been proved that he had one)"], and, finally, poetry itself ("Verse—unabashedly bold—is appropriate"). In the process, Moore challenges the primacy of a male literary heritage. Even as she assures Saint Valentine of her intention to make us "think of you and not me," her ironic renaming of his "memento" for a female precursor in fact situates her poem within a literary tradition newly engendered as female. Moreover, Moore here inscribes a meditation on language that supports Sandra Gilbert and Susan Gubar's recent discovery that modernist women writers often encode their claim to literary authority in "fantasies about the possession of a mother tongue" ("Sexual Linguistics" 527).

For "Saint Valentine" is fundamentally a poem about etymology. Moore's portrait of Vera, once named—"It could be a vignette"— immediately recalls its origins to produce a "vinelet" border. Transformed into a "mere flower," lexical and alliterative associations call forth a "violet," a playful anagram (love it) whose metaphoric sense —"said to mean the / love of truth or truth of / love"—establishes a revised etymology that claims the truth (verity) of the connection between gender (Vera) and poetry (verse). Moore's specific focus in her final stanza on the writing process confirms her revisionary intentions: "Any valentine that is *written* / Is as the *vendange* to the vine. / Might verse not best confuse itself with fate?" Moore's italicization emphasizes the link between the act of writing and the rethinking of origins. "Vendange" reintroduces the foreign and forgotten ancestor into the English language as Vera, the female poet, reinserts its counterpart into literary history. "Vendange," which shares a common root with "vinelet" and "vignette" (*vinum*), reiterates the parallel between natural and poetic generativity; moreover, its double meaning as both the process of harvesting and the product harvested clearly identifies Moore's valentine as both a text about writing and a written text. Though "verse" too supposedly initiates in *wer*, "to turn, to plow," that is, to harvest, Moore suggests an original (and better) (con)fusion with *wer*, to speak, thus making poetry synonymous with "fate," derived from *bha*, to speak. Thus, Moore's poem not only re-en-genders literary history, but defines female destiny as the production, at once initial and final, of fruitful poetic speech.

In this context, Moore's long association with *The American Heritage Dictionary of the English Language*, on whose usage panel she served until her death, suggests a parallel interest in poetry and lexicography that further clarifies the fascination with etymology and an original language visible in such poems as "Saint Valentine." Indeed, Moore's structuring of language closely resembles that designed by *The American Heritage Dictionary* to illustrate the exis-

tence of an antecedent common language: "the constantly ramifying
nature of lexical creativity, descent, and borrowing is such that many
tens of thousands of modern English words can be proved to be descended from a mere 1,500 Indo-European roots" (XLVII). Moore's
strategy here both complements and significantly contrasts with parallel attempts by other female modernists, in Gilbert and Gubar's
words, to "annihilate the alphabetic basis and bias" of patriarchal
language ("Ceremonies" 36). While Moore's "engendering" of letters and revisionary mythology of linguistic origins connect her to
a distinctively female modernism, her specific choice to rewrite the
"History Book" as the "herstory" of the alphabet and the dictionary
also allows her to undermine from within both male modernism and
the male poetic tradition as a whole, subverting the foundation in
classical education and the science of the word by which they sought
to exclude women writers (see Benstock, *Women* 25–28).

Yet, my reading of Moore also supports Gilbert and Gubar's
insistence elsewhere that the distinction between male and female
usage of similar techniques must be sought simultaneously in the
realm of experience (*Madwoman* 87). What may be unique to self-
generative writing by women is its literalness, that is, its crucial
encoding of the generation of an authentic female self. Thus, far from
reflecting back on themselves, female texts open out onto social
and political reality. Using the title poem of *Nevertheless* as my
principal example, I want to suggest that at least some of Marianne
Moore's associative poetry uses the female body as a primary textual
generator. The parallel creation of a self-defined language and an
autonomous sexual identity now allows Moore to triumph over male
aggression.

"Nevertheless" opens with three parallel objects—a strawberry,
a hedge hog, and a starfish—whose form ("where the fragments
meet") and whose fertility ("the multitude of seeds") announce them
as metaphors for the female genitals. In this initial context and
throughout the poem, the transformation of one image into another
again characterizes female sexuality as fluid and multiple. Moore
seems to take ironic pleasure in selecting metaphors whose prickli-
ness might suggest male fear of the "toothed" vagina; the title of the
poem can be read as announcing an opposition to traditional male
views of female sexuality as well as to comforting male ideas about
the "chastity" of Moore's own poetry. Moore confirms our initial

suspicions about her poetic subject by an even more explicit description of the female genitals ("What better food / than apple-seeds— the fruit / within the fruit—locked in / like counter-curved twin / hazel-nuts?") that operates as both a womb and a vulva image. The choice of the "apple" as the nourishing "food" recalls Eve as the progenitor of the human race and the prototype of productive female sexuality.

In its focus on "stalks" and "roots," the next section of the poem might be read to introduce the contrast of the male genitals. If so, Moore continues her ironic play on male fear of female sexuality, complete with some appropriate punning: connected to "prickly" pears and toothy kok-saghz, these roots are reassured of their power to "grow" in "frozen ground." But, given the emphasis the imagery places on the hidden and the transformative, these lines can also be read as a further exploration of female sexuality. Indeed, the root-supported plants might be seen as metaphors for the ankh.[5] The carrot, moreover, forms the branched "mandrake," whose form, if not its name, suggests the female body, and the ram's-horn root, already associated with the female in "The Paper Nautilus," curves back on itself.

Still, male sexuality does enter the poem, at the very latest, with the grape whose multiple "knots" immobilize its passive partner. In contrast to "The Fish," the encoding of male sexual dominance now leads Moore to an openly ironic ending, marked by the use of exclamations. In a direct contradiction of the conventional view of appropriate female behavior, Moore's line break defines passive endurance as the nonsense it is ("What is there / like fortitude! What sap"). The poem then closes with a derisive attack on male potency and sexual pride ("What sap / went through that little thread") that turns out, moreover, to be thwarted. Moore returns to female sexuality with the "cherry" whose redness suggests both female blood and revolution and whose untouched virginity confirms the original definition of the virgin as a strongly self-defined woman. As Moore says elsewhere, "What of chastity? It confers a particular strength. Until recently, I took it for granted as a universally regarded asset, like avoiding 'all drugs' " (*Reader* 196).

The stress Moore places on the self-fertilizing cherry, the last in a long series of plants all characterized by reproductive autonomy, again affirms the crucial connection she makes between gender and language in her use of modernist textual strategies. As in "A Carriage from Sweden" and "Saint Valentine," the final line of "Nevertheless" ("What sap / went through that little thread / to make the cherry red!") reasserts the power of self-generative language to create new forms and identifies the poem as the self-reflective account of this process. Moore's phonetic play (red/read) asks us to reread the poem as an illustration of its own composition. Moreover, by defining the ink flowing through her pen as the ultimate source of the transformations described in "Nevertheless," Moore ironically undermines Western culture's metaphorical equation of pen and penis (Gilbert and Gubar, *Madwoman* ch. 1–2)—a dissociation of male sexuality and male literary power that is reinforced by her usurpation of the male's sexual and poetic right to "make." In so doing, Moore not only refuses the traditional dichotomy between the literary creativity of the male and the biological creativity of the female, but reclaims the analogy between reproductive and linguistic generativity for the female. Indeed, the resilient virginity that Moore's cherry metaphor associates with female sexuality/textuality foresees Suzanne Lamy's wonderfully appropriate characterization of contemporary female autogenerative practice as textual "parthenogenesis" (31).

Moreover, Moore's parallel embedding of the female genitals and the poetic process also challenges the customary focus on similar images of female eroticism as containment and impenetrability, what even Susan Gubar views—citing Moore, Levertov, and H. D.— as, at best, "emblem[s] of defensive survival in a hostile world" (203). Rather, Moore's lubricating "sap" revalidates the enclosed and the hidden as fertile and dynamic metaphors of both resistance and change. Moore's interest in rethinking etymology may well operate here too to recall the alternate meaning of "sap" (from old French "sappe," an undermining) as an underground trench that protects only to allow one to advance, thus subordinating its defensive to its offensive function even as it serves both simultaneously. Moore answers Gubar and Gilbert's query—"If the pen is a metaphorical penis, with what organ can females generate texts?" (*Madwoman* 7)—by transforming female sexuality itself into a liberating instrument of creativity.

Moore also asserts in other late poems that female sexuality is "never-the-less," never lesser than male sexuality. In "A Jellyfish," one of her most explicitly erotic poems, Moore overturns the title associations of weakness to reaffirm the strength of the self-sufficient female.

> Visible, invisible,
>   a fluctuating charm
> an amber-tinctured amethyst
>   inhabits it, your arm
> approaches and it opens
>   and it closes; you had meant
> to catch it and it quivers;
>   you abandon your intent.

Here the female's successful resistance to male aggression ironically justifies images of the dangerous vagina. Moreover, the poem also invites either a masturbatory or a lesbian reading. The jewel image celebrates female pleasure, as the female, now totally self-defined, experiences orgasm.

Yet, throughout her work, Moore argues a third position even more radical than either the negative critique of male sexual oppression or the positive assertion of female sexual independence. I have already suggested that the central section of "Nevertheless" simultaneously encodes male and female sexuality and that images combining female circularity and male verticality function throughout the poem and throughout Moore's poetry. Indeed, what I earlier read as a womb/vagina image ("the fruit / within the fruit—locked in / like counter-curved twin hazel-nuts") applies equally well in form, function, and linguistic playfulness to the male testes. This parallelism may better answer Moore's query: "What better food / than appleseeds"? What, indeed, can promise more than the fruit shared by Adam and Eve at the original moment of their accession to full humanity? The equal emphasis Moore places on seeds and roots establishes the concept of origin as an unresolved and irresolvable fusion of male and female reproductive capacities. The seed is both the fertilizing sperm and the fertilized ovula; the root, simultaneously male and female in its shape, offers both male support and female nurturance.

While still recalling the "struggle" of male and female sexuality in its opening lines, "Nevertheless," as its title suggests, moves in the course of the poem to challenge the dualistic structures on which gender opposition is based. Moore's first definition of sexual

"victory" encodes female orgasm as an ambivalent gesture of assertion and submission: "Victory won't come / to me unless I go / to
it." But in the following image of domination, which initially seems
to privilege passive surrender ("so / the bound twig that's under- /
gone and over-gone, can't stir"), Moore begins to break down traditional associations of passivity and activity by a startling reversal
of the meaning of the two verbs. The apparently active *go* has been
transformed by both voice and vocabulary into a state of passive
subjection.

Similarly, in the maxim that follows ("The weak overcomes
its / menace, the strong over- / comes itself"), the key sexual term
come now has the form and meaning of active triumph. Indeed, by
etymology, the word *come* itself encodes the ambivalence, the inclusiveness, and the paradoxicalness that Moore's poem attributes
to the parallel concept; it derives from the Indo-European root *gwa-*,
meaning, appropriately, "to go, come." To insist that we read beyond
conventional meaning, Moore uses not only inverted repetitions but
parallel line-break emphasis of *come* and *go* and of *under-* and *over-*;
the interruption of these hyphenated second terms calls our attention to the central role hybridization plays in overcoming traditional
dichotomies. Importantly, the poem's conclusion asks to be read in
several different ways simultaneously. "The weak overcomes its /
menace" may refer either to the apparent weakness of the female
who nonetheless triumphs over the male by "fortitude" or to the
male who reveals his own weakness in the need to resist the threat
of female sexuality. Similarly, "the strong over- / comes itself": the
strong male may be overcome by his self-defeating attempt at domination; the strong female may triumph over obstacles by the fluid
process of self-transformation that the poem recounts; or, most radically, strength may mean the ability for both male and female to
surmount the crippling limits of gender identity.

That this poem both clearly alludes to male and female experience and yet never allows us to identify with certainty any particular set of images as only male or only female, as well as un-
ambivalently positive or negative, seems to me crucially important
to Moore's revolutionary project. The strategy of superimposition
ultimately undermines our very notion of what is masculine or feminine by eliminating the structure of opposition that alone allows us
to define the two categories. Moreover, in choosing to make specifically sexual images simultaneously and inseparably male and

female, Moore rewrites gender at the original level of the biological division into two sexes where most people argue that the very notion of duality originates. It is hardly surprising then that Moore's poetry, as many commentators have noted, so frequently describes images of protective covering, for the self Moore so carefully seeks to defend against both biological and cultural onslaught is a radical hybrid, the offspring of genetically dissimilar male and female parents, which itself lies beyond gender differentiation. Moore, I believe, makes the astonishing assertion that the human self is indeed human.

Moore's project of crossbreeding to produce a new human hybrid illuminates the analogy she often makes between the scientist and the poet. In response to Donald Hall's assertion that "most people" consider the two to be opposed, Moore emphasizes the similarity of poetic and scientific methodology: "The objective is fertile procedure. Is it not? Jacob Bronowski says in the *Saturday Evening Post* that science is not a mere collection of discoveries but that science is the process of discovering. In any case it's not established once and for all; it's evolving" (*Reader* 273–74). Moore's interest in "fertile procedure" makes of her a kind of verbal geneticist.[6] Her two favorite poetic techniques—the series of hyphenated words and the collage of quotations—mark her concern with hybridization; similarly, the visibility she insistently grants to the creative process calls our attention to her interest in origination and generation.

"The Monkey Puzzle" is typical of this aspect of Moore's work. In this poem about crossbreeding and origins, Moore defines literature as the locus of genetic experimentation and rebirth. The endless metamorphosis of the poetic subject whose identity "defies one" takes place "in a kind of Flaubert's Carthage." The transformation of a monkey in rapid succession from a "pine-lemur" to a "Paduan cat with lizard" to a "Foo dog" to a "pine-tree" to a nondog ("more than a dog"; "not a dog") to a jade "conifer" produces an absolute hybrid, "an interwoven somewhat," that the reader cannot possibly identify with certainty as either a tree or a real animal or an objet d'art. It is just such a "true curio in this bypath of curio-collecting" that Moore equates with "beauty." The final stanza reasserts Moore's poetic project: "One is at a loss, however, to know why it should be here, / ... / to account for its origin at all; / but we prove, we do not explain our birth." The function of Moore's poetry is to "prove," to provide evidence, for the existence of hybrid forms.

As we have seen, images of the metamorphic process often appear in Moore's poetry. Her fascination with the mobile, multiple self, able to take on incompatible forms both successively and simultaneously, looks forward to the similar challenges to dualistic and hierarchical thought now prevalent in all fields of feminist theory. More importantly, Moore's notion of the human hybrid may point the way beyond the current insistence that continuous mutability characterizes only the female self. To this end Moore's poetry uses recurrent images of birth and mothering. That Moore periodically attributes this reproductive and nurturing function to the male may best illustrate her intention to transcend gender dichotomization. In "He 'Digesteth Harde Yron,'" for example, the hybrid camel-sparrow "watches his chicks with / a maternal concentration—and he's / been mothering the eggs / at night six weeks—." Similarly, in "The Plumet Basilisk," a poem about the human project of metamorphosis ("the basilisk portrays / mythology's wish / to be interchangeably man and fish"), the mother dragon who lays nine eggs, since "a true dragon has nine sons," identifies Moore's own goal—"O to be a dragon"—as the male-female hybrid.

Moore's explicit focus on the reproductive process also supports the primacy we have seen her grant to linguistic structure and justifies her insistent characterization of herself as "a worker with words" (Sprague 185). Indeed, what Moore specifically saw as "analogous to the laboratory scientist's classification of species in botany or geology" was precisely the investigation of language (Steinman 221) that becomes, in much of her poetry, not only the medium of generative change but its very method. If this reconceptualization of our genetic heritage as essentially linguistic rather than biological might seem to eliminate any concern with the specifically male or female, Moore's conviction that language mediates false dichotomies and allows opposites to coexist clearly has implications for our understanding of gender.

Although Moore's extraordinary poem "Marriage" deserves an essay of its own, we can use it in conclusion as a microcosmic representation of Moore's major poetic concerns. The poem is unique in Moore's work for its overt focus on an intangible abstraction, one, moreover, that allows Moore to connect her interest in language directly to her concern with gender. This discursive poem on the concept of marriage recovers the etymological meaning of *discourse* as a "running back and forth," a continuous and fluid process of mediation. Moore's choice of poetic structure specifically identifies language as the instrument of mediation; in a pattern recurrent in Moore's poetry, "Marriage" takes the form of a dictionary definition of its title concept (and, ironically, of the poet herself)—"turn to the letter M." Gilbert and Gubar note that "the complex process of reinventing, relearning, or reviewing the alphabet becomes for [women] writers a crucial act of self-definition and self-assertion" ("Ceremonies" 46). Moore's reflections on the letter *M*, referring not only to her own name, Marianne, but also to her mother's name, Mary, specifically recall H. D.'s constant meditation on the letter *H*, signaling "not only her own name, Hilda, but her mother's name, Helen, as well as the names of many of her heroes and heroines" (Gilbert and Gubar, "Ceremonies" 35). In "Marriage," moreover, the common etymology of *marriage* and *Marianne* (both derived from the Virgin Mary) allows Moore to reunite within her own self not only mother and daughter but Eve and Mary, the cultural paradigms of the "good" woman and the "bad," as well.

Moore thus models "Marriage" after the text that encodes the process by which human beings use language, their uniquely characteristic behavior, to understand and to structure the world. In addition, the dictionary, in which language both replaces and creates reality simultaneously, defines language as intrinsically self-referential and self-generative. This may explain why Philippe Hamon explores "the fascination of all descriptive writers for the dictionary" primarily in modernist and postmodernist texts in which what is ultimately described and defined is the act of writing itself (474). Not only does this connection once again allow us to reinstate Moore within the linguistic mainstream of modernism, but it suggests that competing definitions of modernism, alternatively based on the primacy of culture or of language, falsely dichotomize a more unified, if more complex, phenomenon. Moreover, the definition— like the stanza that for Moore replaces the word or the line as the significant unit of poetic structure—at once posits both unity and opposition and mediates between them by grouping several distinct meanings, drawn from different fields of knowledge and different spheres of reality, into a single common category. The specific organization that Moore ascribes to "Marriage" in her notes to the poem —"Statements that took my fancy which I tried to arrange plausibly"—announces the effort (parallel to that of the editors of *The*

American Heritage Dictionary with whom she worked) "to arrange a complex word in a psychologically meaningful order" that makes of her poem a "structured unit" rather than the "string of unrelated senses" most critical readings have suggested (XLVI).

But, as in "Saint Valentine," Moore here alters lexicography, whose cultural and linguistic forms have predominantly served the male poet, by attaching mediation as a category of thought and language to the original coupling of gender opposites. The feminist subtext we have seen elsewhere surfaces again as Moore reassigns the primacy of origin to the female Eve. Eve not only appears first in the poem—indeed, her appearance specifically allows the poet to begin ("Eve: beautiful woman— / I have seen her / when she was so handsome / she gave me a start")—but Moore grants her the command of language (and literature) traditionally assigned to Adam: "able to write simultaneously / in three languages— / English, German and French— / and talk in the meantime." Not only does Adam's appearance follow Eve's and his first words constitute a "repl[y]" to hers, but Adam, described as the passive instrument of divine prophecy, has only a secondary, subordinate relationship to language in general: "Alive with words, / vibrating like a cymbal / touched before it has been struck, / he has prophesied correctly."

Although Moore's acknowledgment of a system of power founded on gender takes at one point the unusual form of explicit assertion ("experience attests / that men have power / and sometimes one is made to feel it"), she also continues her practice of subversively encoding a sexual subtext. Adam "stumbles over marriage" in search of a way to assuage his sexual desire (" 'the illusion of a fire / effectual to extinguish fire' "); and his discovery of "Unhelpful Hymen!" surely refers not only to the god but to the female anatomy, protective of virginity, that ironically thwarts "that experiment of Adam's / with ways out but no way in." As in "Nevertheless," Moore again explicitly connects human sexuality, through its reproductive function, to the initially linguistic concepts of generativity and origin. In marriage, Adam is "unfathered by a woman"; he has lost not only his privileged relationship with God the Father, the Logos, but his own unique right to "father," to originate.

Moore returns as well to her concern with the dual threat to unity embodied in the opposition of gender. Eve illustrates the female's claim to self-sufficiency and autonomy that, however desirable in and of itself, leads inevitably to a demand for separatism. Eve's first words to Adam stress the connection between the assertive female *I*, emphasized by Moore's italicization, and the isolation of the female self: "*I* should like to be alone." In Adam's and Eve's confrontational dialog later in the poem, Eve persistently rejects Adam. Moore's summary of Eve's attitude reconceptualizes the traditional view of female narcissism as a self-containment necessary to allow women to exist: "She loves herself so much, / she cannot see herself enough." For Adam's sense of identity focuses not on an independent assertion of self, but on the effort to transform the other into a submissive, passive reflection of his own self. Adam needs and invents the couple—"I should like to be alone; / why not be alone together?"—as the false unity of Western culture, based in fact on the domination of the male one. To retain his status as "idol," Adam seeks in Eve "the attitude / of an adoring child / to a distinguished parent." He denies her autonomy as both lover and beloved; as Moore concludes: "he loves himself so much, / he can permit himself / no rival in that love."

But while Moore allows Adam and Eve their respective identities and differences, the stress of her title metaphor and of the poetic process falls on their interdependency, on their opposition as contained within the unity of the poem. If marriage as reality represents "this amalgamation which can never be more / than an interesting impossibility," Moore refuses to call "friction a calamity" and associates "truth" with "the *fight* to be affectionate." In the conclusion to the poem, Moore abandons her representational figures ("What can one do for them— / these savages") to return to the mediative function of language and poetry that alone allows the paradoxical combination of "liberty and union" finally located in "the Book on the writing table." The book in question, by a logical extension of Moore's specific reference to Daniel Webster, substitutes the dictionary for the Bible as the original and primary text of human heritage. Moore's adoption as model of a form of discourse that is both anonymous and plural allows her to enact throughout "Marriage" a very different relationship to language from that we have encountered elsewhere in her poetry. Here Moore replaces the dominant male voice of "He Wrote the History Book" with a fluid shift of pronouns that alternate between the first and third persons and between the generalized and the specific. Similarly, the quotes, which in "Silence" function to drown out Moore's own words, now constitute an authentically new collective voice that allows the poet to function within a linguistic system whose shared commonality reflects and creates that of humanity itself.

My reading of Moore's poetry supports the conclusion that Shari Benstock reaches in her recent discussion of other women modernists: "no critique of these women's lives and work that does not pay particular attention to their interest in and experiment with language can hope to account, even partially, for their contributions as women writers" ("Beyond" 20–21). Clearly, Moore's "disruptive verse" (Gilbert and Gubar, *Norton* 1490) belongs to the longstanding tradition of *écriture féminine* that Gilbert and Gubar posit in their own current reinterpretation of modernism as "a battle of the sexes for linguistic primacy" ("Sexual" 523). In this context, moreover, Moore appropriately proves doubly disruptive. An attentiveness to her language connects Moore, on the one hand, to an emerging tradition of female modernism that her work helps to define, and (re)establishes, on the other hand, the centrality of her role within a long dominant tradition of modernism whose newly recognized maleness her work helps to identify.

In contrast, my reinterpretation of Moore's mythic propriety as, in fact, mythical may seem more problematic. If I am right about the importance that she attaches to sexual and gender identity throughout her poetry, why, one might ask, has no one ever seen it before? Although Moore's curiously noncommittal injunction that "one should be as clear as one's natural reticence allows one to be" (*Reader* 171) might provide a sufficient explanation, Moore's interest in genetics, the science of heredity, also comments on her relationship to the poetic tradition. The split in Moore criticism between those who define her poetry as gender-neutral and therefore male and those who interpret her verse as self-effacing and therefore female clearly identifies the poet herself as a product of crossbreeding. Moore's theory of hybridization in which male and female are both mutually exclusive and inseparably superimposed points to the very ambivalence of gender differentiation that criticism of Moore so accurately reflects. As the poet herself says in "Marriage": "One sees that it is rare— / that striking grasp of opposites / opposed each to the other, not to unity."

NOTES

1. My caution in claiming a chronological evolution in Moore's work is, of course, deliberate. As Taffy Martin points out, Moore's "constant process of revision and deletion makes it nearly impossible to chart a single line of development" in her poetry (xii). Although my reading of Moore to date suggests a more consistent emphasis on the negation of male sexual power and male linguistic authority in her early poems and an increased celebration of a female-centered language and sexuality in her later ones, the presence of a poem such as "Marriage" in *The Selected Poems* of 1935 immediately challenges the clarity of any such distinction. Moreover, both attitudes appear simultaneously or in juxtaposition throughout her poetic career; similarly, however, Showalter's affirmation of a clearcut shift from "feminist critique" to "gynocritics" surely oversimplifies past and present critical theory and practice.

2. Moore's suggestions include, for example, "AEROTERRE / fée rapide (aerofère, aero faire, fée aiglette, magifaire) comme il faire / tonnere alifère (wingèd thunder) / aliforme alifère (wing-slender a-wing)" (*Reader* 215–24).

3. Although Martin's critical approach differs significantly from mine, she also characterizes Moore as a "voleuse de langue" (123).

4. The letter *S* figures prominently throughout Moore's poetic world, inhabited by snails, steamrollers, strawberries, salamanders, steeplejacks, sea unicorns, snakes, sycamores, spruces, Spenser, and the like.

5. Images suggestive of the ankh are prevalent in Moore's poetry; note, for example, the occipital horn of "The Snail" or the lady with the unicorn's head in her lap in "Sea Unicorns and Land Unicorns."

6. Moore's training at Bryn Mawr was in biology and she considered a career in medicine. In an unexpected confirmation of the notion of female tradition, which merits further exploration, Barbara McClintock's work, to which Evelyn Fox Keller has recently allowed us access, provides particularly suggestive evidence of a connection between Moore's poetry and the science of genetics. Indeed, Moore's "Nevertheless" could serve as a poetic illustration of McClintock's conception of the genetic organism as a fluid and dynamic structure that reprograms itself to adapt to changing environmental conditions.

JEANNE LARSEN

Text and Matrix:
Dickinson, H. D., and Woman's Voice

> The writing of women is really translated from the unknown, like a
> new way of communicating rather than an already formed language. . . .
> That's it: reverse everything, including analysis and criticism.
> —Marguerite Duras 174

This essay is about voice. *Is* there a uniquely female language? I doubt it. Can the *idea* of one stimulate a woman-writer/
writer-woman? Absolutely. Consider the work of the "new French
feminists": even the most outrageous of their writings can be aes-
thetically satisfying; even the essays that veer dangerously toward
biological determinism create in me the excitement and vision of
good poetry. Consider, too, the poems of Emily Dickinson and Hilda
Doolittle, women who breathed word of this notion—a language
not men's—long before it became the subject of widespread critical
interest.

> We need languages that regenerate us, warm us, give birth to us,
> that lead us to act and not to flee. . . . In order to reconnect the book
> with the body and with pleasure, we must disintellectualize writing.
> The corporality of language stirs up our sensuality, wakes it up, pulls
> it away from indifferent inertia. (Chantal Chawaf 177)

Consider, too, if you will, this essay, that tilts from a language
shaped by rhythm and metaphor to the *patrius sermo* of the academy,
and back again. (See Gilbert and Gubar, 1985, 532.) Too stuffy, at
times, to claim liberation; too lyrical, at others, for the scholars;
bound, somewhere, to offend: despite all this, there were moments
as I wrote it when I had that exhilarating sense of beginning to speak
with a new tongue.

> It's not to be feared that language conceals an invincible adversary,
> because it's the language of men and their grammar. . . . If woman has
> always functioned "within" the discourse of man, . . . it is time for her

to dislocate this "within," to explode it, turn it around, and seize it; to make it hers, containing it, taking it in her own mouth, biting that tongue with her very own teeth to invent for herself a language to get inside of. (Hélène Cixous "Medusa" 257)

The lyric voice arises from within. Whatever air or Word breathes into us—inspires—it is lungs, throat, lips that form the words and push them out. And voice bears self, or says it does: as exhalations are transformed in the muscle-ringed channel of the windpipe and in the chamber of the mouth, what is created is a sibilant, sybilline sign—listen! can you hear me?—that the *I* is there.

Chamber, channel: this is a female metaphor. It is there for anyone, man or woman, who bears a woman-self within. But it especially unleashes power (like the breaking of waters, like the letting-down of blood) for us whom the culture's usual metaphors for *poesis* have denied. The poet need not woo the muse with swollen pen. She herself is matrix of the text; she is mother of her poems, spinning out her webs despite the looming patriarchal *shush*. Dickinson and H. D. teach us this, naming a new language, claiming power through their voices, engendering a woman's right to speak a self.

To see how this is so, look at the offspring the two spun off. First, H. D.'s celebration of a trans-formed language in "The Flowering of the Rod," the final third of her epic, *Trilogy*. She embodies there in an *écriture féminine*, in a fluid newborn tongue, the love for the mother that is a womanly love of self. Then Emily Dickinson's artful and protective lies: some of her poems on fiction, the language that defended her, as did the fictions of her life.[1] Finally, her daring disregard for self-protection, her rejection of certain dogmas of patriarchal theology and theories of language in Poem 1651 ("A Word made Flesh is seldom"). This poem sings at the very roots of language, sings-into-being her radical act of love for words.

The voices of this essay descended from the voices of the poets. (The daughter descants to the mother's tune.) H. D. breaks with the hierarchies of male modernist poetic discourse, reversing the image systems, rereading the myths. She valorizes the female without denying the male, seeking what Woolf called the "man-womanly," the "woman-manly" (102). The natural voice for discussing her work is the androgynous one of the feminist academician, who attempts to merge woman-identified politics with the masculinist (or at least, male-claimed and male-defined) language of conventional literary criticism. With Dickinson, it is different. She breaks away, perhaps breaks through, tearing apart the very systems—syntax, grammar— of rational discourse. And so my own safe, familiar scholarly language must start to unravel itself: *You do not do, you do not do, / Any more, black shoe;* so Plath unlaces Daddy's tongue. (The distinction of voices is, in fact, not quite so clear. I call them "separate," but notice how each insinuates itself, how each exists within the spaces of the other.) To reverse the order of literary history, I decided, is to follow the sequence of development of feminist theory. The move from H. D. to Dickinson is the move from description of image to radical redefinition, from flower to roots, from embracing child to bold and fertile mother.

The Path from Voice to Self in H. D.'s "The Flowering of the Rod"

To understand H. D.'s poetic gestation of a female voice, we first must understand her sexuality as she came to know it, through her revision of insights gleaned from her analysis with Sigmund Freud. Then we must consider what it means that this "perfect bi-" was a poet (H. D., letter to Bryher, Friedman 241).

> According to H. D.'s account, Freud said that she "had not made the conventional transference from mother to father," that her dreams and visions represented her desire for reunion with her mother, the "phallic mother" of the preoedipal stage. Freud believed that the lesbian remains fixated in her early love for her mother, which she projects onto the lovers who serve as mother substitutes. Freud's diagnosis of H. D.'s "mother-fixation" connects her desire for her mother (about which H. D. openly wrote) with lesbianism (about which she did not openly write).
>
> H. D. privately ignored the prescriptive norms that pervaded Freud's concepts of sexuality and his judgment that she could never have been "biologically happy" with a woman. But she fully accepted the theory that her unconscious desire for her mother was projected onto her love for women—predominantly upon Frances Josepha Gregg, the woman with whom she first came to London, and later upon Bryher (Winifred Ellerman), with whom she lived on and off for most of her adult life. . . . But only [H. D.'s] private letters to Bryher reveal that Freud regarded her occult experiences, her love for Bryher, and her desire for her mother as interconnected symptoms of "mother-fixation," the

motivating impulse of her lesbianism. (Susan Stanford Friedman 238;
cites *Tribute to Freud* 136)

> As for so many lyric poets, the psychosexual mode that dominates
> H. D.'s psyche is the earliest: the oral. At her very center, H. D. wishes
> and fears to fuse with . . . her mother. (Norman N. Holland 501–2)

And so, H. D.: daughter, woman-identified woman, poet. Like
her occult experiences, H. D.'s profound sense of being connected
with her female parent informed her poetry, and gave her the very
images that incarnate her vision. (This, despite the denigration of
the mother by the patriarchy, despite the valorization by the masculinist psychoanalytic establishment of male over female patterns
of personality development. See Gilligan.) Her critics tell us so.

> H. D. came to understand the poem not as an assertion of phallic
> desire, but as presentation, *an act of birth*, a means of disentanglement
> from the burden of *inseminating* thought, and a way to recovery of
> *primal* integrity. (Janice A. Robinson 61 [emphasis mine])

> The major distinction between [the first part of *Trilogy*] and H. D.'s
> early poems is that the poem has become a process or act of discovery.
> No longer a closed form, a thing itself, it has become a *generative act*.
> (Joseph N. Riddel 468 [emphasis mine])

H. D.'s work invites a new understanding of human psychosexual development, one that liberates the voice of the female poet by
using the insights of Freud while correcting the errors of his culture-
bound explication of them. He views as pathological the "obstinate
self-assertion" of female homosexuality (caused by a " 'masculinity
complex' "), the "failure" to "arrive at the ultimate normal feminine attitude in which she takes her father as [exclusive] love-object"
("Female Sexuality" 257). He proclaimed (in the notorious article on
female sexuality first published about two years before his analysis of
H. D.) "that in women the development of sexuality is complicated
by the task of renouncing that genital zone which was originally
the principle one, namely, the clitoris, in favour of a new zone—the
vagina. But there is a second change which appears to us no less
characteristic and important for feminine development: the original
mother-object has to be exchanged for the father. We cannot as yet
see clearly how these two tasks are linked up" (252).

Surely the linkage (clitoris/female love-object, vagina/male
love-object), if oversimple, is clear. What is less than obvious is

why there must be a complete "renunciation." Just as many modern sexologists have gone beyond Freud to recognize the validity of both vaginal and clitoral sexual response, so H. D. teaches us to see the usefulness to the poet of a focus on both male and female parents, an identification with both masculine and feminine, an appreciation of the femaleness that the culture would deny. At one point during World War II, the time of *Trilogy*'s composition, H. D. wrote, "Women, WOMAN—this new aquarian age we have been told is well on the way—a woman's age, in a new sense of WOMAN" (Guest 275).

Even the title of "The Flowering of the Rod" celebrates the identification/transformation of the phallic with/to the vulvar. The cross unfurls its head to become the ankh, the female sign, the sign of life. "He [Christ] was the first to wing / from that sad Tree, / but having flown, the Tree of Life / bears rose from thorn" (sect. 11). "The Flowering" begins with Christ transfigured amid the snows and the blue gentians of Mount Hermon (a matrix already linked with Mary in the preceding poem in *Trilogy*, "Tribute to the Angels," sect. 32). But the poem leaves Christ, "the heavenly pointer" (sect. 11), for Mary Magdalene, "the first actually to witness His life-after-death." This Mary is immediately associated with Mary of Bethany (who also cleansed the feet of Jesus), the sister of Lazarus and Martha (sect. 12). The Mary figure is soon further transformed into the "Mary-myrrh" of section 16: Myrrha, mother of Adonis (and, by mythic association, of his brother-gods of death and rebirth, Attis, Tammuz, Jesus) and finally to H. D.'s version of the Christian Virgin Mother.

Look at the poet's own metaphor, her distinctly female image, as she claims for herself the voice of the "Pythoness," the Delphic poet-priestess in section 10 of "The Flowering of the Rod." (And remember the audacity, when H. D. was young, of a woman daring to translate a language generally thought best reserved for the study of males—though of course her "translations" were into words that were her own.) To sing as a poet, she tells us, is to be a woman, a powerfully sexual woman, not one who's cold.

> It is no madness to say . . .
>
> it is not tragedy, prophecy
>
> from a frozen Priestess,
> a lonely Pythoness

who chants, who sings
in broken hexameters . . .

yet it is, if you like, a lily
folded like a pyramid,

a flower-cone,
not a heap of skulls;

it is a lily, if you will,
each petal, a kingdom, an aeon,

and it is the seed of a lily
that having flowered,

will flower again;
it is that smallest grain . . .

The power to generate poet's words is re-presented here as the mother's gift to the daughter: the beautiful, unmutilated female genitals. (The mother was never castrated; she has an*other* power.) H. D. is the girl-child who did not have to protect a threatened sense of sexuality and self by an anxious definition of that self as fundamentally different from the parent with the vulva.[2] (Surely the security that allows an openness of self is useful to a poet. Surely it is advantageous for the poet to value both masculine and feminine.) She never repudiated altogether the primal bond of mouth to breast. She is the poet whose mouth bears words.

H. D. again celebrates the female, and again links it to poetic power, later in "The Flowering of the Rod." The patriarch and "Wise Man" Kaspar, who casts out Mary of Magdala's devils (as did H. D.'s healing "Master" Freud), sees in Mary's hair something that triggers an awesome mystic vision of poetry. It is as clearly vulvar as the image quoted above.

the speck, fleck, grain or seed
opened like a flower.

And the flower, thus contained
in the infinitely tiny grain or seed,

opened petal by petal, a circle,
and each petal was separate

yet still held, as it were,
by some force of attraction

to its dynamic centre . . .

And he heard . . .

words neither sung nor chanted
but stressed rhythmically;

the echoed syllables of this spell. (sects. 30, 31)

Oral, female, oracular, lyrical: "The Flowering," having defined
the origins of poetry in these terms, returns to the mother at the end.
In its final sections, H. D. takes us to the image of another avatar
of Mary, the Mother with her Babe in arms. The poet herself (she
discussed this in her analysis with Freud) was born in Bethlehem,
Pennsylvania. Her hometown was, then, not only Jesus's, but the
ancestral home of Mary. The sessions with Freud revealed H. D. to
be the "descendant of Mary" (Robinson 333); mother and child—or
children, one female, one male—are thus even more closely identified with one another. But who *is* the infant in Mary's arms in the
last line of "The Flowering"? Not Jesus, no man-child, but a "bundle
of myrrh." The reader knows at this point that the myrrh images
Mary herself. Remember section 16, where the mother of Adonis—
read Christ—is transformed into the myrrh tree. "I am Mary . . . /
Mary shall be myrrh . . . / (though I am Mara, bitter) I shall be Mary-
myrrh." For H. D., then, to bear her vision, to voice her poem, is to
learn at last that mother and child are one. ("H. D. suggests [in *Tribute to Freud*] that somehow during the course of her sessions with
Freud she found the mother by becoming the mother, by finding the
mother in herself" [Robinson 332]. "The mother is the Muse, the
creator, and in my case especially, as my mother's name was Helen"
(H. D. *End to Torment* 41, cited in Robinson 4). To speak or inscribe
the poem is to em*body* her vision in a journey of words that leads to
a womanly incarnation of the self.[3]
      A further example of how the poet's bold voicing of female
myth transmutes the fathers' Christian story: sections 21 to 26 tell
how Mary Magdalene defied the restrictions on entering the house
where Jesus was "Guest." In thus claiming for herself, uninvited,
a space in the house of the fathers, she shocks "Simon the host"
with her bold femaleness, her "extraordinary," pagan Siren hair. But
though to poor dull, ugly Simon (the leper "we presume was healed
of his plague, / healed in body" at least) she suggests only debased
sexuality and madness, wise Kaspar knows more.
      The devils he cast out of Mary (presented in section 26 in her

aspect as Mary of Magdala) are still "unalterably part of the picture": the female deities survive in a patriarchal world. Their psychic power is recognized by the magus when he calls them *"daemons"* and names them with non-Christian names that reveal just how strongly mother-identified this great power within the unsilenced woman is. They are: Isis, mother of a sun-god and creator of Osiris's golden penis and the snake that gave her power over Ra himself; Astarte, whose name means "womb" or "she of the womb"; Cyprus, who is both Aphrodite and Aphrodite's birthplace, her mother-land; Ge-meter, literally, "earth-mother"; De-meter, the familiar Ceres, who seeks her daughter; another "earth-mother" too primal to have a more sharply differentiated name; and "Venus / in a star," that is, paranomastically, Venus in the form of Astar/Istar/Ishtar, all variants on the name of Astarte. These are the visionary woman's spiritual powers, embodied in unmistakably female forms.

What is the reader to make of all these shiftings of persons and images from one form to the other? Is the shifting *itself* in any way the expression of a female poetic imagination, of a womanly voice? In H. D.'s striking expression of her poetic ability to flow from one (so-called) entity to another to yet another as part of her search for the articulation of her selfhood, we see a psychological mode that has been judged to be a distinctly feminine one. She can connect. She can be this one, and this one, and this. She need not fear that union will bring the death of self. As Nancy Chodorow argues, "feminine personality comes to define itself in relation and connection to other people more than masculine personality does" ("Family Structure" 44). In union, the poet finds self, and voice.[4]

The spiraling of time that infolds "The Flowering of the Rod" also leads us to a mother-identified poetic self.[5] H. D. clearly denies in her poem the dominant time-myth of Western patriarchal religion, the one-way line of history. Consider her rejection of linear time in the many sections of "The Flowering" that are first-rate examples of lyric timelessness, for example, "I am the first or the last . . . / I have gone forward, / I have gone backward, / I have gone onward from bronze and iron, / into the Golden Age" (sect. 8).

The Golden Age to which the speaker has gone "onward" is chronologically *prior* to those of baser, warlike metals: the paradox smashes the timeline. In this denial of the Graeco-Judeo-Christian patriarchy's concept of historicity, the poet longs with the circling geese of sections 3, 4, and 5—who "remember as they sway and hover," in a movement counter to linear time—for the paradise of the lost culture of Atlantis. As Susan Gubar points out, this "lost center-island," Atlantis, is "a fitting symbol of the time of pre-historic eternity before the fall into patriarchal history" (216). But what would a Kronos-defying return mean in terms of the history of the individual's life? This place that poet and geese "once knew," this place of "bliss," of "the fruit that satisfies," this place that they "hunger" for, may also be the preoedipal realm (vanished yet somehow remaining within the depths of the sea) of oneness with the mother. ("[H. D.'s] mystical and religious wishes hark back to the early mother-child relationship" [Holland 487–88].)

Does H. D.'s articulation and celebration of the female proscribe the male? Clearly not. In Christ, in Kaspar, in the visionary wild gander (section 3) who shows the way, we are given images of maleness that are positive. But they are not supreme. (That way lies Golgotha, crucifixion on a war-born hill of skulls; "The Walls Do Not Fall" has made this clear.) Kaspar / the Arab, when he does not recognize Mary, is haughty and stuffy. Only after he stoops and receives—through the "grain or seed . . . like a flower" nestled in her hair—*his* vision of Atlantis (his own preoedipal unity with the female), can the echoing voice of poetry's spiraling language let him escape his fall into patriarchal history and remember his connection with "the drowned cities of pre-history" (sect. 33). The poem his vision gives him translates itself to speak of the forgiveness of Lilith and Eve *and* "one born before": surely this last is Adam. As a figure of the poet, whose brain *trans*lates, Kaspar serves as a figure of H. D.'s self, the figure we follow to Bethlehem.[6]

So the masculine, too, has a role to play in the journey to the mother. Like the important two-sexed image of "the rain that has lain long / in the furrow" (sect. 2), "this duality, this double nostalgia" (sect. 4) reminds us early in the final part of *Trilogy* that what this bisexual poet seeks is a self that does not blur the two elements of her inward duality, but that also does not deny the speech and power of either one.[7]

H. D., then, talks us back to H.—to Hilda and to her mother Helen—D. As oracular Pythoness (was this female snake her lesbian laugh at Papa Freud?), her mouth brings forth a mystery. It is herself—her strong, articulate self—she bears.[8] But she also bears the mother, by re-creating her in the narrative of the poem. And the mother, in turn, once / still / always gives birth to *her*.

What is borne out by H. D.'s words can nurture us as well. Her method is (like Dickinson's) circuitous, her identity is born of her embrace of transformation. And as H. D. sings, she tells us: the vulva through which we enter the world, the vulva that defines her sexuality, is no gash or snarling wound, but a blossom; the mother from whom she received it is not one who lacks or castrates; the poet, like her mother, bodies forth.

To Lose the Head: Toward a Definition of Emily Dickinson's "écriture féminine"

Dickinson will not hold her tongue, will not sacrifice her head, is no good girl staring mute at the patriarchy's knife. She'll sing herself as H. D. will, and help us lose our heads another way. What's she up to when she defines the poet's problematic playthings, fiction and language? Here are dictionary entries from texts (and "sexts") that might help us see.

1. *To lose the head:* woman silenced.

"If [women] don't actually lose their heads by the sword, they only keep them on condition that they lose them—lose them, that is, to complete silence." (Cixous "Castration" 43)

2. *To lose the head:* a refusal to give (give up the) (give into the) head, a refusal to suck up to phallogocentrism.[9]

"Neither [Dickinson's] personal education nor the habit of her society as she knew it ever gave her the least inkling that poetry is a rational and objective art." (R. P. Blackmur as qtd. in Juhasz *Naked and Fiery Forms* 11)

3. *To lose the head:* to the guillotine with "rational art"!

"If I feel physically as if the top of my head were taken off, I know *that* is poetry." (Dickinson *Letters* II 474)

4. *To lose the head:* to get into the body.

"Just as the lover enters, dismembers, and reassembles the body of the beloved, so the writer must enter and deconstruct patriarchal language/ideology to reconstruct new possibilities." (Wenzel on Wittig 284)

5. *To lose the head:* to get into the female body.

"As for time, female subjectivity would seem to provide a specific measure that essentially retains repetition and eternity . . . there are cycles . . . and unnameable *jouissance* . . . female subjectivity . . . becomes a problem with respect to . . . [the] linear time . . . of language considered as the enunciation of sentences." (Kristeva 16–17)

6. *To lose the head:* to get into the body of the language, the flesh of the tongue.

"All of her passes into her voice . . . Her flesh speaks true . . . In women's speech as in their writing, that element which never stops resonating . . . is the song, first music from the first voice of love which is alive in every woman." (Cixous "Medusa" 251)

Critics like Suzanne Juhasz, Terence Diggory, and Sandra M. Gilbert and Susan Gubar have rightly pointed to the stresses within and around Dickinson or perhaps any woman who weaves an artist's web of words. The sticky threads and loomings of the patriarchy warp her head's reel. (Remember a looming is a mirage. A reel winds spun yarns, it's a dizzy sway, it's running riot, it's a dance.) But it is just as true—as these critics note—that for Dickinson this tension is a creative one. She will not be silenced; she will make the silence itself the weft of her song.

Each of the definitions above bears understandings of alternative language that are threaded through the poems Dickinson made despite the culture's threatening hiss, *be still.* Language as lies (fiction) shields her naked vulnerability from the sword of silence (cf. definition 1).[10] Language incarnate in poems as word-made flesh is ever present and breaks the murderous Kronos-line of grammatical, one-way-linear, rational discourse (cf. definitions 2, 3, 4). Language as she spins her yarns (in lies that net the truth) inscribes a body in its very flesh of resonant vowels and recycled consonants, a body of cyclic time (cf. definitions 5 and 6) that long outlives the one-time penetration into history of (phal)-Logos.

Diggory points out how in poems 666 ("Ah, Teneriffe! . . . I'm kneeling—still—") and 8 ("There is a word / Which bears a sword"), *silence* is for the poet an armor; it "defends against the destructive power of words" (140). But language can protect the poet too, through the "difficulty" of Dickinson's works, and through the fictions it allows her to create. These fictions are her shield. This is the one safe way for women to speak. Thus, Poem 1129 begins, "Tell all the Truth but tell it slant— / Success in Circuit lies." So success lies in going around. (An obsolete meaning of *circuit* is "circumlocution.")

But if we break the straightedge rules of grammar and read *lies* as a noun and *Circuit* as its modifier, what kind of lies are these? Check *circuit* in the *O.E.D.*:

1. Lies of—a favorite word of Dickinson's—*circumference*, of "the act of going around." (Juhasz notes the importance of *circumference* in Dickinson's poems. Her "method . . . is to continually approach . . . which . . . safeguards her from losing herself in the process. Her word for this process is 'Circumference': through circling to delineate essence" [*Naked and Fiery* 21].)

2. Lies of "space enclosed by a circumference." (Woman's inner space? some might rush to say. But consider this instead: her life circum*scribed* by the patriarchy's myths, by *circuit* lies. And consider, then, her gleeful exploitation of what was meant to restrict.)

3. Lies (this definition was obsolete but available to her in *The Merry Wives of Windsor*) of a circlet, a diadem, the crown of the poet-Queen. From poem 195: "Get Gabriel—to tell—the royal syllable — / Get Saints—with new—unsteady tongue— / To say what trance below / Most like their glory show— / Fittest the Crown!" (Thus, the fictions of poetry, the sacred lies that are new-said truth: these crown her Queen.)

I said that language, Emily Dickinson's ringing nonlinear language of interwoven sounds, works against timebound linear thinking; it does this through phonic repetitions that draw the mind again and again back to words gone by. Poem 1,651 shows how this is so. The rich texture, the web, of its soundplay embodies her refusal of patriarchal language ("language considered as . . . noun + verb; topic-comment; beginning-ending": Kristeva [17]) even before we attempt to unravel the poem's twistings of thought and syntax, before we try to catch what it might mean. Listen to the sibilants, the liquid *l*s and *r*s, the tongue-tip *th*s and *t*s and *d*s. (See Burke on the "concealed alliteration" of phonetic cognates [369–71]. And remember *t* hides in *ch*, and *s* in *x*.)

    A Word made Flesh is seldom
2   and tremblingly partook
    Nor then perhaps reported
4   But have I not mistook
    Each one of us has tasted
6   with ecstasies of stealth
    The very food debated

8   To our specific *strength*—
     A *Word that breathes distinctly*
10   *Has not the* power *to d*ie
     Cohesive as the Spirit
12   *It may expire if He*—
     "Made Flesh *and dwelt* among u*s"*
14   *Could* condescension *be*
     Like this consent *of Language*
16   *This loved* Phi*lology.*

The intricate rhyme scheme here is exploded and put back together. It might be schematicized: a b c b c' d c' d' d'' e f g h g i g.
That is: *a b c b* (okay so far, familiar and it pulls the eye along); *c' d
c' d'* (a bit odd, this second "quatrain," which harks back to line 3,
then wobbles when line 8 veers off from a perfect rhyme with 6); *d''
e f g* (hold on, the "progression" has completely disappeared, though
in the one place where one might *expect* a change—when line 9
could mark the close of the 16-line poem's first half by differing from
8—there is a reverberation of "d"); and finally—no, wait, there's a
tidy little quatrain, *f g h g,* in lines 11–14, though that's not where a
quatrain *ought* to be; finally, *h g i g,* just where we hear of a "consent
of language," we return to the pattern of the first four lines.

The words of the poem, too, are shattered, scattered, reassembled. (See definition four again.) The poem is rich in clusters of key
sounds: *s/sh/z* 's, *t/d/th* 's, and *l/r* 's. One example of this patterning: there are four *l*s in the first two calm lines, only two in the
next ten (where the words tear at themselves), and seven (plus one
not pronounced) in the final quatrain, five of them in the liquid and
euphonious last two lines. Another: lines one through ten each have
from three to seven *t*s or *d*s or *th*s, and up to line six (where tone
and meaning also shift) the harshest member of this family—the *t*—
predominates. Then a new language rises. The only line after the
tenth to contain more than two of these sounds is line thirteen, a
quotation interjected from the patriarchy's Word.

But other poets, female and male, alliterate. How does this
poem incarnate its defiance of patriarchal logocentric language; how
does it literally "deconstruct" and "reconstruct" (definition four
again) its very words? Listen to these pairs of pseudo-antonyms: "par-
took/*mi*stook"; "tasted/*de*bated"; "strength/*dis*[s]tinct"; "breathes/
expire"; and "consent/con*de*scension." (Notice, too, how the word-

play and the imagery of coalescence and incarnation summon up "condense" here.) Or look at other mixings and feedback loops, the quasi-anagrams. (Remember an *l* is an *r*, a *t* is a *th* or a *d*.) "*—ly* partook/*reported*"; "*Spirit*/*expire* if"; "has *tasted*/with ecstasies"; "*tasted*/*d*istinct(ly)"; "with ec*stasies*/*stealth*"; and "*stealth*/ *strength*"

And think about the punch line of the poem, the final witty rending of the beloved flesh that makes the poem the claiming of language that it is, "*loved Phil*ology." The words are dismembered and reassembled. The philologist sings of roots. This is Dickinson's radical act of love, her entry into word-made flesh, her quick and raveling text that will not submit to *man*made grammar's rules.

Thus the language Emily Dickinson had to work with is dismantled, re-woven into the phonemic matrix (the mother-ess) of her words. Might there be some other language, one somehow different from the word-system of the patriarchy? The possibility (no certainty) generates the poem. The speaker's voice halts, it stumbles, syntax and grammar break down altogether. But, though she breaks the rules of the Logos-logic of the fathers, she wins through, in the final lines, to the harmonies of her own newborn voice.

What, then, do these woman's-words say to us? Though communion with Logos-language, the "Word made Flesh" of masculinist scripture, is scant, scary, and secretive, ll. 1–3), there is another language. "Each one of us" has known on (her?) tongue another Word: a Word that "breathes" (sounds, in-spires) "distinctly" (differently *and* clearly), a Word that is just right for our strength (limited or great?), when breath is "de- [= not] bated," and allowed to flow. In *this* comm-union there is ecstasy (physical passion, mystic rapture, in-spir-ation; etymologically, being driven *out of one's mind*). *This* "irrational" head-lost Word (or *écriture*?) is eternal, it coheres (cleaves together, as lovers cleave). It could only be killed *if* Logos (whose story—fiction? the quotation marks in line 13 are suggestive —we've heard so much about) could condescend (yield, come down voluntarily) as does *this* "consent" (compliance, or in physiology, "a relation of sympathy between one organ . . . and another"), of language. That is, patriarchal language *could* triumph over this radical new tongue *if* it possessed the same, beloved, capacity to yield, comply, relate.

But wait, it's not so simple. There are glitches, halts, breaks in the speaking voice. Try to parse the sentence beginning on line eleven: this other Word "may expire," "if He . . . could condescension be." The grammar's off. Time's gone astray: not "might" but "may," not "can" but "could." And where does the grammar break down? Just at the audaciously ironic utterance of biblical language, just where Logos enters the poem.

Is this nascent nonpatriarchal, female voice defeated, then? No. Dickinson still gets it said, though the heart of the poem lies not in the words but in the spaces between them, somewhere after that dangling *He.* The "message" is conveyed not by what is said; in those next-to-last lines conventional communication appears to fail. Rather, meaning is conveyed by what is not said, precisely because we are reminded of all that *cannot,* in the only language we have been taught, be conveyed. The poem happens where women have had to speak: on the margins of masculinist culture's discourse, on the blank edge of the page. To speak is to break the rules. So, speaking, the language is broken.[11]

And (read it again, remembering her famous Poem 754, "My Life had stood a loaded gun") perhaps the "power to die" is indeed a power, perhaps as Gelpi suggests in his reading of this other poem, "she is empowered to kill experience and slay herself into art" (131). When we hear that this new Word "may expire" (may breathe out as the counter-language's breath), perhaps we ought not think of its death, its conquest by phallogocentric language, but of the new tongue's birth. Yes, it *may* be ex-pired, delivered from the mouth-womb of the poet's body, delivered to life in the air that rings our listening ears. Proof of the possibility, of course, is this unbeheaded woman's very poem, Emily Dickinson's tour de force exhibition of linguistic grace and power. Her fragmentation of the words of patri-archal language—the words she puns on, splits, and reassembles—subverts our simple faith in the substantiality of signifiers. She dis-mantles the old language to create her own. Despite the patriarchal pressures toward stillness and toward slightness, the zaftig (large-bodied, juicy, germinal) Miss/Myth of Amherst asserts her refusal to be silenced.

And so the poets sing. They sing a mother's song, but it does not lull. They sing in new languages the song of the self. For them, it is the song of the sex that unfurls like a flower, the song of the mouth that brings forth. They speak out of silence. They will not be still. They may wrap themselves at times in fiction's lies, but they will not tell the lie of hierarchy. *Male* and *female* as we have been taught them are a false opposition: one may shift its form into the other. Both may be embraced within the one. In this embrace, the fathers' old language dies. Its rigid dualities, its unquestionable answers, are dissolved at grammar's bourn. Syntax may break and words unravel; still, the voice is borne, not stillborn, but out of stillness, born.

NOTES

1. See the discussion of Dickinson's "life-fictions" in *Madwoman in the Attic*, where Sandra M. Gilbert and Susan Gubar argue that her "posing was not an accident of but essential to her poetic self-achievement, specifically because—as we have suggested—the verse-drama into which she transformed her life enabled her to transcend what Suzanne Juhasz has called the 'double bind' of the woman poet: on the one hand, the impossibility of self-assertion for a woman, on the other hand, the necessity of self-assertion for a poet" (584). Note also their discussion of the large size of "this self-consciously small poet's dress" (614).

2. Nancy Chodorow, in her analysis of the development of gender identity in boys and girls, describes how boys must define themselves as separate, while girls develop more "flexible ego boundaries" ("Family Structure" 59). In her view of human personality development, "First, masculinity becomes and remains a problematic issue for a boy. Second, it involves denial of attachment or relationship, . . . and differentiation of himself from another. Third, it involves the repression and devaluation of femininity on both psychological and cultural levels . . ." ("Family Structure" 51).

3. Janice Robinson's discussion of the "fluid" symbolic language of Moravian hymns suggests a childhood source for H. D.'s visions of a Christ who is both male and female (81–90). The very process of transformation and identification of opposites that generates the materials of *Trilogy* is a process of moving from male images to female ones. Consider the profoundly affecting vision H. D. had on Corfu in 1920 and discussed with Freud during her analysis in the early '30s. There appeared "picture-writing on the wall" of a hotel on Corfu, a succession of pictures formed of light: first, the masculine silhouette of a soldier or airman in a visored cap ("dead brother?"); then the neuter "outline of a goblet or cup, actually suggesting the mystic chalice" and the

alchemist's transforming crucible; and finally, "the stand for a small spirit-lamp," representing the tripod-throne of the poet-prophet*ess* of Delphi (H. D. *Tribute* 44–46).

    Trilogy was written in the forties, while the poet was working on her *Tribute to Freud*. Joseph Riddel has even called the poems of *Trilogy* "companions to *Tribute*" (464). And these three powerful images—and their empowering shift from male to female—are in fact prophetic of the three parts of the epic: the helmeted warrior, of "The Walls Do Not Fall," which begins with life in the war-ravaged London of the Blitz; the chalice, of "Tribute to the Angels," in which many transmutations follow an invocation of "Hermes Trismegistus . . . patron of alchemists"; and the Delphic tripod, of "The Flowering of the Rod," where, as we have seen, the poet valorizes womanly poetic power in the figure of the Pythoness.

4. This is not to say that men cannot operate in this mode. Remember John Keats's "negative capability." But the poets of a patriarchal culture must labor under the devaluation of a way of perceiving and understanding labeled effeminate—unless, like H. D., they can transvalue it, and claim it as their own proud *and* female voice.

5. Robinson suggests a "feminine perspective" in H. D.'s work in general: "she interprets events in terms of the timeless natural world rather than in terms of the historical process" (56). Thinkers like Julia Kristeva or Mary Daly would agree that female time is nature's cyclic time, but Sherry Ortner points out the danger of definitions of femaleness as closeness to nature: "Since it is always culture's project to subsume and transcend nature, if women were considered part of nature, then culture would find it 'natural' to subordinate, not to say suppress, them" (73). To view a nonlinear chronological perspective as *inherently* "feminine" is to accept a dangerous concept grounded in biological determinism, but of course, H. D. may have done so.

6. H. D.'s poem is shaped by her awareness of the one-sidedness of the whole force of the patriarchy, which values *only* analysis. Directly after his liberating vision of Atlantis, Kaspar's mind—that is, reason, as opposed to what the poet presents as the mystic/woman's denial of separations—prompts him "even as if his mind / must sharply differentiate" to frame the thought, *"it is unseemly that a woman / appear at all."* That this is indeed a perversion of the vision is made clear by the narrator: "his spirit was elsewhere . . . he-himself was not there. . . . What he thought was the direct contradiction / of what he apprehended" (sects. 34, 35).

7. "The Master" also wrote, "there can be no doubt that the bisexual disposition which we maintain to be characteristic of human beings

manifests itself much more plainly in the female" (Freud 255). This notion would seem to have been a help to H. D. as she came to terms with who she was.

8. Susan Gubar points out the poem's progress toward self-expression through language: "The final book of the *Trilogy* embodies the emergence of the poet's sustained voice in a story" (211). The importance to H. D. of her art as a possible means of thus finding herself can be seen in a letter the poet wrote to her friend John Cournos during World War I: "I have all faith in my work. What I want at times is to feel faith in my self, in my mere physical presence in the world, in my personality. I feel my work is beautiful, I have a deep faith in it, an absolute faith. But sometimes I have no faith in myself" (Guest 79–80).

9. In his discussion of phallogocentrism, Jonathan Culler cites Jacques Derrida's definition: "the term asserts the complicity between logocentrism and phallocentrism. 'It is one and the same system: the erection of a paternal logos . . . and of the phallus as a "privileged signifier" (Lacan).' . . . In both cases there is a transcendental authority and point of reference: truth, reason, the phallus, 'man' " (172).

10. See Margaret Homans's discussion of the idea of a nondualistic woman's language (216–18), where she writes: "A close reading of Dickinson demonstrates that the best course is to embrace and exploit language's inherent fictiveness, rather than to fight against it" (217). Dickinson's exploration of language's basis in subject-object dualism is further discussed in Homans's later essay, " 'Oh, Vision of Language!' " (Juhasz *Feminist Critics*, 114–17).

11. Cristanne Miller examines other such "subversive" and empowering "disruptions of language" in Dickinson's work in "How 'Low Feet' Stagger" (Juhasz *Feminist Critics* 134–55). For more on how Dickinson "shapes a language that challenges the Western literary tradition's shared assumptions about the very character of figurative language itself," see Joanne Feit Diehl's " 'Ransom in a Voice' " (Juhasz *Feminist Critics* 156–75).

Bibliography

Abbott, Craig S. *Marianne Moore, Reference Guide*. New York: G. K. Hall, 1978.

Abel, Elizabeth. "(E)Merging Identities: The Dynamics of Female Friendship in Contemporary Fiction by Women." *Signs* 6 (Spring 1981):412–32.

——. "Women and Schizophrenia: The Fiction of Jean Rhys." *Contemporary Literature* 20 (1969):155–77.

Ackroyd, Peter. *T. S. Eliot: A Life*. New York: Simon & Shuster, 1984.

Agustini, Delmira. *Poesías Completas*. Ed. Alberto Zum Felde. Buenos Aires: Editorial Losada, 1971.

Aiken, Conrad. *Ushant: An Essay*. New York: Duell, Sloan, and Pearce, 1952.

Allen, Paula Gunn. "The Sacred Hoop: A Contemporary Perspective." *The Sacred Hoop: Recovering the Feminine in American Indian Traditions*. Boston: Beacon Press, 1986.

Anderson, Charles. *Emily Dickinson's Poetry: Stairway of Surprise*. New York: Doubleday Press, 1966.

Auerbach, Nina. *Woman and the Demon*. Cambridge: Harvard University Press, 1982.

Baer, Elizabeth R. "The Sisterhood of Jane Eyre and Antoinette Cosway." In *The Voyage In: Fictions of Female Development*. Eds. Elizabeth Abel, Marianne Hirsch, and Elizabeth Langland. Hanover: University Press of New England, 1983.

Barthes, Roland. *Roland Barthes by Roland Barthes*. New York: Hill and Wang, 1977.

Baym, Nina. "Melodramas of Beset Manhood: How Theories of American Fiction Exclude Women Writers." *American Quarterly* 33 (1981):123–39. Rpt. in *The New Feminist Criticism*. Ed. Elaine Showalter. New York: Pantheon Books, 1985.

——. *Woman's Fiction*. Ithaca: Cornell University Press, 1978.

Beauvoir, Simone de. *The Second Sex*. Trans. H. M. Parshley. 1952; New York: Vintage, 1974.

Belenky, Mary Field, Blythe McVicker Clinchy, Nancy Rule Goldberger, and Jill Mattuck Tarule. *Women's Ways of Knowing.* New York: Basic Books, 1986.

Bell, Barbara Currier, and Carol Ohmann. "Virginia Woolf's Criticism: A Polemical Preface." In *Feminist Literary Criticism: Explorations in Theory.* Ed. Josephine Donovan. Lexington: University Press of Kentucky, 1975. Rpt. from *Critical Inquiry* 1 (1974):361–71.

Benjamin, Jessica. "A Desire of One's Own." In *Feminist Studies, Critical Studies.* Ed. Teresa De Lauretis. Bloomington: Indiana University Press, 1986.

Benstock, Shari. "Beyond the Reaches of Feminist Criticism: A Letter from Paris." *Tulsa Studies in Women's Literature* 3 (1984):5–27.

———. *Women of the Left Bank.* Austin: University of Texas Press, 1986.

Bergonzi, Bernard. *T. S. Eliot.* London and New York: Macmillan, 1972.

Bingham, Millicent Todd. *Emily Dickinson: A Revelation.* New York: Harper and Row, 1954.

Blake, Caesar R., and Carlton F. Wells. *The Recognition of Emily Dickinson.* Ann Arbor: University of Michigan Press, 1964.

Blake, William. *The Poetry and Prose of William Blake.* Ed. David V. Erdman. Com. by Harold Bloom. Garden City: Doubleday, 1965.

Bloom, Harold. *The Anxiety of Influence: A Theory of Poetry.* New York: Oxford University Press, 1973.

———. *Blake's Apocalypse: A Study in Poetic Argument.* Garden City: Doubleday, 1963.

———. *Figures of Capable Imagination.* New York: Seabury Press, 1976.

———. "Interview with Robert Moynihan." *Diacritics* 13 (1983):57–68.

———. *A Map of Misreading.* New York: Oxford University Press, 1975.

———, ed. *Modern Critical Views: T. S. Eliot.* New York: Chelsea House, 1985.

———. "A New Poetics." Rev. of *Anatomy of Criticism* by Northrop Frye. *Yale Review* 47 (1957):130–33.

———. *The Ringers in the Tower: Studies in Romantic Tradition.* Chicago: University of Chicago Press, 1971.

———. *Shelley's Mythmaking.* New Haven: Yale University Press, 1959; rpt. Ithaca: Cornell University Press, 1969.

———. *The Visionary Company: A Reading of English Romantic Poetry.* Garden City: Doubleday, 1961. Rev. and enl. Ithaca: Cornell University Press, 1971.

———. *Yeats.* New York: Oxford University Press, 1970.

Bombal, María Luisa. "Las islas nuevas." *La última niebla. La amortajada.* Barcelona: Seix Barral, 1984.

Borges, Jorge Luis. "The Library of Babel." *Ficciones.* Ed. and Trans. Anthony Kerrigan. New York: Grove Press, 1962.

Bornstein, George. *Transformations of Romanticism in Yeats, Eliot, and Stevens.* Chicago: University of Chicago Press, 1976.

Brontë, Charlotte. *Jane Eyre.* 1847; New York: Bantam, 1981.

Burke, Carolyn. "Irigaray Through the Looking Glass." *Feminist Issues* 7 (1981):288–306.

Burke, Kenneth. "On Musicality in Verse." In *The Philosophy of Literary Form: Studies in Symbolic Action.* 1941; Baton Rouge: Louisiana State University Press, 1967.

Cameron, Sharon. *Lyric Time: Dickinson and the Limits of Genre.* Baltimore: Johns Hopkins University Press, 1979.

Campos, Julieta. "Mi vocación literaria." *Revista Iberoamericana* 51 (1985): 467–70.

Chase, Richard. *Emily Dickinson.* New York: William Sloane Associates, 1951.

Chawaf, Chantal. "Linguistic Flesh." Trans. Yvonne Rochette-Ozzello. In *New French Feminisms: An Anthology.* Eds. Elaine Marks and Isabelle de Courtivron. New York: Schocken Books, 1981.

Chodorow, Nancy. "Family Structure and Feminine Personality." In *Woman, Culture, and Society.* Eds. Michelle Zimbalist Rosaldo and Louise Lamphere. Stanford: Stanford University Press, 1974.

———. *The Reproduction of Mothering: Psychoanalysis and the Sociology of Gender.* Berkeley: University of California Press, 1978.

Cixous, Hélène. "Castration or Decapitation?" Trans. Annette Kuhn. *Signs* 7 (1981):41–55.

———. "The Laugh of the Medusa." Trans. Keith Cohen and Paula Cohen. In *New French Feminisms: An Anthology.* Eds. Elaine Marks and Isabelle de Courtivron. New York: Schocken Books, 1981. Originally published as *"Le Rire de la méduse." L'Arc* (1975):39–45.

———. "Sorties" from *La jeune née.* Trans. Ann Liddle. In *New French Feminisms: An Anthology.* Eds. Elaine Marks and Isabelle de Courtivron. New York: Shocken Books, 1981.

Cleary, Vincent J. "Emily Dickinson's Classical Education." *English Language Notes* 18 (1980):119–29.

Cooper, James Fenimore. *The Last of the Mohicans: A Narrative of 1757.* 1826; New York: Signet Books, 1962.

(Cornillion), Susan Koppelman, ed. *Images of Women in Fiction: Feminist Perspectives.* Bowling Green, Ohio: Bowling Green University Popular Press, 1973.

Cortázar, Julio. *Hopscotch.* Trans. Gregory Rabassa. 1963; New York: Pantheon Books, 1966.

Costello, Bonnie. *Marianne Moore: Imaginary Possessions.* Cambridge: Harvard University Press, 1981.

———. "The 'Feminine' Language of Marianne Moore." In *Women and Language in Literature and Society*. Eds. Sally McConnell-Ginet, Ruth Borker, and Nelly Furman. New York: Praeger, 1980.

Cuddy, Lois A. "The Influence of Latin Poetics on Emily Dickinson's Style." *Comparative Literature* 13 (1976):214–29.

———. "The Latin Imprint on Emily Dickinson's Poetry: Theory and Practice." *American Literature* 50 (1978):74–84.

Culler, Jonathan. *On Deconstruction: Theory and Criticism after Structuralism*. Ithaca: Cornell University Press, 1982.

Cunningham, Adrian. "Continuity and Coherence in Eliot's Religious Thought." In *Eliot in Perspective: A Symposium*. Ed. Graham Martin. New York: Macmillan, 1970.

Darió, Rubén. "Mía." *Prosas Profanas. Poesías Completas*. Madrid: Aguilar, 1968.

Dash, Cheryl. "Jean Rhys." In *West Indian Literature*. Ed. Bruce King. London: Macmillan, 1979.

Davison, Ned. *The Concept of Modernism in Hispanic Criticism*. Boulder, Colorado: Pruett Press, 1966.

de Man, Paul. *Blindness and Insight: Essays in the Rhetoric of Contemporary Criticism*. New York: Oxford University Press, 1971.

Derrida, Jacques. "Freud and the Scene of Writing." *Yale French Studies* 48 (1972):73–117.

———. *Spurs/Éperons*. Trans. Barbara Harlow. Chicago: The University of Chicago Press, 1979.

Diamond, Arlyn, and Lee R. Edwards, eds. *The Authority of Experience: Essays in Feminist Criticism*. Amherst: University of Massachusetts Press, 1977.

Dickinson, Emily. *The Complete Poems of Emily Dickinson*. Ed. Thomas H. Johnson. Boston: Little, Brown, 1960.

———. *The Letters of Emily Dickinson*. Eds. Thomas H. Johnson and Theodora Ward. 3 vols. Cambridge: Belknap Press, 1958.

———. *The Letters of Emily Dickinson*. Ed. Mabel Loomis Todd. New York: World Publishing Company, 1951.

———. *The Poems of Emily Dickinson*. Ed. Thomas H. Johnson. 3 vols. Cambridge: Belknap of Harvard University Press, 1955.

Diehl, Joan Fiet. " 'Come Slowly—Eden': The Woman Poet and Her Muse." *Signs* 3 (1978):572–87. Rpt. as the first chapter of *Emily Dickinson and the Romantic Imagination*. Princeton: Princeton University Press, 1980.

———. "Dickinson and Bloom: An Antithetical Reading of Romanticism." *Texas Studies in Literature and Language* 23 (1981):418–41.

Diggory, Terence. "Armored Women, Naked Men: Dickinson, Whitman, and Their Successors." In *Shakespeare's Sisters: Feminist Essays on Women Poets*. Eds. Sandra M. Gilbert and Susan Gubar. Bloomington: Indiana University Press, 1979.

Dillard, Annie. *Teaching a Stone to Talk: Expeditions and Encounters*. New York: Harper & Row, 1982.

Dinnerstein, Dorothy. *The Mermaid and the Minotaur: Sexual Arrangements and Human Malaise*. New York: Harper & Row, 1976.

Doolittle, Hilda. *Collected Poems, 1912–1944*. Ed. Louis L. Martz. New York: New Directions, 1983.

———. *Tribute to Freud*. 1974; New York: New Directions, 1984.

Douglas, Ann. *The Feminization of American Culture*. New York: Random House, 1977.

DuPlessis, Rachel Blau. "For the Etruscans." In *The New Feminist Criticism: Essays on Women, Literature and Theory*. Ed. Elaine Showalter. New York: Pantheon Books, 1985.

Duras, Marguerite. "Interview." Trans. Susan Husserl-Kapit. In *New French Feminisms: An Anthology*. Eds. Elaine Marks and Isabelle de Courtivron. New York: Schocken Books, 1981.

Eagleton, Terry. *Literary Theory—An Introduction*. Minneapolis: University of Minnesota Press, 1983.

Eisenstein, Hester, and Alice Jardine, eds. *The Future of Difference*. New Brunswick: Rutgers University Press, 1980.

Eliot, T. S. *After Strange Gods: A Primer of Modern Heresy*. New York: Harcourt Brace Jovanovich, 1934.

———. *Collected Poems, 1909–1962*. London: Faber and Faber, 1963; New York: Harcourt, Brace and World, 1963.

———. "Marianne Moore." *Dial* 75 (1923):594–97.

———. *Poems Written in Early Youth*. London: Faber and Faber, 1967.

———. *Selected Essays*. 3rd ed., enlarged. London: Faber and Faber, 1951; New York: Harcourt, Brace and Company, 1932.

———. *To Criticize the Critic*. New York: Farrar, Straus, and Giroux, 1965.

———. *The Use of Poetry and the Use of Criticism*. London: Faber and Faber, 1933.

Emerson, Ralph Waldo. *Essays: First Series*. In *The Collected Works of Ralph Waldo Emerson*. Eds. Joseph Slater, Alfred R. Ferguson and Jean Fergusson Carr. 2 vols. Cambridge: Belknap Press, 1979.

Faulkner, William. *Absalom, Absalom!* New York: Random House, 1936.

Felman, Shoshana. "Women and Madness: The Critical Phallacy." *Diacritics* 5 (1975):2–10.

Fiedler, Leslie. *Love and Death in the American Novel*. 1960, revised 1966; New York: Stein and Day, 1975.

Fite, David. *Harold Bloom: The Rhetoric of Romantic Vision*. Amherst: University of Massachusetts Press, 1985.

Fitzgerald, F. Scott. *The Great Gatsby*. 1925. Study Guide Edition. New York: Scribner's, 1962.

Flynn, Elizabeth A., and Patrocinio P. Schweickart, eds. *Gender and Reading: Essays on Readers, Texts, and Contexts*. Baltimore: Johns Hopkins University Press, 1986.

Forché, Carolyn. "Burning the Tomato Worms." In *Gathering the Tribes*. New Haven and London: Yale University Press, 1976.

Freud, Sigmund. *The Complete Introductory Lectures on Psychoanalysis*. Ed. James Strachey. 1959. New York: W. W. Norton, 1966.

———. "Female Sexuality." Trans. Joan Riviere. Vol. 5 of *Collected Papers*. Ed. James Strachey. 6 vols. New York: Basic Books, 1959.

———. *The Standard Edition of the Complete Psychological Works of Sigmund Freud*. Ed. James Strachey. London: The Hogarth Press, 1961.

Friedman, Susan Stanford. "'I go where I love': An Intertextual Study of H. D. and Adrienne Rich." *Signs* 9 (1983):228–45.

Frye, Joanne. *Living Stories, Telling Lives*. Ann Arbor: University of Michigan Press, 1986.

Frye, Northrop. *Anatomy of Criticism: Four Essays*. 1957; Princeton: Princeton University Press, 1969.

———. "Ministry of Angels." 1953. Rpt. in *Northrop Frye in Culture and Literature: A Collection of Review Essays*. Ed. Robert Denham. Chicago: University of Chicago Press, 1978.

———. *The Well-Tempered Critic*. Bloomington: Indiana University Press, 1963.

Gallop, Jane. *The Daughter's Seduction: Feminism and Psychoanalysis*. Ithaca: Cornell University Press, 1982.

———. "Reading the Mother Tongue: Psychoanalytic Feminist Criticism." *Critical Inquiry* 13 (1987):314–29.

Gallup, Donald. *T. S. Eliot: A Bibliography*. London: Faber and Faber, 1969.

Gardiner, Judith Kegan. "On Female Identity and Writing by Women." In *Writing and Sexual Difference*. Ed. Elizabeth Abel. Chicago: University of Chicago Press, 1982.

Gardner, Helen. *The Art of T. S. Eliot*. Oxford: Cresset Press, 1949.

Garner, Shirley Nelson, Claire Kahane, and Madelon Sprengnether, eds. *The (M)other Tongue: Essays in Feminist Psychoanalytic Interpretation*. Ithaca: Cornell University Press, 1985.

Gelpi, Albert. "Emily Dickinson and the Deerslayer: The Dilemma of the Woman Poet in America." In *Shakespeare's Sisters: Feminist Essays on Women Poets*. Eds. Sandra M. Gilbert and Susan Gubar. Bloomington: Indiana University Press, 1979.

Gelpi, Barbara Charlesworth. "A Common Language: The American Woman Poet." In *Shakespeare's Sisters: Feminist Essays on Women Poets*. Eds.

Sandra M. Gilbert and Susan Gubar. Bloomington: Indiana University Press, 1979.

Gelpi, Barbara Charlesworth, and Albert Gelpi. "Introduction." *Adrienne Rich's Poetry*. New York: W. W. Norton, 1975.

Gilbert, Sandra M. "The American Sexual Poetics of Walt Whitman and Emily Dickinson." In *Reconstructing American Literary History*. Ed. Sacvan Bercovitch. Cambridge: Harvard University Press, 1986.

————. "Costumes of the Mind: Transvestism as Metaphor in Modern Literature." In *Writing and Sexual Difference*. Ed. Elizabeth Abel. Chicago: University of Chicago Press, 1980.

————. "'Life's Empty Pack': Notes toward a Literary Daughteronomy." *Critical Inquiry* 11 (1985):355–84.

Gilbert, Sandra M., and Susan Gubar. "Ceremonies of the Alphabet: Female Grandmatologies and the Female Authorgraph." In *The Female Autograph*. Ed. Domna Stanton. New York: The New York Literary Forum, 1984. For a history of the composition of this article, see note under "Sexual Linguistics."

————. "'Forward into the Past': The Complex Female Affiliation Complex." In *Historical Studies and Literary Criticism*. Ed. Jerome J. McGann. Madison: University of Wisconsin Press, 1985. Enlarged and substantially revised as Chapter 4 of *No Man's Land*, Vol. I.

————. *The Madwoman in the Attic: The Woman Writer and the Nineteenth-Century Literary Imagination*. New Haven: Yale University Press, 1979.

————. *No Man's Land: The Place of the Woman Writer in the Twentieth Century*. Vol. I. *The War of the Words*. New Haven: Yale University Press, 1988.

————, eds. *The Norton Anthology of Literature by Women: The Tradition in English*. New York: W. W. Norton, 1985.

————. "Sexual Linguistics: Gender, Language, Sexuality." This working paper, which began as an essay written by Sandra M. Gilbert, entitled "Speaking in Mother Tongues: Woman's Sentence and Women's Sentencing," evolved into a collaborative project, which resulted in two essays: "Sexual Linguistics: Gender, Language, Sexuality," which appeared in *New Literary History* 16 (1985):515–43, and "Ceremonies of the Female Alphabet." These two essays were recombined with added material to form Chapter 5 of *No Man's Land*, Vol. I.

————, eds. *Shakespeare's Sisters: Feminist Essays on Women Poets*. Bloomington: Indiana University Press, 1979.

————. "Tradition and the Female Talent." Paper presented at the School of Criticism and Theory at Northwestern University. Also published in *Proceedings of the Northeastern University Center for Literary*

Studies 2 (1984):1–27. Revised to form Chapter 3 of *No Man's Land*, Vol. I.

Gilligan, Carol. *In a Different Voice: Psychological Theory and Women's Development*. Cambridge: Harvard University Press, 1982.

Gordon, Lyndall. *Eliot's Early Years*. New York: Oxford University Press, 1977.

Graves, Robert. *The White Goddess*. 1948. Amended and enlarged. New York: Farrar, Straus and Giroux, 1966.

Greene, Gayle, and Coppélia Kahn, eds. *Making a Difference: Feminist Literary Theory*. London: Methuen, 1985.

Gubar, Susan. "'The Blank Page' and the Issues of Female Creativity." Rpt. in *The New Feminist Criticism*. Ed. Elaine Showalter. New York: Pantheon Books, 1985. Originally published in *Critical Inquiry* 8 (1981):243–63.

―――. "The Echoing Spell of H. D.'s *Trilogy*." In *Shakespeare's Sisters: Feminist Essays on Women Poets*. Eds. Sandra M. Gilbert and Susan Gubar. Bloomington: Indiana University Press, 1979.

―――. "Mother, Maiden, and the Marriage of Death: Women Writers and an Ancient Myth." *Women's Studies* 6 (1979):301–15.

Guest, Barbara. *Herself Defined: The Poet H. D. and Her World*. Garden City: Doubleday, 1984.

Haggard, H. Rider. *Heart of the World*. New York: McKinlay, Stone & Mackenzie, 1894.

―――. *She*. New York: Books, Inc., 1886.

Haller, Evelyn. "Virginia Woolf's Use of Egyptian Myth." In *Virginia Woolf: A Feminist Slant*. Ed. Jane Marcus. Lincoln: University of Nebraska Press, 1983.

Hamon, Philippe. "Qu'est-ce qu'une description?" *Poétique* 12 (1972):465–85.

Harjo, Joy. *She Had Some Horses*. New York: Thunder's Mouth Press, 1983.

Heath, Stephen. "Difference." *Screen* 19 (1978):51–112.

Higgins, David. *Portrait of Emily Dickinson*. New Brunswick: Rutgers University Press, 1967.

Holland, Norman N. "H. D. and the 'Blameless Physician.'" *Contemporary Literature* 10 (1969):474–506.

Hollander, John. "The Devil's Party." Rev. of *The Anxiety of Influence*. *Poetry* 122 (1973):298–303.

Holloway, John. *The Chartered Mirror*. London: Routledge and Kegan Paul, 1960.

Homans, Margaret. *Women Writers and Poetic Identity: Dorothy Wordsworth, Emily Brontë, and Emily Dickinson*. Princeton: Princeton University Press, 1980.

Irigaray, Luce. *Speculum of the Other Woman*. Trans. Gillian C. Gill. Ithaca:

Cornell University Press, 1985. Originally published in French under the title *Speculum de l'autre femme*, © 1974 by Les Éditions de Minuit.

———. *This Sex Which Is Not One*. Trans. Catherine Porter with Carolyn Burke. Ithaca: Cornell University Press, 1985. Originally published in French under the title *Ce sexe qui n'en est pas un*, © 1977 by Éditions de Minuit.

Jacobus, Mary. "The Difference of View." In *Women Writing and Writing about Women*. Ed. Mary Jacobus. London: Croom Helm; New York: Barnes and Noble, 1979.

James, Louis. *Jean Rhys*. Thetford, England: Longman, 1978.

JanMohamed, Abdul R. "The Economy of Manichean Allegory: The Function of Racial Difference in Colonialist Literature." *Critical Inquiry* 12 (1985):59–87.

Jay, Gregory S. *T. S. Eliot and the Poetics of Literary History*. Baton Rouge: Louisiana State University Press, 1983.

Johnson, Thomas H. *Emily Dickinson: An Interpretive Biography*. Cambridge: Belknap Press, 1955.

Jones, Ann Rosalind. "Writing the Body: Toward an Understanding of *L'Écriture Féminine*." *Feminist Studies*, 7 (1981):247–63. Rpt. in *The New Feminist Criticism*. Ed. Elaine Showalter. New York: Pantheon Books, 1985.

Jones, Gayl. *Corregidora*. New York: Bantam Books, 1976.

Juhasz, Suzanne, ed. *Feminist Critics Read Emily Dickinson*. Bloomington: Indiana University Press, 1983.

———. *Naked and Fiery Forms: Modern American Poetry by Women, A New Tradition*. New York: Harper and Row, 1976.

Kaiser, Daniel. Rev. of *A Map of Misreading*. *Studies in Romanticism* 15 (1976):320–26.

Kammer, Jeanne. "The Art of Silence and the Forms of Women's Poetry." In *Shakespeare's Sisters: Feminist Essays on Women Poets*. Eds. Sandra M. Gilbert and Susan Gubar. Bloomington: Indiana University Press, 1979.

Katz-Stoker, Fraya. "The Other Criticism: Feminism vs. Formalism." In *Images of Women in Fiction: Feminist Perspectives*. Ed. Susan Koppelman (Cornillon). Bowling Green, Ohio: Bowling Green University Popular Press, 1972.

Keller, Evelyn Fox. *A Feeling for the Organism: The Life and Work of Barbara McClintock*. San Francisco: W. H. Freeman, 1983.

Kelley, Mary. *Private Woman, Public Stage*. New York: Oxford University Press, 1984.

Kenner, Hugh. *The Invisible Poet: T. S. Eliot*. New York: McDowell, Obolensky, 1959.

Kermode, Frank. *The Romantic Image*. New York: Random House, 1967.

———. *The Sense of an Ending: Studies in the Theory of Fiction*. New York: Oxford University Press, 1967.

King, Bruce, ed. *West Indian Literature*. London: Macmillan, 1979.

Knust, Herbert. "Sweeney among the Birds and Beasts." *Arcadia* 2 (1967): 204–17.

Kolodny, Annette. "Dancing Through the Minefield: Some Observations on the Theory, Practice, and Politics of a Feminist Literary Criticism." *Feminist Studies* 6 (1980): 1–25. Rpt. in *The New Feminist Criticism*. Ed. Elaine Showalter. New York: Pantheon Books, 1985.

———. *The Land before Her: Fantasy and Experience of the American Frontiers, 1630–1860*. Chapel Hill: University of North Carolina Press, 1984.

———. *The Lay of the Land: Metaphor as Experience and History in American Life and Letters*. Chapel Hill: University of North Carolina Press, 1975.

———. "A Map for Re-Reading: Or, Gender and the Interpretation of Literary Texts." *New Literary History* 11 (1980): 451–67. Rpt. in *The New Feminist Criticism*. Ed. Elaine Showalter. New York: Pantheon Books, 1986.

Kramer, Hilton. "The Triumph of Misreading." *The New York Times Book Review*, 21 August 1977, 3, 28.

Krieger, Murray. *The New Apologists for Poetry*. Bloomington: Indiana University Press, 1963.

Kristeva, Julia. *Desire in Language: A Semiotic Approach to Literature and Art*. Ed. Leon S. Roudiez. New York: Columbia University Press, 1980.

———. "Women's Time." Trans. Alice Jardine and Harry Blake. *Signs* 7 (1981): 13–35.

Kuhn, Annette. "Introduction to Hélène Cixous's 'Castration or Decapitation?'" *Signs* 7 (1981): 36–40.

Lacan, Jacques. *Écrits: A Selection*. Trans. Alan Sheridan. New York: W. W. Norton, 1977.

———. *Le Séminaire: Livre XX: Encore*. Paris: Éditions du Seuil, 1975.

Lamy, Suzanne. *d'elles*. Montréal: l'hexagone, 1979.

Lanser, Susan Sniader, and Evelyn Torton Beck. "[Why] Are There No Great Woman Critics? And What Difference Does It Make?" In *The Prism of Sex: Essays in the Sociology of Knowledge*. Eds. Julia A. Sherman and Evelyn Torton Beck. Madison: University of Wisconsin Press, 1979.

Lattin, Vernon E. "The Quest for Mythic Vision in Contemporary Native American and Chicano Fiction." *American Literature* 50 (1979): 625–40.

Lawrence, D. H. *Studies in Classic American Literature*. 1923; New York: Penguin Books, 1977.

Leibman, Sheldon. "The Turning Point: Eliot's *The Use of Poetry and the Use of Criticism.*" *Boundary 2* 9 (1981):197–218.

Lemaire, Anika. *Jacques Lacan.* Trans. David Mackey. London: Routledge and Kegan Paul, 1977.

Lewis, Gordon K. *Main Currents of Caribbean Thought: The Historical Evolution of Caribbean Society in Its Ideological Aspects, 1492–1900.* Baltimore: Johns Hopkins University Press, 1983.

Lipking, Lawrence. "Aristotle's Sister: A Poetics of Abandonment." *Critical Inquiry* 10 (1983):61–82.

Litz, A. Walton. "'That strange abstraction,' Nature": T. S. Eliot's Victorian Inheritance." In *Nature and the Victorian Imagination.* Eds. U. C. Knoepflmacher and G. B. Tennyson. Berkeley: University of California Press, 1977.

Lobb, Edward. *T. S. Eliot and the Romantic Critical Tradition.* London: Routledge and Kegan Paul, 1981.

McConnell-Ginet, Sally, Ruth Borker, and Nelly Furman, eds. *Women and Language in Literature and Society.* New York: Praeger, 1980.

Marks, Elaine, and Isabelle de Courtivron, eds. *New French Feminisms: An Anthology.* New York: Schocken Books, 1981.

Marsh, R., and Tambimuttu, eds. *T. S. Eliot: A Symposium.* London: Editions Poetry; Chicago: Regnery, 1948.

Martin, Mildred. *A Half-Century of Eliot Criticism: Annotated Bibliography of Books and Articles in English, 1916–1965.* Lewisburg: Bucknell University Press, 1972.

Martin, Taffy. *Marianne Moore, Subversive Modernist.* Austin: University of Texas Press, 1986.

Matthiessen, F. O. *The Achievement of T. S. Eliot: An Essay on the Nature of Poetry.* New York: Houghton Mifflin, 1935.

———. *American Renaissance.* New York: Oxford University Press, 1941.

Mellown, Elgin W. "Character and Themes in the Novels of Jean Rhys." *Contemporary Literature* 23 (1972):458–74.

Miller, Christanne. "How 'Low Feet' Stagger: Disruptions of Language in Dickinson's Poetry." In *Feminist Critics Read Emily Dickinson.* Ed. Suzanne Juhasz. Bloomington: Indiana University Press, 1983.

Miller, James E. *T. S. Eliot's Personal Wasteland: Exorcism of the Demons.* University Park: Pennsylvania State University Press, 1977.

Miller, Nancy K. "Emphasis Added: Plots and Plausibilities in Women's Fiction." *PMLA* 96 (1981):36–48. Rpt. in *The New Feminist Criticism.* Ed. Elaine Showalter. New York: Pantheon Books, 1985.

Miller, Ruth. *The Poetry of Emily Dickinson.* Middletown, Conn: Wesleyan University Press, 1968.

Mitchell, Juliet, and Jacqueline Rose. *Feminine Sexuality: Jacques Lacan and the école freudienne.* New York: Pantheon Books, 1982.

Moers, Ellen. *Literary Women: The Great Writers.* Garden City: Doubleday, 1976; New York: Oxford University Press, 1985.

Mohr, Eugene. "The Pleasures of West Indian Writing: An Introduction to the Literature." *Caribbean Review* 11 (1982):33–36.

Moi, Toril. *Sexual/Textual Politics: Feminist Literary Theory.* London and New York: Methuen, 1985.

Montefiore, Janet. "Feminine Identity and the Poetic Tradition." *Feminist Review* 13 (1983):69–84.

Moore, Marianne. *The Complete Poems of Marianne Moore.* New York: Macmillan, 1981.

——. *A Marianne Moore Reader.* New York: Viking, 1961.

——. "A Note on T. S. Eliot's Book." *Poetry* 12 (1918):36–37.

Moraga, Cherríe, and Gloria Anzaldúa, eds. *This Bridge Called My Back.* Watertown, Mass: Persephone, 1981.

Morrison, Toni. *Sula.* New York: Knopf, 1973.

Mossberg, Barbara Antonia Clarke. *Emily Dickinson: When a Writer is a Daughter.* Bloomington: Indiana University Press, 1982.

Mulvey, Laura. "Visual Pleasure and Narrative Cinema." *Screen* 16 (1975):6–18.

Nebecker, Helen. *Jean Rhys: Woman in Passage: A Critical Study of the Novels of Jean Rhys.* Montreal: Eden, 1981.

O'Hara, Daniel. " 'The Unsummoned Image': T. S. Eliot's Unclassical Criticism." *Boundary 2* 9 (1980):91–124.

Ong, Walter J. *Fighting for Life: Contest, Sexuality, and Consciousness.* Ithaca: Cornell University Press, 1981.

Ortner, Sherry B. "Is Female to Male as Nature Is to Culture?" In *Women, Culture, and Society.* Eds. Michelle Zimbalist Rosaldo and Louise Lamphere. Stanford: Stanford University Press, 1974.

Ostriker, Alicia. *Stealing the Language: The Emergence of Women's Poetry in America.* Boston: Beacon Press, 1986.

Paz, Octavio. *Children of the Mire: Modern Poetry from Romanticism to the Avant-Garde.* Trans. Rachel Phillips. Cambridge: Harvard University Press, 1974.

Pinkney, Tony. *Women in the Poetry of T. S. Eliot: A Psychoanalytic Approach.* London: Macmillan, 1984.

Plante, David. *Difficult Women: A Memoir of Three: Jean Rhys, Sonia Orwell, Germaine Greer.* New York: Obelisk-Dutton, 1984.

Plath, Sylvia. *Ariel.* New York: Harper and Row, 1966.

Poe, Edgar Allan. *The Complete Poems and Stories of Edgar Allan Poe.* Eds. Arthur Nelson Quinn and Edward O'Neill. 2 vols. New York, 1946.

Poirier, Richard. *A World Elsewhere.* New York: Oxford University Press, 1966.

Polansky, Steven. "A Family Romance—Northrop Frye and Harold Bloom." *Boundary 2* 9 (1981):227–45.

Porter, David. *Dickinson: The Modern Idiom*. Cambridge: Harvard University Press, 1981.

Puig, Manuel. *Kiss of the Spider Woman*. Trans. Thomas Colchie. New York: Alfred A. Knopf, 1979.

Rama, Angel. *Rubén Darío y el modernismo*. Caracas: Universidad Central de Venezuela, 1970.

Ramchand, Kenneth. *An Introduction to the Study of West Indian Literature*. Middlesex, England: Nelson, 1976.

Rhys, Jean. *After Leaving Mr. Mackenzie*. London: Cape, 1930.

———. *Complete Novels*. New York: W. W. Norton, 1985.

———. *Good Morning, Midnight*. London: Constable, 1939.

———. Interview. "Fated to Be Sad." With Hannah Carter. *The Guardian*, 8 August 1968, 5.

———. *The Left Bank: Sketches and Studies of Present-Day Bohemian Paris*. London: Cape, 1927.

———. *The Letters of Jean Rhys*. Edited and selected by Francis Wyndham and Diana Melly. New York: Viking, 1984.

———. *Sleep It Off, Lady*. London: Deutsch, 1976.

———. *Smile Please: An Unfinished Autobiography*. Berkeley: Creative Arts, 1979.

———. *Tigers Are Better Looking*. London: Deutsch, 1968.

———. *Voyage in the Dark*. 1934; New York: W. W. Norton, 1982.

———. *Wide Sargasso Sea*. 1966; New York: W. W. Norton, 1982.

Rich, Adrienne. *The Dream of a Common Language: Poems 1974–1977*. New York: W. W. Norton, 1978.

———. "Vesuvius at Home: The Power of Emily Dickinson." In *Shakespeare's Sisters: Feminist Essays on Women Poets*. Bloomington: Indiana University Press, 1979.

———. "When We Dead Awaken: Writing as Re-Vision." In *On Lies, Secrets, and Silence: Selected Prose*. New York: W. W. Norton, 1979. Originally published in *College English* 34 (1972):19–30.

Rich, B. Ruby. "Anti-Porn: Soft Issue, Hard World." *Feminist Review* 13 (1983):56–67.

Richards, I. A. "On Mr. Eliot's Poetry." In *Principles of Literary Criticism*. 2d ed. London: K. Paul; Trench, Trubner, & Co., 1926.

Ricks, Beatrice. *T. S. Eliot: A Bibliography of Secondary Works*. New Jersey: Scarecrow, 1980.

Riddel, Joseph N. "H. D. and the Poetics of 'Spiritual Realism.'" *Contemporary Literature* 10 (1969):447–73.

Robinson, Janice A. *H. D.: The Life and Work of an American Poet*. Boston: Houghton Mifflin, 1982.

Robinson, Marilynne. *Housekeeping*. New York: Farrar, Straus and Giroux, 1981.

Rosenfeld, Claire. "The Shadow Within: The Conscious and Unconscious Use of the Double." In *Stories of the Double*. Ed. Albert J. Guérard. Philadelphia: Lippincott, 1967.

Sands, Kathleen, ed. "A Special Symposium Issue on Leslie Marmon Silko's *Ceremony*." *American Indian Quarterly* 5:1 (1979).

Sarduy, Severo. *Escrito sobre un cuerpo*. Buenos Aires: Ed. Sudamericana, 1969.

———. *From Cuba with a Song*. In *Triple Cross*. Trans. Suzanne Jill Levine. New York: E. P. Dutton, 1972.

Scharfman, Ronnie. "Mirroring and Mothering in Simone Schwarz-Bart's *Pluie et Vent sur Télumée Miracle* and Jean Rhys' *Wide Sargasso Sea*." *Yale French Studies* 62 (1981):88–106.

Schneiderman, Stuart. *The Death of an Intellectual Hero*. Cambridge: Harvard University Press, 1983.

Sewall, Richard B. *The Life of Emily Dickinson*. 2 vols. New York: Farrar, Straus and Giroux, 1974.

———, ed. *Emily Dickinson: A Collection of Critical Essays*. Englewood Cliffs: Prentice-Hall, 1963.

Showalter, Elaine. "Critical Cross-Dressing: Male Feminists and the Woman of the Year." *Raritan* 3 (1983):130–49.

———. "Feminist Criticism in the Wilderness." In *Writing and Sexual Difference*. Ed. Elizabeth Abel. Chicago: University of Chicago Press, 1982. Reprinted from *Critical Inquiry* 8 (1981):179–205. Also rpt. in *The New Feminist Criticism*. Ed. Elaine Showalter. New York: Pantheon Books, 1985.

———. "Toward a Feminist Poetics." Rpt. in *The New Feminist Criticism: Essays on Women, Literature and Theory*. Ed. Elaine Showalter. New York: Pantheon Books, 1985. Originally published in *Women Writing and Writing by Women*. Ed. Mary Jacobus. London: Croome Helm, 1979.

———. "Literary Criticism: Review Essay." *Signs* 1 (1975):435–60.

———. *A Literature of Their Own: British Women Novelists from Brontë to Lessing*. Princeton: Princeton University Press, 1977.

———, ed. *The New Feminist Criticism: Essays on Women, Literature and Theory*. New York: Pantheon Books, 1985.

Sigourney, L. H. *Letters to Young Ladies*. New York: Harper & Brothers, 1833.

Silko, Leslie Marmon. *Ceremony*. New York: Signet Books, 1977.

Southam, B. C. *A Student's Guide to the Selected Poems of T. S. Eliot.* London: Faber, 1968.

Spacks, Patricia Meyer. *The Female Imagination.* New York: Camelot-Avon, 1972.

Sparks, Elisa Kay. "Sons of the Father: Critics of Romanticism and Romantic Critics." Ph.D. diss. Bloomington: Indiana University, 1980.

Spender, Dale. *Man Made Language.* London: Routledge and Kegan Paul, 1980.

Spivak, Gayatri C. "Displacement and the Discourse of Woman." In *Displacement: Derrida and After.* Ed. Mark Krupnick. Bloomington: Indiana University Press, 1983.

———. "Three Women's Texts and a Critique of Imperialism." *Critical Inquiry* 12 (1985):243–61.

———. "Unmaking and Making in *To the Lighthouse.*" In *Women and Language in Literature and Society.* Eds. Sally McConnell-Ginet, Ruth Borker, and Nelly Furman. New York: Praeger Publishers, 1980.

Sprague, Rosemary. "Marianne Moore." In *Imaginary Gardens: A Study of Five American Poets.* New York: Chilton, 1969.

Staley, Thomas. *Jean Rhys: A Critical Study.* Austin: University of Texas Press, 1979.

Stead, C. K. *The New Poetic.* London: Hutchin, 1964.

Steinman, Lisa M. "Modern America, Modernism, and Marianne Moore." *Twentieth Century Literature* 30 (1984):210–30.

Stimpson, Catharine R., and Ethel Spector Person, eds. *Women: Sex and Sexuality.* Chicago: University of Chicago Press, 1980.

Storni, Alfonsina. *Obra poética completa.* 2d ed. Buenos Aires: Sociedad Editora Latinoamericana, 1964.

Sudol, Ronald A. "Elegy and Immortality: Emily Dickinson's 'Lay this Laurel on the One.'" *ESQ: Journal of the American Renaissance* 26 (1980): 10–15.

Tennyson, Alfred. *The Poems of Tennyson.* Ed. Christopher Ricks. London: Longman Group Limited, 1969.

Todorov, Tzvetan. "Critical Response III: 'Race,' Writing, and Culture." Trans. Loulou Mack. *Critical Inquiry* 13 (1985):171–81.

Tomlinson, Charles, ed. *Marianne Moore: A Collection of Critical Essays.* Englewood Cliffs: Prentice-Hall, 1969.

Tompkins, Jane P. *Sensational Designs: The Cultural Work of American Fiction, 1790–1860.* New York: Oxford University Press, 1985.

Van Doren, Mark. "Introduction." In *The Letters of Emily Dickinson.* Ed. Mabel Loomis Todd. New York: World Publishing Company, 1951.

Virgil [P. Vergili Maronis]. *Aeneidos: Liber Sextvs.* Commentary by R. G. Austin. Oxford: Oxford University Press, 1977.

Visca, Arturo Sergio. *Correspondencia íntima de Delmira Agustini y tres versiones de "Lo Inefable."* Montevideo: Biblioteca Nacional, 1978.

Walker, Alice. *The Color Purple.* New York: Washington Square Press, 1982.

Walsh, John Evangelist. *The Hidden Life of Emily Dickinson.* New York: Simon and Schuster, 1971.

Weisbuch, Robert. *Emily Dickinson's Poetry.* Chicago: University of Chicago Press, 1975.

Wenzel, Hélène Vivienne. "The Text as Body/Politics: An Appreciation of Monique Wittig's Writings in Context." *Feminist Studies* 7 (1981): 264–87.

Whicher, George Frisbie. *This Was a Poet: A Critical Biography of Emily Dickinson.* New York: Scribner's, 1938.

Woolf, Virginia. "Response to 'Affable Hawk' (Desmond MacCarthy)." In *Women and Writing.* Ed. Michèle Barrett. New York: Harcourt, Brace and World, 1979.

———. *A Room of One's Own.* 1929; New York: Harcourt Brace Jovanovich, 1957.

Wolfe, Peter. *Jean Rhys.* Boston: G. K. Hall, 1980.

Wyndham, Francis. "Introduction." *Wide Sargasso Sea.* By Jean Rhys. New York: W. W. Norton, 1966.

Ziff, Larzer. *The American 1890s: The Life and Times of a Lost Generation.* New York: Viking, 1966.

Zum Felde, Alberto. *Proceso intelectual del Uruguay y crítica de su literatura.* Montevideo: Imprenta Nacional Colorado, 1930.

———. "Prólogo." *Delmira Agustini. Poesías completas.* Buenos Aires: Losada, 1971.

Notes on the Contributors

TEMMA F. BERG is assistant professor of English at Gettysburg College, where she also teaches in the Women's Studies Program. She has guest edited an issue of *Reader: Essays in Reader-Oriented Theory, Criticism, and Pedagogy* on the interrelationship between reader-response theory and deconstruction, and contributed the essay on reader-response theory to the anthology *Tracing Literary Theory*. She has published many essays on the subject of reading, especially of women reading, in *Studies in the Novel*, *Criticism*, and *Canadian Review of Comparative Literature*. She has been working on an anthology of women's literary theory.

STEPHEN H. CLARK completed his dissertation on William Blake and rationalism in 1986 at Cambridge University. His recent work includes an introduction to the thought of Paul Ricoeur; articles on Locke, Pope, and Philip Larkin; and an article on poems by Akenside, Macpherson, and Young. He is presently working on a study of misogyny in English poetry and compiling an anthology of contemporary British poetry. He currently teaches at Harlaxton College, Grantham.

CAROLYN A. DURHAM is Inez K. Gaylord Professor of French at the College of Wooster, where she also teaches in the Women's Studies and Comparative Literature programs. She is the author of *L'Art romanesque de Raymond Roussel* and of numerous articles on the works of Claudine Hermann, Simone de Beauvoir, Marie Cardinal, William Styron, Denis Diderot, and others. She is currently completing a book-length manuscript on the works of Marie Cardinal that focuses on the connections between Anglo-American and Francophone feminist theory.

ANNA SHANNON ELFENBEIN, an associate professor of English at Southern Illinois University, teaches American literature and Women's Studies. Her first book, *Women on the Color Line*, examines the treatment of mixed-race women characters in the fiction of George W. Cable, Grace King, and Kate Chopin. She has also written on Elinor Wylie, Olive Tilford Dargan, and Toni Morrison and has been at work on a book examining the dialogue on race and women's place in nineteenth- and twentieth-century American fiction.

LEIGH GILMORE is assistant professor of English at the University of Southern Maine, where she also teaches Women's Studies. She has written on the connection between French feminist theory and medieval mystical writing, and on self-representation and women's writing. She has been working on a book on women's autobiography.

JEANNE LARSEN is associate professor of English at Hollins College. She is the author of a book of poetry, *James Cook in Search of Terra Incognita*, and a book of literary translations from Chinese, *Brocade River Poems: Selected Works of the Tang Dynasty Courtesan Xue Tao*. Her poems and short stories have appeared in numerous literary magazines. She has also published an article on H. D.'s *Helen in Egypt*, and several on medieval Chinese literature. Her forthcoming novel is set in eighth-century China, Taoist heaven, and Buddhist hell.

MARILEE LINDEMANN is a doctoral candidate in English at Rutgers University. She has published articles on fiction by American women in *Praxis* and the *Willa Cather Pioneer Memorial Newsletter*, and has taught English and Women's Studies at Rutgers and Northern Arizona University. For 1987–88, she was awarded an American Fellowship from the American Association of University Women to work on her dissertation, "Women Writers and the American Romance: Studies in Jewett, Gilman, and Cather." She was also awarded a research grant in women's studies from the Woodrow Wilson National Fellowship Foundation.

SUSAN JARET McKINSTRY is assistant professor of English at Carleton College. She has published articles on T. S. Eliot, Emily Brontë, Ann Beattie, Margaret Atwood, and Emily Dickinson, as well as several poems and short stories. She has completed a book on contemporary theory, and is co-editing a book on feminist dialogism.

ADRIANA MÉNDEZ RODENAS is associate professor of Spanish at the University of Iowa, where she also teaches in the Women's Studies and Comparative Literature programs. She is the author of *Severo Sarduy: el neobarroco de la transgresión* and of numerous articles on contemporary Caribbean and Latin American literature. She has also published an essay on Mexican novelist Elena Garro and is working on a psychoanalytical study of the novels of the Chilean María Luisa Bombal. Currently she is researching a book on women's travel narrative and historical memoirs in nineteenth-century Spanish America.

LAURA NIESEN DE ABRUÑA has taught at the University of Texas at Austin, the University of Puerto Rico at San Juan, and Ithaca College, where she is an assistant professor of English. She is the author of *The Refining Fire: Herakles and Other Heroes in T. S. Eliot's Works* and articles on Jean Rhys, Mark Twain, Edith Wharton, T. S. Eliot, and Caribbean literature. She has been working on a book-length manuscript on twentieth-century women writers of the English-speaking Caribbean.

MARÍA ROSA OLIVERA-WILLIAMS studied law at the Universidad de la República, in Montevideo, Uruguay. She has published a book on gaucho poetry, *La poesía gauchesca de Hidalgo a Hernández: respuesta estética y condicionamiento social*, and is the author of numerous articles on such writers as Pablo Neruda, Mario Benedetti, Cristina Peri-Rossi, Delmira Agustini, Alfonsina Storni, and Florencio Sánchez. At present, she is working on a manuscript for her second book on Uruguayan literature in exile. Since 1982 she has been an assistant professor at the Department of Modern and Classical Languages of the University of Notre Dame.

ELISA KAY SPARKS is an assistant professor of English at Clemson University, where she directs the Freshman Composition Program and helps with Women's Studies as well as teaches literary criticism and science fiction. She has published several articles on science fiction and fantasy writers, and is finishing an annotated bibliography on contemporary critical theory for G. K. Hall.

Index